In a Time of Monsters

By the same author
The Unravelling

In a Time of Monsters

Travels Through a Middle East in Revolt

Emma Sky

Atlantic Books
London

First published in Great Britain in 2019 by Atlantic Books, an imprint of
Atlantic Books Ltd.

1 2 3 4 5 6 7 8 9

A CIP catalogue record for this book is available from the British Library.

Except where noted, all photographs are taken by the author.

Map artwork by Jeff Edwards.

Hardback ISBN: 978-1-78649-560-0
E-book ISBN: 978-1-78649-561-7
Paperback ISBN: 978-1-78649-562-4

Printed in Great Britain by Bell and Bain Ltd, Glasgow

Atlantic Books
An imprint of Atlantic Books Ltd
Ormond House
26–27 Boswell Street
London
WC1N 3JZ

www.atlantic-books.co.uk

For fellow travellers

The old world is dying, and the new world struggles to be born:
now is the time of monsters
Antonio Gramsci

Who lives sees, but who travels sees more
Ibn Battuta

CONTENTS

Preface

A new Middle East constantly struggles to be born. But each attempted birth is abortive, with visions of utopia replaced by dystopia. After two decades of working in the region, I set out to make sense of the great upheavals taking place. Between 2010 and 2016, I travelled from Tahrir Square in Cairo to the Qandil mountains in Kurdistan; from the markets of Damascus to the marshes of Mesopotamia; from tea shops in Antakya to shopping malls in Saudi Arabia; from pyramids to petroglyphs; from the Persian Gulf to the Dead Sea to the Mediterranean; from Baghdad to Bukhara; from Khartoum to Carthage; from mosque to church to synagogue. I witnessed how dreams of new political orders based on rights and justice were shattered in wars and fragile states – and demons unleashed upon the world.

The overthrow of Saddam Hussein's authoritarian regime in 2003 by a US-led coalition did not herald a new regional democratic order as envisaged by its Western architects. Instead, Iraq's civil war sowed disorder beyond its borders. Furthermore, the collapse of the Arab counterweight that kept the Islamic Republic of Iran in check upended the balance of power in the region, fueling competition that continues to destabilize the Middle East.

The 'new' Iraq remains hamstrung by weak institutions and kleptocratic elites. Poor public services and rampant corruption have led to cycles of protests, violence and insurgency against the government. Elections are held regularly, but have not brought about meaningful change. Despite not winning the 2010 elections, Nuri al-Maliki, a Shia Islamist, still secured a second term as prime minister and subsequently marginalized his Sunni political opponents, consolidated power and implemented sectarian policies. This created the conditions that enabled the Islamic State – otherwise known as Daesh, or ISIS – to rise up out of the ashes of al-Qaeda in Iraq and proclaim itself as the protector of Sunnis.

In 2011, the youth of the Middle East sprang up in squares and streets across the region to protest injustice, call for better governance and demand jobs. However, sclerotic regimes proved incapable of reform. They either clung on to power or collapsed.

In Syria, the violent response of President Bashar al-Assad to the peaceful protests propelled the country's descent into civil war. He falsely proclaimed that he was the only bulwark against terrorism – and through his use of terror he made his prophecy come true. The United States and its allies called for Assad to go – but gave minimal support to force his departure. Segments of the Syrian opposition took up arms and sought external support in their domestic conflict. Turkey,

Saudi Arabia, the United Arab Emirates and Qatar provided weapons and funds to competing Sunni groups. Iran deployed its military advisers, as well as Shia militias from Lebanon, Iraq and Afghanistan, to prop up Assad's embattled regime. Russia supplied it with air power.

Iraq and Syria became one battlefield. The lands once renowned for prophets, laws and the first organized states became synonymous with sacralized conflict, evil and anarchy. Black-clad figures – poisonous seeds germinated by corrupt elites and nourished by external intervention – planted the flag of Daesh in cities, *souqs* and *saharas*. Ancient trading metropolises, centres of culture and cosmopolitanism, were reduced to rubble. Thousands were decapitated or enslaved in the wake of a caliphate intent on imposing an austere, intolerant, patriarchal monoculturalism – the fantasy of fundamentalists throughout the ages.

A US-led coalition mobilized to counter ISIS. In 2016 alone, the US dropped 24,287 bombs on Iraq and Syria. The military campaign crushed Daesh – but it also destroyed cities, killed thousands of innocent civilians, enabled the proliferation of militias, shored up autocratic regimes and facilitated Iran's development of land corridors across Iraq and Syria to Israel's borders.

The outflow of refugees and terrorism from the Middle East contributed to the British vote to leave the European Union and the rise of Donald Trump, whose tirades against Muslims and immigrants – and pledges to protect Americans from ISIS, the bastard child of the Iraq War – helped propel him to the White House.

Pax Americana is dying; America's post-Cold War triumph-alism crashed and burned in the Middle East. The very notion of an international community has waned and withered. The Iraq War was the catalyst of this decline; the failure to stop the bloodshed in Syria the evidence. The international system is transitioning from a unipolar to a multipolar world, with the Middle East one of multiple competing spheres of influence. A revanchist Russia seeks to weaken the US-led liberal world order by supporting Assad in Syria and flooding the European Union with refugees fleeing its aerial bombardment. A rising and dissatisfied China pursues 'One Belt, One Road' for the acquisition of minerals and energy, building infrastructure including oil and gas pipelines across the region. Middle Eastern powers, for their part, are adjusting and competing to shape a regional order in flux.

In a Time of Monsters relates my encounters with young people calling for reforms and others seeking revolution; insurgents willing to die for a cause and ordinary citizens simply seeking to live in security; pilgrims walking to Karbala and refugees headed for Germany; and Western diplomats trying to mediate peace overseas while polarization increases back home. It endeavours to contribute to a better understanding of a region in transition during a time of changing world order. In writing *In a Time of Monsters*, I hope to encourage others to explore the unknown, build bridges, and be fearless seekers of our common humanity.

If the book imparts any of the virtue and value of travel, then it has served its purpose.

In a Time of Monsters

The Middle East

Slavonski Brod

CROATIA
BOSNIA
& HERZ.
★ Sarajevo
ITALY
★ Belgrade
SERBIA

★ Skopje
FYROM
● Idomeni
Thessaloniki ●
Istanbul

★ Ankara

TURKEY

GREECE
★ Athens

Black Sea

Sidi Bou Said
Tunis ★ ● Carthage
Kairouan ● ● Hammam Sousse
TUNISIA ● Gargour
● Jerba
Tataouine ●
★ Tripoli

Mediterranean Sea

HATAY
● Apaydin
Antakya
SYRIA ● Palmyra
R. Euphrates

★ Damascus
Zaatari ●
Jerash ● ★ Amman
JORDAN

Alexandria ●
Cairo ★

LIBYA

EGYPT

Med

CHAD

R. Nile

Red Sea

SUDAN

● Meroe
Musawarat ●
Omdurman ● ★ Khartoum

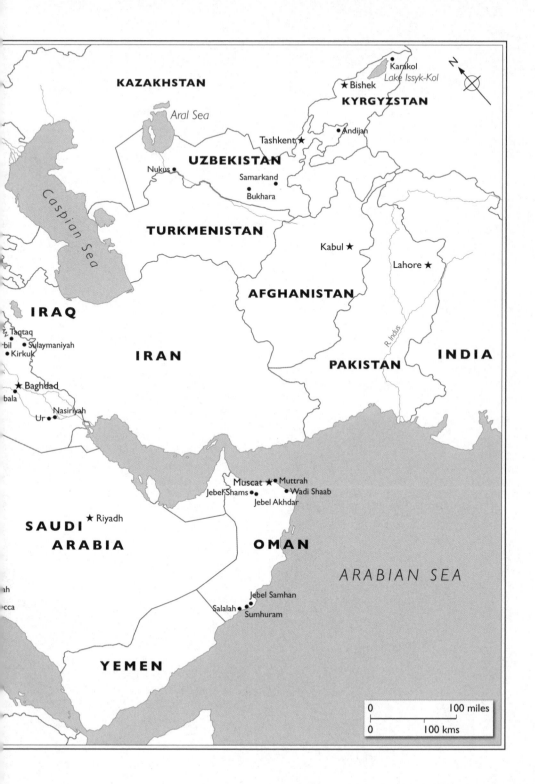

What had it all been for?

…how does it feel?
To be on your own, with no direction home
A complete unknown

Bob Dylan

I had not told anybody I was coming home.

There were no direct flights from Baghdad, so I hung out for a few days in Istanbul before flying on to London. I unlocked the front door of my house in Battersea and walked straight over the mountain of mail. The air was musty and stale. I opened the shutters in the living room to let in the light, and then threw open the back door for fresh air. I walked around the house, taking in the black-and-white photos of the Old City of Jerusalem, the rugs that I had brought back from Afghanistan, the prints from Egypt and Yemen, the Armenian pottery, the Moroccan tagine and the books stacked on the shelves. This was my home, full of my belongings and the mementos I had collected in faraway places.

The house was neglected and cold. But it felt safe. A refuge after years working in war-torn Iraq.

I texted Daniel Korski that I had just got back. Korski was born in Denmark to Polish Jewish refugees, had long since made London his base and had been involved in initiatives to stabilize countries post-conflict, including in Iraq and Afghanistan. He invited me to meet up with him that night at a pub in Notting Hill. So, a couple of hours later, I was drinking wine and deep in discussion with Korski and his friend, Tom Tugendhat, an army officer. Conversation was easy and animated – we had our wars to talk about and government policy to chide.

At the end of the evening, Tom gave me a ride across London on the back of his bike. Giggling and drunk, I managed to cling on to his waist as we cycled down the Portobello Road and into Hyde Park, past the memorial to Princess Diana and along the Serpentine. He dropped me off at the bus stop near Wellington Arch.

The next morning, I went to my local Sainsbury's supermarket to stock up on food. What did I want to eat? I didn't know. I hadn't cooked myself a meal in years. Did I want full-fat, half-fat or skimmed milk? Did I want free-range, corn-fed, organic or caged eggs? Did I want white, brown, wheat, wholegrain, thin-, medium- or thick-sliced bread? Marmite. I wanted Marmite. And at least with Marmite I didn't have to choose between different brands – there was only one. And Heinz beans. I would eat Marmite on toast, beans on toast and boiled egg on toast until I felt more inclined to cook.

*

In the weeks after my return, I was not sleeping well. I would wake up anxious in the middle of the night. I had no job, no income, no direction.

I took an inventory of my situation. I was in good health. I had a house to live in – and some savings to live off. I had friends. But the only people I connected to were those who had been to war. Here in London, I was bored. No one needed me. I had nothing to do.

I had no idea what I wanted to do next.

*

Most of my adult life had been spent in the Middle East. I fell in love with the region the first time I set foot in it, aged eighteen. I found something there that was lacking in the West. The warmth, the interconnectedness, the sense of belonging, the history.

It was in the Middle East that I discovered a sense of purpose, a passion for promoting peace.

My interest in the region had been sparked during a gap year spent working on a kibbutz in Israel. The secularism and socialism of the kibbutz was a stark contrast to the Christianity and conservatism of Dean Close, the British boarding school in Cheltenham that I had attended on scholarship. While by the 1980s many kibbutzim had become privatized, Kfar Menahem still held on to the vision of its founders.

I was assigned to work in the cowshed. I got up at dawn to milk cows, and at night I gathered around the campfire with young people from all over the world, discussing the meaning of life and how to bring about world peace. To me, it appeared an ideal community, where people from different backgrounds lived in harmony, with each person contributing what they could and receiving full board and lodging in return. I observed how, in a safe and equitable environment, people of different cultures could co-exist. The experience – at such an impressionable age – turned me into a humanist. Having been accepted to read Classics at Oxford, I changed course to Middle East Studies at the end of my first term, when the first Palestinian intifada broke out.

I spent the nineties in Jerusalem working in support of the Middle East peace process, managing projects on behalf of the British Council with the aim of building up the capacity of the Palestinian authority and fostering relations between Israelis and Palestinians. But by 2001, the Oslo Accords faltered and then failed, and the second intifada was in full swing. The projects I had been working on closed down, and I returned to the UK.

Although opposed to the 2003 Iraq War, I responded to the request of the British government for volunteers to administer the country after the invasion. I wanted to go to Iraq to apologize to Iraqis for the war, and to help them rebuild their country. My assignment was only supposed to be for three months – but it ended up spanning seven years. I found myself governing the province of Kirkuk, and then going on to serve as the political adviser to the top leaders in the US military.

While I had gone out to Iraq in June 2003 on secondment from the British Council, to continue working there I had to resign from my permanent and pensionable job and move on to short-term consultancy contracts – initially with the UK's Department for International Development, and then, after the British government withdrew its forces and lost interest, with the United States Army. And so on my return to the UK in September 2010, I was no longer part of any organization.

No one in British officialdom showed any interest in me or what I had been doing. As a civilian returning from war, there was no parade or band – or even a debriefing.

I did not feel any real sense of homecoming. London was alien to me. I could not cope with congested streets and overcrowded shops. I jumped at loud noises. I looked for escape routes. I was hyper-aware, constantly scanning for suspicious-looking people. With so many different styles and cultures in London, I could not tell who looked out of place. Many people looked odd to me – some very odd!

I found it hard to concentrate or to sit still. I tried reading books, and my eyes went over the lines, page by page, but I retained little. When I reread a paragraph, I had no recollection of having seen it before.

I searched the Internet for news of Iraq. I sent emails and text messages via Viber to Iraqi friends, eager to hear from them, to check that they were still alive, to tell them I was missing them.

I felt like an Iraqi exile, yearning to be back in Baghdad.

*

Every morning, I jogged around Battersea Park. On one occasion, as I was stretching after my run, I spotted a young man with two prosthetic blade-runner legs. He had the upright demeanour of a soldier, so I approached him.

'Hey, how did you lose your legs?' I asked casually, as if it were no big deal.

'I stood on a bomb,' he responded, while miming the explosion with his hands.

'Iraq or Afghanistan?'

It had been in Helmand, Afghanistan. The province that had taken the lives and limbs of numerous British soldiers and US marines. I told him I had served in Afghanistan in 2006 with ISAF (NATO's International Security Assistance Force), and in Iraq before and after. We shook hands and introduced ourselves. He told me his name was Harry Parker, a captain in the Rifles regiment.

After we'd been chatting for a while, he asked if I had ever met his dad, General Nick Parker. I had not. But we soon realized that we had someone in common: his father's close friend, General Sir Graeme Lamb, the former head of the SAS. 'Lambo', as he was generally known, had retired to the countryside. But he had got in contact with me on my return to make sure I was doing OK and we had met up for a drink. He'd told me all about Harry and how well he was coping with his injuries. And here in Battersea Park, by chance, Harry and I had met.

Harry told me he was trying out his new running legs. It was not easy to balance on them at the beginning. It took time, he explained, as he rocked back and forth. His eyes sparkled, and he was quick to smile, masking the pain and suffering he had been through.

'When you see Lambo,' I said, 'tell him I beat you running!'

Harry grinned. In previous years, a mixture of awkwardness and embarrassment would have deterred me from speaking to someone with prosthetic legs. I would not have had any connection to them, would not have known what to say. But now, all around me, I saw veterans of our wars, returning reshaped by their experiences, many confident and proud but some as fragments of their former selves. It was veterans I could relate to the most.

When I got home from the park that day, the tears started to pour down my face. And then I broke into deep sobs.

What had our wars been for?

*

I continued to mope around at home, wondering how I was going to find new purpose, to rekindle my passion for life, to feel part of something bigger than myself.

My tried-and-tested method of rebooting was to go on a trip. I had been interested in travel for as long as I could remember. I loved the research, the poring over guidebooks and examining maps. As a child, my imagination had been sparked by Tolkien's *Lord of the Rings*, photos in the *National Geographic*, and the memoirs and biographies of adventurers who had sought the sources of rivers or scaled uncharted peaks.

Travelling solo to distant lands was the ultimate challenge. I'd started off with trips of two to four weeks, and built up to journeys that lasted months – then, after university, years. Each time I set out, I felt sick with anxiety. But with experience, I grew more confident in embracing uncertainty and coping with whatever was thrown at me.

I knew I needed to get away from the UK. I needed a distraction, to go somewhere that promised adrenaline and adventure, new places and faces. So I approached the Sudanese embassy in St James's in London for a visa. During my interview, the consular official asked me why I wished to visit his country. The embassy did not receive many requests for tourist visas, as Sudan was under international sanctions and the UK government's travel advice did not encourage visits.

It did not seem appropriate to confess that I was bored, bitter and twisted – and that Sudan promised escape and escapades. I responded that I had read *Season of Migration to the North* by the Sudanese novelist Tayeb Salih, and wished to visit the homeland of the great author. The consular official smiled, and stamped a visa into my passport.

Two months after my return from Baghdad, I packed a small red rucksack, walked out my front door and got on a plane to Khartoum.

*

Bilad as-Sudan, the Land of the Blacks. Here was a country of dust and danger, of blue skies and yellow sands, a place I had never visited before but which in so many ways felt familiar. My senses were reawakened by the sound of the muezzin calling the faithful to prayer, the sight of merchants in markets and the smell of kebab. I felt alive again.

I went out to Omdurman, a city on the west bank of the Nile facing Khartoum, to visit the camel market. Hundreds and hundreds of camels for sale, along with sheep and goats, all congregated on the edge of the desert.

'Hello *khawaja*!' a trader shouted out to me. I was the only white person, and a source of great interest.

When I shot back a response in Arabic he invited me over, giving me a white plastic chair to sit on before pouring me a cup of well-sugared tea. 'Where are you from?' asked the trader, who was wearing a white *jalabiya* (thobe) and a white *imama* (turban).

'England. Britain,' I responded.

'Ah, Gordon Pasha,' he said, with a grin that revealed a half dozen teeth. 'We killed him!'

I smiled back at the reference to Gordon of Khartoum. When travelling, my identity was typically reduced to my nationality, with all the history that it evoked. In the late nineteenth century, London had appointed General Gordon – renowned for putting down the Taiping Rebellion in China during the Opium Wars – as Governor-General of Sudan, where he worked to suppress revolts and eradicate the local slave trade. In 1884 he was instructed by London to evacuate Khartoum, but instead hung on with a small force. Mohamad Ahmed bin Abd Allah, who had pronounced himself the Mahdi (the prophesized redeemer) and declared jihad against foreign rule, besieged Khartoum with his fundamentalist followers. General Gordon was hacked to death on the steps of the palace. The Mahdi ordered his head to be fixed between the branches of a tree.

After the Mahdi's death from typhoid six months later, his three deputies fought among themselves until one emerged as *al-khalifa*, the caliph, seeking to further the vision of the Mahdi through jihad – under the banner of black flags. In 1898, General Kitchener defeated the caliph at Omdurman, mowing down with Maxim guns the Mahdist soldiers who were armed only with spears, swords and old rifles. Avenging the murder of Gordon, Kitchener ordered the destruction of the tomb of the Mahdi and for his bones to be thrown into the

Nile. Winston Churchill, a young army officer at the time, was scandalized by Kitchener taking the Mahdi's head as a trophy.

The camels in the market each had a front leg tied back, to hobble them so that they could not wander off. The trader explained that some brokers were purchasing for the Egyptian market and others for the Gulf, where camel racing was very popular. He pointed to different dromedaries, extolling their virtues as he tried to gauge my interest. I asked if he had one that would carry me as far as London. 'We have camels that go on land and sea,' he enthused. 'I have one that is a very good swimmer. I give you a very good price.'

I was not tempted to make an offer – not even for a moment.

*

Khartoum seemed a safe city and I was happy to walk on my own along its streets, which were apparently planned out using the design of the Union Jack.

Setting out to explore, I ambled down Nile Street, parallel to the Blue Nile River. I eyed the presidential palace in which Omar al-Bashir had installed himself after he came to power in a military coup in 1989. Despite his indictment by the International Criminal Court for war crimes and crimes against humanity for the deaths of over 300,000 in Darfur, Bashir remained firmly ensconced in power, winning presidential elections yet again in 2010.

Although they had since fallen out, Bashir's key ally when he first came to power was the Islamist Hassan al-Turabi. It was Turabi who was credited with turning Sudan into an Islamic state – and a state sponsor of terror. In 1991, he established the Popular Arab and Islamic Congress, which attracted to its conference militants from across the world. At his invitation, Osama bin Laden took up residence in Khartoum, investing in local infrastructure and agriculture businesses – and in international terrorist networks. It was the 1998 bombings of US embassies in Tanzania and Kenya, killing 224 people, that marked the emergence of bin Laden and his al-Qaeda organization onto the world stage. In retaliation, President Bill Clinton ordered cruise missile strikes on the Shifa pharmaceutical factory in Khartoum (in the mistaken belief that it was making chemical weapons) and on al-Qaeda bases in Afghanistan, where bin Laden had relocated to.

I then spotted 'Gaddafi's Egg', the conspicuous five-star Corinthia Hotel whose construction the Libyan leader had funded. At one stage, Gaddafi had sponsored the 'Islamic Pan-African Legion' as part of a scheme to unify Libya and Sudan. Gaddafi went through pan-Arab, pan-Islam and pan-African periods during his four-decade rule of Libya. He controlled the country through fear, protected by a nasty security apparatus. He assassinated those he did not like, supported rebels in different countries and allowed the Irish Republican Army and Palestinian militants to train in camps in Libya.

Gaddafi's relations with the West deteriorated further after the 1988 bombing by Libyan officials of Pan Am Flight 103 over Lockerbie, killing 270 people. However, following the invasion of Iraq in 2003, he feared he might suffer the same fate as Saddam and so gave up the nuclear capabilities he had purchased from A.Q. Khan, a Pakistani nuclear scientist. In response, international sanctions against him were lifted.

A little further down the road was the People's Friendship Cooperation Hall, a massive structure that included a conference

room, theatre and banquet facility. It was a gift from China, the
largest investor in Sudan. China was building dams, railways,
roads, power plants and pipelines, and it was Sudan's biggest
trade partner. The first China–Sudan oil deals were signed in
1995 and the main oil refinery was a joint venture between the
two countries. Oil had long since replaced cotton as Sudan's
main commodity: 95 per cent of its exports were oil – sold
mostly to China.

I took a *raksha* – a three-wheeled taxi – to Souq al-Arabi, a
densely packed maze of stalls, carts and shops in the commercial
heart of Khartoum, south of the Great Mosque. 'Are you
Chinese?' the driver asked me. What a bizarre question, I
thought. I do not look in the slightest bit Chinese. By way of
explanation, the driver went on to tell me there were many
Chinese working in Sudan.

Wandering through the Arab market, I passed the gamut of
small businesses, all thronging with merchants and customers.
Every imaginable item could be found in these stalls, from
curtains to cement mix, table mats to musical instruments,
spices to saucers, gauze to gold. I spotted a number of Chinese
people. And lots of cheap Chinese produce.

*

Late in the afternoon on a Friday, I went back to Omdurman
to visit the tomb of Hamed al-Nil, a nineteenth-century Sufi
of the Qadiriyya order. Sufism, a mystical practice within
Islam, had first come to Sudan in the sixteenth century.
It was prevalent across the country, although rejected by
fundamentalist Muslims.

The smell of incense was strong in the air. Around a hundred Sufis were gathered in a large circle, swaying back and forth, clapping their hands and reciting *dhikr*, the remembrance of Allah, accompanied by drums and cymbals.

'*La ilaha illa allah* [There is no god but Allah],' the dervishes chanted, dressed in green, with long dreadlocked hair and beads wrapped around their necks.

'*La ilaha illa allah*,' the crowd, in white, intoned back.

The dervishes whirled around and around, robes flowing and limbs swinging, chanting and spinning in a hypnotic display of religious devotion. After about an hour or so, the mystical Muslims, smiling in ecstasy, reached a state of trance.

The spectacle was mesmerizing. It was only when the evening call to prayer rang out that the spell was finally broken.

*

After a few days in Khartoum, I set out northwards by car along the road that Osama bin Laden had built in the 1990s, passing convoys of military vehicles, trucks and armoured personnel carriers.

It took half a day to make the 150-mile trip north-east to the Meroe pyramids. That night, I camped out in a tent. The desert was freezing. I climbed fully clothed into my sleeping bag, poking my head out of the flap of the tent to look at the glittering sky. Millions of stars shone brightly, and I could see them in their full glory without pollution or electric lights obscuring my vision. It took me a few seconds to locate the Pole Star and the Plough. As I gazed up at the galaxy, my world telescoped out. I realized, at that moment, that the Iraq War would assume a different perspective with the passage of time and distance. Despite the destruction and devastation that humans inflicted, the universe was so much bigger than us.

The cold kept me awake most of the night. I rose before dawn and climbed on top of a sandbank to watch the sun rise over the desert, turning the dunes a rusty orange. There was not a soul in sight as I wandered among the pyramids. They had narrow bases and steep sides, some about twenty feet tall, others rising to almost a hundred feet. They were smaller than the ones in Egypt but much more numerous – there were over two hundred of them, separated into three sprawling groups. Built between 720 and 300 BC as tombs for Nubian royals, they had weathered the test of time until an Italian explorer decapitated forty of them in the 1830s in search of treasure. Idiot.

Back on the road, I stopped at Musawarat, the largest Meroitic temple complex in Sudan, dating back to the third century BC. The caretaker approached me and asked me where I was from. When I told him, he responded: 'Ah, Britain, you used to rule the world.' He showed me around, pointing out the elephant training camp, college and hospital. As he noted that a certain artefact was missing, he looked me straight in the eye with one eyebrow raised. 'It is in the British Museum,' he announced.

I winced. This then became a running gag between us as we walked around.

'This piece is missing,' he would say, pointing to another empty space.

'We're keeping it safe for you in the British Museum,' I responded with a grin.

He told me that his father had been the caretaker before him, and his grandfather before him. His family had lived there for generations.

Along the Nile between Aswan in Egypt and Khartoum, there are a few shallow stretches of river with white water, known as the cataracts. After leaving Musawarat, I stopped the car at the Sabaluqa Gorge, the sixth cataract. I lunched at a rudimentary restaurant on the riverbank, where fish was cooked over coals in front of me.

A boatman agreed, for a reasonable price, to take me out on his wooden vessel. It was painted blue and green, with a canopy that provided protection from the sun. I sat down towards the front on the wooden slats, while the boatman sat at the back next to the motor.

As we made our way through a granite canyon, I asked him if he had spent his whole life on this stretch of the river. Much to my surprise, he told me he had been a guest worker in Iraq for years, working in mortuaries. He remembered his time there fondly, and reminisced about the places he had visited: Najaf, Ramadi, Baghdad, Basra... He had been able to save money to send to his family back home, too. Iraq had been so modern, he told me, and he had loved it. He showed me photos of his sons, whom he had named Saddam, Qusay and Uday. Even his daughters were named after members of Saddam's family!

'Saddam was a good leader and did a lot for Iraq,' he claimed, before lamenting how the Iraqi president had turned *majnun* (crazy) in later years, invading neighbouring countries and killing so many of his own countrymen. The boatman compared him to Colonel Gaddafi, who he said had started out as *majnun* but had recently become more normal.

I thought about Gaddafi's meetings in his lavish Bedouin reception tent, his female bodyguards and the plastic surgery that had transformed his face. I was not sure at all that he had become less *majnun*.

*

Back in Khartoum, the British defence attaché, Colonel Chris Luckham, hosted me in the comfortable apartment he shared with two tortoises and his teenage son, who had tattooed on one arm 'My name is Ozymandias, king of kings'. Chris and I had served together in Afghanistan in 2006. He had taken up his post in Khartoum in 2009 and was facilitating security negotiations between the government of Sudan and the Sudan People's Liberation Movement, in order to implement the 2005 Comprehensive Peace Agreement to end the civil war that had caused the death of around two million people.

Chris was convinced that the problems of Sudan were resolvable. 'It's all about economics,' he told me. 'Sudan has potential: oil fields, the fertile Nile valley and Port Sudan, one of the five major access points to Africa. The challenge is the distribution of wealth – and migration to sustainable areas of Sudan.'

However, it seemed inevitable that north and south were headed towards separation. A referendum on the independence of the south was scheduled for 2011, vociferously supported by American evangelists, as well as film stars such as George Clooney.

On Remembrance Sunday, I accompanied Chris to the Commonwealth war cemetery in south-east Khartoum. Around two hundred people had gathered to pay tribute to the dead. It was a simple ceremony, held under bright blue skies. When it was over, I wandered the rows of immaculately kept graves, reading the names and dates from the two world wars. I reflected that while our soldiers continued to die overseas, these days their bodies were brought home – and not left buried in foreign fields.

On my last day in Sudan, Chris and I went out in his two-man kayak to where the White Nile meets the Blue Nile, the confluence known as *al-Mogran*. As we paddled, we kept close to the shores of Tuti Island, which supplies Khartoum with much of its fruit and greens. I had spent a day walking through the island's citrus orchards and around its fields of vegetables. Now I was viewing it from a different angle.

Khartoum means 'elephant trunk' in Arabic, and it was apparently so named due to the shape of the river around Tuti Island. From the water, I could not tell where in the trunk we were. I was tired of paddling and my arms were aching. Chris admonished me to paddle harder, warning me that if I did not do so, we would not get back to shore in time and I would miss my flight.

'Oh fuck,' I responded, somewhat sarcastically. I would have been quite happy to stay longer.

But the trip had done the trick. Sudan had acted as a defibrillator, bringing me back to life and reviving my interest in the world.

*

In January 2011, I testified in London before the Chilcot Inquiry into the Iraq War. I sat on one side of the table facing the commissioners: Sir John Chilcot, a career diplomat and senior civil servant who chaired the inquiry; Baroness Usha Prashar, a member of the House of Lords; Sir Roderic Lyne, a former ambassador; and two historians, Sir Lawrence Freedman and Sir Martin Gilbert. I felt quite apprehensive. It was my first interaction with British officialdom since leaving Baghdad. But it also meant that, at last, someone wanted to hear my views on the situation in Iraq, what had happened and why things had gone so wrong.

At the end of the session, Sir Lawrence Freedman approached me and handed me his business card. He proposed that I come teach about Iraq at King's College London where he was Professor of War Studies. But Harvard was in my sights by now. On my return from Khartoum, I had received notification that my application for a 'spring semester' fellowship was successful.

A few days after testifying, I touched down in the US at Boston Logan Airport. I stood in line at passport control and presented my British passport.

'Ma'am, why were you in Sudan?' the Transportation Security Administration (TSA) official inquired.

'I went there on holiday,' I responded.

'Ma'am, nobody vacations in Sudan.' He had already pressed a buzzer. Another humourless TSA official was quickly at the counter, instructing me to follow him. I was taken off to a special room to the side and told to sit. Mexicans, Muslims and me. Officials barked at us to remain silent and not to use our cell phones.

After thirty minutes or so, a security official returned with my passport. He leafed through the pages. 'Ma'am, what were you doing in Sudan?' he asked in a firm manner. I repeated that I had been on holiday. But he showed no interest in camel markets, whirling dervishes and Nubian pyramids.

He went on: 'Ma'am, why were you in Eye-rak?'

'I was working for the US military.'

'Ma'am' – his voice was now more aggressive – 'you are British!'

Oh God. How was I going to explain how I had come to work for the US military? It was a long story.

The official was most unfriendly. My stamps from faraway places were not ones that the TSA coveted – they were setting off alarm bells. I wondered if he had ever set foot outside the United States.

I presented all my Harvard documentation and he went off with it, presumably to show it to one of his superiors. Did I really now fit the profile of a terrorist? I began to have serious concerns that I was going to be denied entry into the US.

An hour later, I was released. They had checked with Harvard and googled me. Yes, I had been accepted on a fellowship. Yes, I had indeed worked with the US military in Iraq.

As to why I had gone to the Sudan? That was something that, for them, was left unexplained.

*

Harvard was heaven. There were six of us selected to be resident fellows at the Institute of Politics at the John F. Kennedy School of Government; to be interesting people about campus in order to inspire students to pursue careers in public service. I ran a series of workshops on the wars in Iraq and Afghanistan under the banner 'Post 9/11 wars – national security or imperial hubris?' The discussions on whether the wars had made us safer or created more enemies appealed to a wide range of students: those in the military, Muslims, Republicans and Democrats alike. General Odierno, my former boss in Iraq, came to speak to the students prior to taking up his post as chief of staff of the US Army. General Petraeus Skyped into the class from Kabul, where he was commander of ISAF.

Students were assigned to help me organize my events and social life. Jimmy was chubby, long-haired and bearded before he became lean, cropped and clean-shaven; he had a girlfriend before he turned to boys. And Gavin was a football player, tall and chiselled and as straight as can be. Our last evening together, at the end of the semester in early May, we went to see the musical *Hair* in Boston, and rushed up on stage at the end to dance to 'Aquarius/Let the Sunshine In'. It seemed a fitting send-off for Gavin, who signed up for the Marines the next day.

But while I was reliving student life in my forties in Cambridge, Massachusetts, great upheavals were taking place in the Middle East. In Tunisia, Mohamad Bouazizi's self-immolation pushed President Ben Ali to flee the country. In Egypt, mass protests led to President Mubarak's resignation and arrest. In Yemen, there were large-scale demonstrations calling for Ali Saleh to step down. In Libya, Gaddafi threatened to hunt people alley by alley – *zenga zenga* – which led to a UN Security Council resolution authorizing a no-fly zone over the country and 'all necessary measures' to protect civilians. In Bahrain, protestors gathered at the Pearl Roundabout. In Syria, thousands congregated in Damascus, Aleppo, Homs and Hama.

Across the Middle East, young people were going onto the streets to demand dignity and justice. They seemed to be speaking with one voice – in unity across the Arab world – angered at regimes that did little for their people and treated public goods as private possessions. Arabs were no longer saying they were hapless victims and that the West was to blame for all the ills afflicting their region. They were mobilizing – and using the Internet and social media to great effect. Dictators were fleeing in the face of popular protests rather than foreign intervention. The wall of fear was coming down, and at long last, positive changes appeared to be on the horizon for the Middle East, generated from inside the countries themselves.

A huge drama was playing out. And, even in the United States, I felt caught up in it. I followed it obsessively on the Internet and on TV, and posted incessantly about it on Facebook.

I yearned to experience the energy and camaraderie of the revolutions. And I wanted to find out whether democracy was really coming to the Middle East – and what influence, if any, the Iraq War had had on the region.

I decided to travel the Arab Spring.

CHAPTER 1

Hold your head up, you're an Egyptian!

Egypt

May 2011

'*Ash-sha'b yurid isqat an-nizam!*' the Egyptians chanted over and over again.

I joined in with them, cautiously at first and then more enthusiastically. '*Ash-sha'b yurid isqat an-nizam!* [The people want the fall of the regime!]' There was something so rebellious, so enrapturing, so empowering in those words. It was intoxicating.

It was May 2011, and although President Mubarak had been removed three months previously, Friday demonstrations had turned into a weekly ritual. Egyptians waved flags, their hands and faces painted in its colours of red, white and black. I read the slogans on the banners: 'Bread, freedom and social justice', 'Muslims and Christians – we are all Egyptians', 'The army and the people are one hand'.

In the circle in Cairo's Tahrir Square that day, protesters were angered by rumours that Mubarak was being offered amnesty on the condition that he returned the money he

had taken and also apologized to the Egyptian people. They
scoffed that his wife, Suzanne Mubarak, had only admitted
to assets worth $4 million, and they demanded she be jailed.
There were posters depicting Mubarak trying to run off with
the wealth of the Egyptian people; on another, Zakaria Azmi,
his chief of staff, was portrayed as a tortoise and accused of
'Corruption, blood and slow governance'; yet more showed
the entire Cabinet with vampire teeth.

Further details of the dishonesty of the old regime were
coming to light. The former tourism and housing ministers
were both in jail awaiting trial, accused of selling off plots of
prime real estate for virtually nothing to their cronies, who then
made millions. Businessmen close to the regime had received
government contracts and loans, while most Egyptians had
few economic opportunities.

A man, who I presumed from his beard was one of the
Ikhwan, the Muslim Brotherhood, led the crowd in chants.
Everyone joined in. Then it was the turn of a young clean-
shaven man, who chanted the revolutionary slogan 'Hold
your head up, you're an Egyptian'.

I moved towards another area. A young woman, wearing a
baseball cap and a black-and-white chequered keffiyeh scarf
around her neck, stood on a platform singing before a group
of female activists. There had been reports of horrible sexual
assaults in Tahrir Square, but this woman stood boldly in front
of the crowd. She shrieked the lyrics, inviting her audience
to shout back. Her confidence was extraordinary. What she
lacked in musical talent, she made up for in enthusiasm.

I looked around me. Mubarak's National Democratic Party

building had been gutted by fire. Guards now appeared to be protecting the red neoclassical Egyptian Museum, repository of some of the finest ancient treasures in the world. It had been broken into on 28 January 2011 – the 'Day of Rage' – with some of the displays damaged and artefacts looted. The fourteen-storey Mogamma building, which housed myriad government agencies, had been left untouched. I hated that place. As a student, I had once queued there for hours and hours, waiting for a permit to visit the Western Desert oases. A 1992 Egyptian movie *Al-irhab wal kabab* (*The Thief and the Kebab*) tells the story of a man who takes people in the Mogamma building hostage after trying unsuccessfully for weeks to complete paperwork. Everyone wants to know about the big political statement he's making, but there is none. He was simply hungry and wanted a kebab – and justice. I found it odd that this building had been spared. Perhaps it was because so many Egyptians were on the public-sector payroll.

I struck up conversation with the man standing next to me. 'The situation is much better since the revolution,' he told me. 'There is more freedom. No police knocking on doors in the night and taking people away.'

After years of passive compliance, the Egyptian people were no longer accepting their lot in life. It was they – not Western intervention – who had removed an autocratic regime. The power of the people.

Egypt, *Umm al-Dunya* (Mother of the World), was once more leading the region. New identities were being created. New friendships were being formed. In Tahrir Square, people helped each other: they collected the trash, they provided drinks, they administered first aid. I had never witnessed such a spirit in all the years that I had been visiting Egypt. They were fearless in their demands for dignity. And my heart was with them.

*

The British ambassador, Dominic Asquith, had kindly offered to host me during my stay in Cairo, after I emailed him asking if he might have time to meet. It was his last month in Egypt, and he was packing up.

I had first got to know Dominic in Baghdad in 2004, when we both lived in 'Ocean Cliffs', the name ironically bestowed on the trailer accommodation in an underground car park that protected us from incoming rockets. The great-grandson of British prime minister H.H. Asquith, Dominic certainly looked more at home in the substantial stone building in Cairo than a containerized housing unit in Baghdad.

Built in 1894, the ambassador's residence served as a reminder of Britain's former prestige and power. It was here that General Kitchener planned the expedition to the Sudan to avenge General Gordon's death. In fact, Dominic's desk was the very one he used. The bedroom assigned to me was where Churchill used to stay during his visits. It was larger than my whole house in London. And when I opened the shutters, I looked out upon the Nile.

Over dinner and wine, Dominic explained the events that had led to the revolution. Khaled Said, a young middle-class man with an interest in computing, had been arrested in a cybercafé in Alexandria by two detectives on 6 June 2010.

They smashed his head against a door, beat him to death and stuffed drugs down his throat. Photos of the battered body went viral. Dominic said that Egyptians had been furious that the police would no doubt escape with impunity. He pointed out that if such an end could come to an innocent-looking kid from Alexandria, then no Egyptian felt safe.

Shortly after the killing, Wael Ghonim, a Google marketing executive, set up a Facebook group called 'We are all Khaled Said'. Wael's postings, in colloquial Egyptian dialect, initially complained of police brutality. However, influenced by events in Tunisia, his postings started to call for action to bring about change in Egypt, urging people to gather in Tahrir Square on 25 January – National Police Day – to protest the police state. (National Police Day commemorates the attack on Ismailia police station by British forces on 25 January 1952, in which fifty policemen were killed. Six months later, on 23 July, the Free Officers Movement led by Mohamad Naguib and Gamal Abdel Nasser staged a coup that marked the Egyptian revolution. King Farouk was exiled, Egypt was declared a republic and the Brits were driven out.)

The British residence was located in the Garden City neighbourhood of Cairo, close to Tahrir Square. On 25 January, Dominic had watched thousands of Egyptians congregating. There were calls for the Minister of Interior to step down, complaints about the secret police making arrests, and demands for a higher minimum wage. Dominic had wandered into the square and spoken with some of the protestors. They had chanted the same slogans as the people in Tunisia, calling for the fall of the regime and for Mubarak to get on a plane like the Tunisian president Ben Ali. But they had not really expected to start a revolution, Dominic stressed.

However, when some demonstrators were killed in Suez, those in Cairo took the decision to continue going to Tahrir Square in order to honour their memory. Family members urged them to remain home and stay out of trouble, assuring them that their voices had been heard. But Mubarak responded by dispatching *baltagiyya* (thugs) – some of whom were on camels – to attack the protesters. His speeches to the nation came too late and were tone-deaf, showing how completely out of touch he was with public sentiment.

Anger increased and more people came to the square. From 2 February onwards, the protesters began in earnest to demand that Mubarak should go. The Muslim Brotherhood, who had not participated in the demonstrations at the start, turned out to man the barricades, pushing back the police, protecting the protestors and providing basic services. And thus the relationship between the Ikhwan and the secularists developed through a common cause in the square.

*

I really did not know what to make of what I was seeing in Egypt. I'd had a conflicted relationship with the country since my first visit – a year spent at the University of Alexandria studying Arabic as part of my Oxford degree. I had wonderful memories of visiting Siwa and oases in the Western Desert, of floating on a *felucca* down the Nile, of riding on horseback through palm groves to the pyramids, and of hanging out in the hippy resort of Dahab on the Sinai Peninsula.

However, by the end of that year I had concluded that our cultures were very different, and that when brought into contact they frequently clashed. There were, for example, the awful attitudes towards women. Over 90 per cent of women had been subjected to female genital mutilation – a practice that was supposed to discourage them from adultery. Total contempt was shown to me, and I was frequently humiliated. I had men rub up against me on buses, and hands thrust between my legs as I walked down the street.

Egyptians also asked me endless questions about the British author Salman Rushdie. At that time the Supreme Leader of Iran, Ayatollah Khomeini, had issued a fatwa calling for him to be killed for blasphemy for his novel *The Satanic Verses*. I responded that I respected Rushdie's right to express his views, even if I disagreed with them. Countless Egyptians argued back that no one had the 'right' to insult the prophet – and Rushdie should be punished by death.

But the greatest vitriol, I discovered, was directed at Jews and the 'Zionist entity' (as Israel was habitually referred to), despite the formal peace treaty Egypt had signed with its neighbour following the Camp David Accords of 1978. At bookstores, I saw covers with caricatures of Jews and swastikas, and copies of the *Protocols of the Elders of Zion*, a notorious anti-Semitic forgery about a Jewish plan to dominate the world.

Towards the end of my course in Alexandria, the most bizarre incident took place. Hans, a fellow student, and I had decided to drop in for a drink at the Radio Bar. Small and dingy, with smelly toilets, it was our regular haunt as it was downtown and served alcohol – a rarity in this highly conservative city.

Sometimes we would sit in the corner wearing monster masks, looking like aliens from another planet – which was exactly how we felt. But more often than not we would drink away our time discussing the crazy experiences of the day. On this particular afternoon, the bar was empty except for an overweight, middle-aged Egyptian sat in the corner on his own drinking beer.

'Hello, welcome,' he called out loudly to us in English when we entered. 'Where are you from?'

'England,' I responded.

'Germany,' Hans replied.

The Egyptian jumped to his feet, giving Hans a Nazi salute. 'Heil Hitler!' he blasted out excitedly. 'Hitler was a good man. He killed six million of them!' Hans had frequently received this sort of response in Egypt whenever he mentioned his nationality, but he still found it mortifying. A number of my Jewish relatives had died in the Holocaust. Before coming to Egypt, I had never heard anyone praise Hitler.

Hans and I tried to ignore him as we sat down at a table, ordered drinks and got stuck into our own conversation. But the Egyptian man had started to cough. And the coughing turned to choking. He collapsed, red in the face and gasping for breath. The barman rushed over to help. I suggested we lay him on the ground on his side in the recovery position.

'No! An Egyptian man does not lie on the ground!' the barman shouted at me animatedly. He and his assistant instead put a couple of chairs next to each other and laid the man on his back on top of them. Then the barman

proceeded to thump him on his chest, yelling repeatedly
'*Wahad Allah*!' One God. He pulled the man's ears hard.

By this stage, the man had gone strangely silent. I took his
pulse, checked his eyes and held a mirror to his mouth. I then
pronounced him dead.

'*Inna lillahi wa inna ilayhi raji'un* [We are all from Allah and
to him we return],' the barman declared. He and his assistant
debated what to do next, saying that they could not admit the
man had died in the bar.

Hans and I told them we would go to the nearby hospital to
notify medical staff so they could come and take the body away.
Hans turned the sign on the door to 'Closed' as we walked off
in shock. We returned about forty minutes later with a doctor
to find the sign on the door had been turned to 'Open'. We
went in. The place was full of customers.

Hans called the barman over and asked, 'Where's the body?'

'What body?' the barman responded, straight-faced. He then
went on to explain to the doctor that there had been a man who
had fainted but he had recovered and gone home. Hans and I
looked at each other, astounded. There was only one exit from
the bar – out the front of the building. They could not have put
the body in the toilets, because people were constantly going in
and out. So they must have put him in the kitchen, we reasoned.
While the barman and doctor talked, I walked to the back and
peered through the crack in the kitchen door. I could see the
body propped up against the fridge.

The doctor believed the barman and left. Hans and I headed
out to the waterfront. It was now dark. We stood in silence,
looking out at the sea.

And then we began to talk it through. An Egyptian man had died due to an unintended consequence of his interaction with us. If we had not gone to the bar that afternoon, then the Egyptian most likely would have finished his beer and gone home.

We guessed that, later that night, after everyone left, the barman and his assistant would take the corpse and dump it in the sea. The body would later wash up on the shore and his family would never know the circumstances of his death.

'Perhaps it was divine intervention?' Hans contemplated.

*

It was over twenty years since my student days in Egypt. Could the country really have changed so much, I wondered. Had globalization Americanized Egyptians? The young Egyptians in the square seemed so like the young Americans who had mobilized to elect Obama. Were they representative of the country as it was now, or was I only encountering educated elites? I needed to explore beyond Tahrir Square.

As the sun set and the call to prayer rang out once more across Cairo, I walked down the Corniche towards the Maspero television building (named after the French archaeologist who had been chairman of the Egyptian Antiquities Authority), to where the Copts were demonstrating. Egypt's Coptic community constitutes over 10 per cent of the population and is the largest Christian community in the Middle East, but its numbers are on the decline.

The central police, dressed in black, prevented the traffic from driving down the Corniche. A couple of Copts insisted on checking everyone walking down the street. I joined the women's line, got patted down and had my bag searched. Hundreds of Copts had gathered, some standing and holding big crosses, others lying on rugs on the ground. The area smelled of urine. There was none of the carnival spirit of Tahrir Square here. I took a photo and was immediately approached by two young men who tried to stop me.

'Why are you here?' one asked me.

'I'm visiting Cairo to see the country after the revolution,' I responded.

'Do you know who we are and why we are demonstrating?' the other man quizzed me.

'You're Christians and you're angry with the Salafists. Your church has been burned down.' I had read about it in the newspaper. Salafists – ultra-conservative Muslims – were being blamed.

They nodded, satisfied with my response. The Ministry of Interior and numerous police stations had been trashed during the days of the revolution, as people lashed out at symbols of oppression. But Egyptians were so used to living within a police state, they were now worried about increased crime and lawlessness and complained of chaos. Traffic was more congested, with less police to control it. And it was the Copts who were the most nervous about these changes.

'Things were much better under the old regime. Never had a church been burned down before. Since the fall of the regime, seven churches have been burned down,' the first man said. He looked and sounded scared. Rumours were rife, increasing the sense of fear and suspicion.

'You must let the outside world know what is happening.'

He then told me that he suspected that some members of the old regime were trying to create problems between Muslims and Christians to show that things were better before and that they were needed again to restore order.

The second man added that he wanted the army to do more to protect Christians. The other Copt scoffed at this, saying the head of the military, General Tantawi, was in bed with the Salafists.

The next day, I stumbled across another demonstration near Tahrir Square. Around a hundred bearded men were holding up posters demanding the release of Sheikh Omar Abdel-Rahman from US custody. The Egyptian police and army prevented the crowd from moving any closer to the US embassy.

I asked one of the demonstrators who Sheikh Omar was. He responded that he was a blind old sheikh who had served eighteen years in solitary confinement in the United States. He did not mention that the sheikh had been associated with the terrorist organizations the Islamic Group and Egyptian Islamic Jihad – and had been jailed for his role in inspiring the 1993 bombing of the World Trade Center in New York.

Back at the British ambassador's residence, I expressed my surprise at all the beards I was seeing. Dominic explained that, since the removal of Mubarak, many Egyptians had grown beards, no longer afraid to openly show their religiosity. I was not yet able to discern from the style of beard who was religious, who was Islamist and who was just hip.

We discussed the decades-long struggle in Egypt between authoritarian rulers and Islamists. Dominic told me that, among Egyptians – particularly those of an older generation – there lingered a nostalgia for Gamal Abdel Nasser and the pride he had made them feel, despite his huge policy failures. The charismatic colonel had become president in 1956, and one of his first actions was to nationalize the Suez Canal. Britain coordinated an attack with France and Israel to seize control of the canal and overthrow Nasser. However, the United States condemned the invasion and pressured Britain and France to accept a United Nations ceasefire and a humiliating retreat. It was an inglorious ending to Britain as a great power.

Nasser's *Sawt al-Arab* (Voice of the Arabs) radio broadcasts had connected Arabic speakers across national boundaries. With his anti-imperial credentials and calls for Arab solidarity, he was the champion of Arab nationalists across the region, inspiring the (short-lived) union of Egypt and Syria in the United Arab Republic as well as the overthrow of the Hashemite monarchy in Iraq in 1958. But the massive defeat of the Arab armies by Israel in 1967 was a huge embarrassment, and weakened the appeal of Arab nationalism.

The main competition to the secular Arab nationalism espoused by Nasser, Dominic elaborated, came from the Muslim Brotherhood, who claimed that 'Islam is the solution'. Founded in Cairo in 1928 by an Egyptian schoolteacher named Hassan al-Banna, the Ikhwan asserted the role of religion in society, condemning the Westernizing and secularizing tendencies of the political elite. Oppressed and pushed underground, the views of the Ikhwan were further radicalized in the 1950s and

1960s by a charismatic Egyptian, Sayyid Qutb, who became convinced that it was impossible to work within the existing political system, and that revolutionary politics and armed struggle were necessary in order to achieve social justice in the Muslim world. He had spent two years in America, which left him with contempt for Western materialism and what he saw as the dearth of spiritual values.

After members of the Ikhwan attempted to assassinate Nasser in 1954, Qutb was jailed, tortured and sentenced to fifteen years of hard labour. In prison, he wrote *Milestones*, a radical commentary on the Quran and a call for the promotion of a genuine Islamic society. Qutb categorized Muslims as living in *jahiliyya*, a state of ignorance, having abandoned God's eternal message. Qutb believed that Islam was the only route to human freedom. He argued that when the state itself was perceived to be effectively in the hands of 'unbelievers' – defined as unrighteous, irreligious, corrupt, arrogant puppets of the West – then nearly all means of overcoming the state were justified, including armed struggle (jihad). The only valid laws were God's laws, as enshrined in Sharia. Qutb was released from jail in 1964 but the following year he was re-arrested for conspiring against the Egyptian state, convicted and executed.

Dominic stressed that the leaders of the Muslim Brotherhood in Egypt had dissociated the movement from Qutb's more radical theses and reverted to al-Banna's less revolutionary outlook. They had adopted a gradualist and non-violent perspective, achieving a modus vivendi with the Egyptian state. And they had developed a large network around the country. 'Where the government is not,' Dominic said, referring to slums and rural areas, 'there the Ikhwan are.' Many of their members were doctors and engineers who had found in political Islam a way to embrace modernity without having to abandon their values and beliefs. However, Qutb's ideas had gone on to influence successive generations of radical Islamists.

When Anwar Sadat succeeded Nasser in 1970, he sought to move Egypt away from Soviet-style, state-led socialism towards Western capitalism, and opened the door to foreign direct investment. But while the new *infitah* policy enabled those close to the regime to become rich, it failed to create a free market economy and was met by resistance from those whose wages remained stagnant.

Sadat was a devout Muslim. He rehabilitated the Ikhwan as a social and religious movement, using the Islamists to balance the leftists in the country. But radical Islamists condemned him for failing to implement Sharia, for being a tyrant, and for being a traitor by making peace with Israel at Camp David. He was assassinated on 6 October 1981 – at the annual victory parade of the Egyptian army to commemorate the 1973 war – by an officer who was secretly a member of Egyptian Islamic Jihad and who proclaimed 'I have killed the Pharaoh!'

Hosni Mubarak, Sadat's vice president, assumed the presidency and continued with Egypt's integration into the global economy. But the subsequent structural adjustment programme, mandated by the International Monetary Fund (IMF), scaled back the public sector, leading to a decrease in jobs and services. The Ikhwan filled the vacuum.

Like his predecessors, Mubarak kept close tabs on the Muslim Brotherhood and their more radical offshoots. Dominic believed the president let the Ikhwan expand in order to convince Western governments that they were a real threat and that he needed to be allowed a freer rein to crack down on all dissent. As with other authoritarian rulers in the region, Mubarak constantly claimed that the choice was him or the Islamist terrorists. Fear that the Islamists were the only alternative to authoritarian rule had led the middle class, up until now, to support the status quo.

'I am hoping that the Arab uprisings will show that a third way is possible,' I said.

Dominic raised an eyebrow. He was not overly optimistic, he told me, pointing out that the attempts to forge a consensus between the disparate groups were going nowhere. There seemed to be few leaders with stature and foresight who were willing to make compromises and bridge divides. The Ikhwan were by far the best-organized party in Egypt, established across the country and also dominant in professional associations. To assuage the fears of others, they had promised they would not seek the presidency. Meanwhile the Salafists, who had not taken part in the revolution and who had hitherto refused to participate in politics, were setting up a new political party, al-Nour.

Secular groups were divided and splintered. They had been able to mobilize against Mubarak, but they lacked the organization and leadership to effectively coalesce around an agenda for the future. They were concerned about the influence that the Ikhwan would have over the constitution, and were fearful of the Muslim Brotherhood's demand for Sharia to be the only source of legislation. Secularists were worried that the Ikhwan would sweep to power through elections, and 'democracy' would be reduced to 'one person, one vote, one time'.

Dominic had spoken to several Egyptians who confessed their hope that the elections would be delayed. They looked towards the military – who had taken 'temporary' power – as the guardian of the state. But Dominic told me he was concerned that the longer the military remained in power by delaying the elections, the more difficult it would be to shift them and establish civilian rule.

*

I set out to visit old haunts. I walked from Tahrir Square towards Talaat Harb Square (named after the economist who founded the Bank of Egypt), passing landmarks that brought back so many memories. Felfela was still serving *fuul* (fava beans) and *taamiya* (falafel). Groppi's tea room had seen better days. I had once sat there at a table next to Egypt's most famous writer, Naguib Mahfouz, whose accounts of life in Cairo had revealed so much that I did not see. The Madbouly bookstore still sold his work. I passed endless rows of shoe shops. Everything looked so familiar. Little had changed in two decades.

I turned right and walked until I reached al-Azhar Mosque. Completed in 972, it had once been regarded as the seat of Islamic learning. But since its nationalization under Nasser, it had been brought under government control and no longer functioned as a space for critical thinking. Its reputation had long since declined.

I took off my shoes, donned a hijab and entered. An old man sitting in the courtyard asked me where I was from, and then went on to recount the visit of Prince Charles to al-Azhar and how he had made a very positive impression due to his respect for and knowledge of Islam. The old man then told me he had watched Prince William's wedding on TV.

I walked barefoot through the carpeted halls, and came across a young man sitting reading, with an English book on Islam to his side. I greeted him and he responded, introducing himself as Ahmed. He was in his mid-twenties with a long beard, and said he was happy to talk about Islam with non-Muslims. I asked him what his father thought of him having such a beard. He giggled and admitted that his father was concerned. Every time he visited home, he shaved off his beard! Ahmed told me he was deeply religious but not a Salafi; he did not follow any particular clique. We got on to the subject of Islam and women. He told me, with a cheeky smile, that women needed to pray separately from men, as men would be distracted by the sight of women's bottoms sticking up in the air when their foreheads touched the ground.

'Do you believe in Allah?' he asked. I replied that I did believe in some greater essence. Then he asked whether I considered the Quran as the direct revelation of Allah. I avoided answering. To doubt the divine origin of the Quran was to question the existence of God.

'Would Allah put us on Earth without a guidebook?' Ahmed continued. I left it as a rhetorical question and again did not respond. I liked Ahmed, and did not want to upset him. He appeared a devout, well-educated and open-minded Muslim. And quite funny.

I left al-Azhar and stopped for lunch at a restaurant in the bazaar of Khan al-Khalili. I ordered a plate of *fuul*, which came with bread and pickles, and a glass of sweet tea. Revitalized, I wandered through Islamic Cairo. At Bab Zuwayla, the massive tenth-century gate, I detoured into the *qasaba* and walked down the street of the tentmakers. A few men called out to me, inviting me to look at their brightly coloured cushion covers, bedspreads and huge tents. 'No charge for just looking!'

I walked through the twisting narrow alleys of al-Darb al-Ahmar to the Citadel, passing shops selling drums, copper, brass, shisha pipes, baskets, tools and spices. Everything was exactly as I remembered it. The same smells and sounds. I was sure that a photo of me walking this route ten years ago, or twenty years ago, would reveal the same stores being run by the same people, or their fathers and grandfathers.

I looked for a café in which to watch Obama deliver a speech on the Middle East from Washington. Most TVs were showing local sports or soap operas. But I finally found one tuned to the US president, with simultaneous translation into Arabic. I sat down next to the one other person watching it.

'The greatest untapped resource in the Middle East and North Africa is the talent of its people. In the recent protests, we see that talent on display, as people harness technology to move the world,' Obama said. He went on: 'And now we cannot hesitate to stand squarely on the side of those who are reaching for their rights, knowing that their success will bring about a world that is more peaceful, more stable, and more just.'

When Obama had finished, I asked the man next to me what he thought. He responded: 'They were good words – but we have seen little action from his last set of good words.' He was referring to the address Obama had delivered in June 2009 at Cairo University, calling for a new beginning between the US and the Muslim world based on mutual interest and respect; and promising to support the peace process between Israel and the Palestinians, to end the war in Iraq and to invest in economic opportunities, education and innovation.

For decades, the United States had supported autocratic regimes in the Middle East to maintain the status quo, fearful of the alternative. Now people in the region were rising up against those same regimes, and Obama wanted to be on the right side of history. It was clear that Mubarak would not be able to regain control of the country. Against the counsel of his advisers, in particular Hillary Clinton, Obama had decided to push for Mubarak's early exit after watching the Egyptian president's defiant televised speech to the nation. He did not want to see the dreams of young activists, such as the Google executive Wael Ghonim, crushed. But he harboured no illusions that the transition would be easy.

The man watching with me, who told me he was an accountant, liked Obama and described him as a 'good man'. 'But,' he went on, 'he is only one man – and he will not be able to change America.' He then reflected for a moment and said Obama was 'merely an employee, carrying out the orders of Congress'. He said that the United States had controlled Egypt through its puppet, Mubarak. Now Egyptians would determine their own future. The US was becoming increasingly irrelevant, he continued. It could not keep running around the world knocking people on the head, behaving as the global policeman. That was not good behaviour.

In his speech, Obama had talked of how the US had killed Osama bin Laden earlier in the month. The accountant turned to me and asked why Obama had mentioned him. 'Bin Laden is not representative of Islam,' he said. Then he told me he was not optimistic about the future, because Egypt was going through a popular revolution with no leaders or political parties to take it forward.

Seeking a place of tranquillity away from the bustle of the city, I jumped in a taxi and asked to be taken to Ibn Tulun Mosque. The taxi driver complained about the economic situation. He told me that if he was lucky, he could earn around $80 a month. Lack of money was putting strain on his relationship with his wife. They lived in cramped conditions with their immediate and extended families.

He wanted the energies of the new regime to be focused on investment. He explained that the real issue was poverty. The population was growing at a rapid rate, with an estimated 12 million living in Cairo. Young people could not afford to get married, and there was insufficient housing. Corruption was endemic, as salaries were so low. To make matters worse, tourism, which normally constituted around 13 per cent of the GDP, had dropped dramatically since the revolution. All this was putting tremendous pressure on Egyptians.

The driver dropped me at Ibn Tulun, the oldest mosque in Cairo – and my favourite. I crossed the large courtyard, then climbed up the minaret using the outer spiral staircase and stood staring out across the city. Ahmad ibn Tulun, born a

Turkic slave in Baghdad, had gone on to become the governor of Egypt and founder of the Tulunid dynasty. Missing his homeland, he modelled the mosque's minaret on the Malwiya Minaret in the Iraqi city of Samarra, which I had climbed a few years previously. Like Ibn Tulun, I was homesick for Iraq.

As I gazed across the sprawling city, I reflected on my conversations during the day. When I'd asked one shopkeeper how he was finding life in the new, post-revolution Egypt, he interrupted me by saying: 'Excuse me, madam, Egypt is a very old country. Our civilization goes back seven thousand years!' His response kept reverberating in my head. When I posed the same question to the muezzin of al-Hakim Mosque, he looked me in the eye and said, 'It even took Allah a week to make the world. It is going to take Egyptians much longer to bring about real change!'

I had not come across any of the revolutionary fervour and excitement I'd felt in Tahrir Square. Instead, I had encountered Egyptians who were not caught up in the events that were being amplified in the media and who were struggling just to make ends meet.

*

On my last day in Egypt, I climbed up Mokattam Hill to the medieval Islamic fortification that housed the military history museum. Display after display depicted Egypt's wars, and so many of them were with Israel. It helped explain how the military had achieved its elevated role in Egyptian society – a role that went well beyond the realm of security. Military industries and holdings constituted a significant percentage of the Egyptian economy. And military men had ruled Egypt from 1952 on.

At the museum, I saw a large statue of Mubarak, and paintings depicting him in military settings. It was the first time I had seen any image of him since my arrival in Cairo. In every office and shop in the country, a nail in the wall marked the place in which his portrait had once hung. No one knew whose photo would go up next.

But I was hopeful that the future would be better than the past. The optimism of the young Egyptians in Tahrir Square was infectious. And they had Tunisia to look to for inspiration.

CHAPTER 2

Dégage!

Tunisia

June 2011

I strode down Avenue Habib Bourguiba, named in honour of Tunisia's first president, past the cafés packed with Tunisians sipping espressos. I could have believed I was strolling along the Champs-Élysées in Paris if it weren't for the barbed wire and tanks. Graffiti proclaimed *dégage* (get out) and *vive la révolution* (long live the revolution).

Passing the Porte de France, I moved seamlessly between Europe and the Middle East. I wandered through the Medina of Tunis, feasting my eyes on the stores selling jewellery, pouffes, leather goods and perfumes. The shop owners greeted me with calls of '*Bonjour madame!*'

One merchant tried to entice me to buy perfume. Jasmine was for the house, he said; orange was for the bath. As I sat drinking mint tea, he advised vigilance as I navigated the market. 'Be careful of your handbag. Always carry it in front of you. There are many thieves in the narrow alleys. *Zenga zenga!*' He made snaking movements with his arms.

Laughing, I asked, 'Do Tunisians actually say *zenga zenga?*'
I had not heard the expression until Colonel Gaddafi used
it in a televised address a few weeks earlier, calling on his
supporters, from a balcony in the Libyan capital of Tripoli,
to fight those protesting his forty-two-year rule.

'We took it from Gaddafi,' he answered me, smiling. 'He
gave that speech about hunting down enemies, alley by alley,
zenga zenga.' He raised his arms above his head, imitating the
leader of Tunisia's eastern neighbour. The catchphrase had
gone viral thanks to an Israeli in Tel Aviv who'd used clips of
Gaddafi's speech, with him raising one arm in the air while
pounding his other fist on the podium, to create an electro
song which he'd uploaded onto YouTube. In the bottom
corners of the screen was a woman dancing in a tank top and
skimpy shorts, representing Gaddafi's penchant for female
bodyguards.

I walked on until I reached the Zitouna Mosque, the
oldest in Tunis, at the centre of the Medina. I sat down on
the cool flagstones, appreciating the peace and quiet after
the melee of the market. The mosque once hosted one of
the most renowned universities in the history of Islam. It
was founded in 737, more than two hundred years before
Cairo's al-Azhar University. Its most famous graduate was
Ibn Khaldun, who was one of the greatest philosophers of
the Middle Ages – and a great traveller. Born in Tunis in
1332, he wrote the *Muqaddimah,* one of the first works to
deal with social sciences and the philosophy of history. His
central concept was *asabiyyah,* or tribalism, the bond of
cohesion and solidarity that could bring a certain group to

power. He observed that a group generally ruled for three generations before becoming so corrupt that it lost support and was replaced by another.

*

The next day, I climbed into the back seat of a taxi with Greta Holtz, the US deputy assistant secretary of state for the Middle East, who I had come to know well in Iraq. The driver quickly struck up conversation with us.

'All Tunisians are very happy that Ben Ali is gone,' he declared. 'We are proud that we brought about our revolution ourselves – and peacefully.' He noted that Mubarak, who had ruled for thirty years, had tried to cling on to power in Egypt, cracking down violently on the protestors. In contrast, Ben Ali had fled Tunis on 14 January 2011, ending his twenty-three-year rule without bloodshed.

Ben Ali had become president back in 1987, when he deposed Habib Bourguiba in a bloodless coup, declared him senile, unfit to rule, and incapable of addressing the problems facing the country. It was Bourguiba, president since independence in 1957, who had built up Tunisia's strong bureaucracy, promoted women's rights (including birth control), heavily invested in education to ensure universal literacy, and separated religion and state. But he had stayed in power too long – over thirty years. And criticism of his rule had become widespread. Ben Ali promised change. He had joined the Tunisian army in 1958, training in France at the military academy of Saint-Cyr and at the artillery school at Châlons-sur-Marne and studying engineering in the United States. He became head of Tunisian

military security, then served as the military attaché at the
Tunisian embassy in Morocco prior to being appointed head
of national security, interior minister and prime minister. As
president, Ben Ali won re-election in 1989, 1994, 1999, 2004
and 2009 – each time by a massive margin.

'It is clear that Ben Ali was an agent of the United States,' the
driver went on. 'He kept the Islamists at bay for America, and in
return the US kept him in power.' Greta looked at me and rolled
her eyes. She was used to people in the region claiming that the
US controlled everything and was responsible for all their ills.

The driver dropped us off in a middle-class neighbourhood
of Tunis, at the home of Radhia, a retired local embassy staffer.
Greta had previously spent three years working at the embassy
in Tunis, and was pleased to be back visiting the country. Radhia
and her daughter, Dima, were delighted to see Greta again,
greeting her like a relative. Soon we were seated around the
table, drinking tea and eating cake. After the initial catch-up
on family news, the conversation turned to the monumental
events taking place in Tunisia.

Dima was a judge in her thirties. She described how on
17 December 2010, in the town of Sidi Bouzid, Mohamad
Bouazizi had doused himself with petrol and set himself
alight. The twenty-five-year-old Tunisian fruit and vegetable
vendor had been protesting the confiscation of his produce
and harassment by local officials.

She then explained that Bouazizi was one of many who worked
in the informal economy without insurance or healthcare. But
his act of defiance had sparked a revolution, galvanizing young
people to change the status quo. Using Facebook and Twitter,

they organized and mobilized to demand dignity. The youth were better educated than their parents, and increasingly connected with the rest of the world. Through the Internet, they saw how people in other societies lived. And they learned more about the situation at home: the corruption of the elites, the inability of the government to deliver public services, the lack of freedom to express themselves, the dearth of opportunities and jobs.

Dima recounted how protests had spread across the country as people vented their frustration at the widespread unemployment and corruption. They wanted justice, she stressed. The president and his circle were getting richer and richer – at the expense of the rest of the country.

'Why should the president think himself better than other Tunisians?' Dima asked rhetorically. 'He does not have better qualifications. He humiliated Tunisians.'

As anger increased, Ben Ali made speeches, promising changes and firing ministers. But on 14 January, professionals in the capital – who were members of civil associations and unions – turned out to demonstrate. Dima described how she and a group of fellow lawyers had joined in, and how Ben Ali's police entered the hotel, near the Ministry of Interior, where she and other protesters were holed up.

'It was terrifying,' she said. Her phone had been low on battery and she did not know who to call. 'A woman was raped. The police beat people with batons and fired tear gas. I could hear shouting.' She had really feared for the worse.

'Fortunately, Ben Ali did not have the support of the army,' Dima went on. General Rachid Ammar, the chief of staff of the

Tunisian armed forces, refused to give the army orders to fire on civilians. By that evening, Ben Ali realized the game was up and escaped on a plane to Saudi Arabia. Some of his associates also fled.

Radhia then described how, in the aftermath of Ben Ali's departure, Tunis temporarily became lawless. Scared to leave their homes, people set up neighbourhood watches to guard their communities, wearing white scarves around their necks.

The police were now back doing their jobs. But Tunisians continued to complain about the *fawda* (chaos) in the country. People were not stopping at traffic lights and were parking anywhere. Intersections were gridlocked. They were building without planning permission. They were setting up stalls illegally in the streets.

'For many,' Radhia said, 'the overthrow of tyranny means doing whatever you like.'

I told Radhia and Dima about my flight to Tunisia. While I had been standing in line at Heathrow, waiting to board my plane, I had heard a bunch of young guys speaking in the strongest London vernacular and turned around to find out who they were. At first I could not see them. It took me a little while to realize that I was actually listening in on the conversation of the seriously bearded twenty-somethings right behind me. They spoke like the native-born Londoners that they were. But they were dressed like Salafis, with long shirts over baggy trousers. On landing, the young British Muslims were met by women dressed in black cloaks and gloves, wearing hijab and niqab, their faces fully covered.

Radhia told me how Rached Ghannouchi and his supporters had returned from exile in London. His Islamist party – Ennahda

– was now the most prominent political party in the country. Ben Ali had banned Ennahda, and so it had been forced to operate underground for years. But now, post-revolution, it was out in the open, with branches across the country. Many predicted that the party would win the elections.

Dima was not concerned. She noted that Ghannouchi had a reputation for being wise and willing to compromise. In exile, he had written articles highlighting the Islamic virtues of *ijma* (consensus) and *shura* (consultation), and the Quranic injunction against compulsion in matters of religion. He had agreed that the will of the people was the source of legitimacy of the state.

'Ennahda will have to be moderate and willing to share power with others in order to gain and maintain the support of Tunisians,' Dima said.

Her mother explained that, before the revolution, men with beards had been watched by the police; young women had not been allowed to wear veils at university; and imams had to have their sermons approved ahead of time. The revolution had changed all that, and Tunisians were now able to practise their religion freely. There were more beards in the streets, as religious men were permitted to grow facial hair without fear of being detained. After prayers, the mosques remained open and people could stay and read. Imams were free to speak and no longer feared secret police sitting within the audience. More women were wearing the veil than ever before – but there were still plenty whose heads were uncovered and who wore fashionable Western clothes.

*

The White House was struggling with how to respond to what was being dubbed the Arab Spring. Greta told me there was an internal debate over whether it should be regarded as a regional phenomenon which required a regional strategy – or whether the United States should respond to events on a country-by-country basis. Greta had been dispatched to Tunisia, with a budget of $400,000, to help the embassy increase its outreach to Tunisians. The US, Greta went on, was keen to help Tunisians strengthen the rule of law and to encourage entrepreneurship and innovation.

For years, the Tunisian regime had limited the US embassy's access to officials and required them to get permission to visit universities, as well as permits to travel within the country. Despite these constraints, the embassy's political section had kept Washington informed of the excesses of Ben Ali and the corruption of his cronies. As WikiLeaks revealed, the embassy was well aware of what Ben Ali's regime was doing. One cable sarcastically noted: 'Whether it's cash, services, land, property, or yes, even your yacht, President Ben Ali's family is rumored to covet it and reportedly gets what it wants.' Another recounted a lavish dinner hosted by Sakher El Materi, the son-in-law of Ben Ali: 'After dinner, he served ice cream and frozen yogurt he brought in by plane from Saint Tropez...' It went on: 'El Materi has a large tiger on his compound, living in a cage. He acquired it when it was a few weeks old. The tiger consumes four chickens a day.'

Since the revolution, embassy officials had been able to meet with whomever they liked and travel wherever they wanted. And Tunisians appeared keen to receive US support.

Greta invited me to join her and her colleagues for dinner with Tunisian activists at a very swish restaurant in La Marsa, an elegant suburb of Tunis. Over seafood, I chatted with a twenty-seven-year-old Tunisian man wearing a Superwoman T-shirt. 'I am ready to die for the revolution,' he told me. He had put his money in the bank in his brother's name before going out to protest.

He was a geek from a privileged background. He described how he had been exposed to US culture through Disney, Marvel and Hanna-Barbera. He traced his personal development in stages: from 1996, he'd communicated in Internet Relay Chat (IRC); from 2004, he was involved in blogs and forums; and from 2009 he was active on social media. Via these platforms, he had been involved in discussions criticizing the regime for a decade.

He thought the first ten years of Ben Ali's rule had been all right. It was censorship of the Internet that had driven him to action against the regime. He really believed in open government. He'd organized a TEDx event in Tunisia, telling people: 'Don't wait for Jack Bauer to come and save you – do it yourself.' Half the cultural references he made were lost on me, but I nodded encouragingly.

Also at the dinner was a former Serbian special forces soldier, who had worked in many different countries for an American NGO that supported the development of political parties. It was fascinating listening to him share his experiences of transition in the Balkans and the challenges they had faced there.

The owner of the restaurant came to the table to show us the largest lobster any of us had ever seen. It was a beast. Even though we were full, we ordered it to keep our conversation going longer. In the background, a Tunisian singer tirelessly performed golden oldies in Arabic, English and Spanish. I sang along to the Egyptian singer Dalida's '*Helwa ya baladi*' – remembering dancing to it during my student days in Alexandria. It was a wonderful evening, with the Tunisians expressing their hopes for the future.

Then the bill arrived and Greta went unusually quiet. We had been charged $1,000 for the lobster.

Greta's budget was not going to go far at this rate.

*

One morning, Greta, Radhia and I headed off south in a black US embassy SUV, to visit various projects that the United States was interested in supporting.

About halfway to Tataouine, our driver took advantage of our diplomatic number plate to overtake a long line of stationary cars. But we were brought to a halt by youths blocking the road and barring any vehicles from passing in either direction. Suddenly, they swarmed the SUV, sitting on our bumper and knocking on the windows. I had no idea what was going on but thought it best to smile and wave – and not reveal any fear of us being dragged from the car and lynched. The driver locked all the doors. The kids refused to budge. The driver opened his window a crack to speak to a tall boy who seemed to be the ringleader. He wanted to know who we were.

'They are foreigners… Belgians… just visiting the country…' the driver responded. It was smart of him to pass us off as Belgians. No one had grudges against Belgians in the Arab world.

Still, the youth was not to be persuaded and refused our request to pass. He told us that he and his friends were from the nearby village of Gargour, which had 17,000 people and no water. They were stopping all traffic from passing until 5 p.m. that day, in an effort to gain the government's attention. He asked that we go back and explain their plight to 'people in Tunis'.

We had no choice but to turn around and try to find an alternative route south. A few miles down the road, we saw some police at a traffic circle and informed them that the youths of Gargour were blocking the road because their village lacked water. The police appeared to know about the situation. But they shrugged their shoulders, apparently not regarding it as their problem.

We passed the village of Hammam Sousse, where Ben Ali was born. I noted the high quality of the main roads, the electricity pylons, the gas stations. Olive trees stood in formation, mile after mile. There were fields of wheat, and sheep were grazing close to the road. Factories were visible. Radhia pointed out the international airport, which had ceased operating after the president's departure from the country. She told us that, off the main roads, the villages were only connected by dirt tracks, and some lacked basic infrastructure. She pointed out donkeys carting water in big plastic tubs on small carts. She described the staggering gap in development between Tunisia's big cities and the rural areas in the middle and south of the country.

It took us eight hours to drive the 330 miles to Tataouine. On arrival later in the afternoon, an impressive young Tunisian woman showed us around her US government-funded NGO, where she ran English-language classes after school. The walls were covered with messages of peace, love and freedom. The children had put up letters to the Peace Corps, to thank them for the work they had done in Tunisia before they were pulled out in the 1990s. I asked the kids their favourite actors. They told me: Brad Pitt and Angelina Jolie. As for their favourite football team, there were different responses: Arsenal, Manchester United, Chelsea...

The young teacher had been selected for a Fulbright scholarship and would spend the coming year in the United States. 'Tunisians demonstrated against Ben Ali to remove oppression and inequality,' she told us. 'I was so happy to see the US Congress come out in support of the Tunisian people.' She had always wanted to establish an NGO, but had not been able to do so before as it required a permit from Tunis, which had been difficult to get. But as soon as Ben Ali departed, she had set up her organization.

She took us to meet a group of young adults so we could hear their hopes and aspirations. She introduced Greta as a State Department official. Greta then turned to introduce me, and I could tell by the look on her face that she was struggling with how to describe me.

'Emma is... a blogger,' Greta announced.

All heads turned towards me. I was now regarded with greater interest than the ambassador. 'A blogger, wow!' one of them commented. They were fascinated. Blogging had taken on such an elevated status since the Arab Spring began. Bloggers told the truth. Bloggers shone the spotlight on government corruption.

'What do you blog on?' one asked. 'And where do you post your blogs?'

I mumbled a bit in my response. The Tunisians probably thought I was being modest. In truth, I had at this stage only written one blog, and it was about my trip to Egypt. Tom Ricks had posted it as part of his 'Best Defense' column on the *Foreign Policy* magazine website.

I wanted to get the conversation back to the Tunisians, so I asked them questions about themselves. They all appeared well-educated and keen to use their skills – but few had jobs and there were not many employment opportunities in the area. They all wanted to start their own NGOs – but had few ideas as to what they would actually do. They had heard that foreigners were coming to Tunisia to fund NGOs – and they wanted the money.

We heard how generous the people of Tataouine were towards Libyan refugees fleeing the conflict in their country. Official figures estimated between 250,000 and 300,000 Libyans had taken refuge in Tunisia. Tunisians put the number higher, at around half a million. They had taken them into their homes, providing toys and books for the children. The Islamic Relief organization was helping with food distribution. But Tunisia had its own difficulties. The economy was dependent on Libya, and had been hit hard by the ongoing war. In addition, around 100,000 Tunisians had been forced to quit their jobs in Libya and return home.

The next day, we drove north out of Tataouine for two hours before we reached the coast. We took the ferry over to Jerba, paying nothing for our tickets as they had been free of charge since the revolution.

It was to Jerba that strong winds had blown Odysseus during his long journey home after the Trojan War. He'd sent some of his men ashore, where they ate lotus flowers and became so forgetful that they lost all desire to continue their voyage. But Odysseus was a man on a mission, and was not to be distracted from reasserting his place as the rightful king of Ithaca. He refused to eat the lotus plants, dragged the crew back to the ship and chained them to the oars, forcing them away from the temptations of the island.

It was clear that the island still had its charms. While tourism elsewhere in the country had dried up, Jerba's golden beaches continued to lure Europeans to its shores. And the island was also home to a Jewish community that, according to tradition, had settled there over 2,500 years ago, following the destruction of the First Temple in Jerusalem.

At the El Ghriba synagogue, I saw Jewish men and little children gathering for the Shabbat service. I struck up conversation with the leader of the Jewish community, who told me they numbered around 1,200 and followed the Torah to the letter. On Shabbat, they did not use money or drive. He asserted that there were no problems between Arabs and Jews on Jerba. As proof, he mentioned that some Tunisian Jews who had migrated to Israel had returned. But, he added with a sigh, 'Nowhere in the world do people really like Jews.'

Leaving the synagogue, I noted a devout Muslim standing outside. I asked him about relations between Jews and Muslims. He responded: 'Those who know the true Islam have no problems with Jews. The Prophet Mohamad lived among Jews, had Jews as neighbours and traded with them.'

The next day we visited the Institute of Technology, where the director told Greta that he was keen to set up exchanges of professors and students with universities in the United States. He and other members of the faculty had studied in America and Europe, and had benefited from the experience.

The director had built up strong relations with the Tunisian ministry of labour, as well as with industry, and reckoned that 70 per cent of his students found work upon graduation. He described how the revolution had impacted the students. They appeared much more empowered now, and were helping Libyans, working harder at their studies, and interacting with their teachers in a more mature manner. His initial fears that things might get out of hand had proved unwarranted. He had even directed the faculty to make some concessions on discipline.

Many of the students were female, and most now wore black abayas and headscarves – but there were still some girls who were not covered, and they all mixed together with ease.

Once our business in Jerba was done, we drove back towards Tunis, stopping off at Kairouan to visit the seventh-century Great Mosque of Uqba. Greta, Radhia and I climbed up onto the roof of a carpet shop and got an amazing view of the mosque: the flagstone courtyard, the arched porticoes and pillars, and the minaret that was over a hundred feet high. The tiles for the *mihrab* (the niche indicating the direction of Mecca), as well as the wood for the *minar* (the pulpit), had been imported centuries ago from Baghdad.

It was hard to imagine that this city, now so isolated, had once attracted scholars from across the Muslim world, and had received envoys from Charlemagne and the Holy Roman Empire. Radhia told us that it had once been regarded as the fourth-most holy city in Islam, after Mecca, Medina and Jerusalem. It was said that seven pilgrimages to its Great Mosque were the equivalent of one to Mecca.

Radhia also explained that from the eighth century onwards, Kairouan had been renowned for stipulating monogamy in the marriage contract – despite Islam allowing a man to take up to four wives.

*

One afternoon, Greta suggested we visit Carthage, which was around ten miles east of Tunis. On the way there, she pointed out the former residence of Abu Jihad, who had been the deputy to the Palestine Liberation Organization leader Yasser Arafat. The PLO had been based in Tunisia from 1982 to 1993, and Abu Jihad had directed military activities against Israel from this house. One evening, assassins had approached the villa pretending to be a couple out for a late-night stroll. They shot one of the bodyguards in the head before rushing inside and shooting Abu Jihad dead in front of his wife and son, who were left unharmed. Given the professionalism of the assassins, the media assumed they had to be Israeli.

I told Greta that I had met Abu Jihad's wife and son in Gaza in the nineties, when I was working there for the British Council. They, along with the PLO leadership, had returned from exile in Tunisia as part of the terms of the Oslo Accords, signed in Washington on 13 September 1993 by Yasser Arafat and Israeli prime minister Yitzhak Rabin on the White House lawn. There had been such optimism back then of achieving a two-state solution to the Israel–Palestine conflict. The PLO and Israel had recognized each other and agreed to resolve their outstanding differences by peaceful means. Negotiators had envisaged the land being shared based on the 1967 borders, with some land swaps, Jerusalem as the capital of both countries, and the right of return of both Palestinians and Jews to their respective states.

But that hope and goodwill had long since disappeared. No mechanisms had been put in place to monitor or address violations of the letter – or the spirit – of the Accords. Extremists on both sides had sought to undermine the trust and confidence necessary to make such a historic compromise. I was at the peace rally in the square in Tel Aviv that fateful night of 4 November 1995, when a religious Jewish radical shot Prime Minister Rabin. In the weeks following his assassination, Palestinian terrorists carried out a series of bombings. Without Rabin's leadership, Israelis succumbed to their fears. Arafat preferred no agreement to concessions on what he regarded as Palestinian rights. The second intifada broke out in 2000 – and the peace efforts of a decade were destroyed.

As we walked around the ruins of Carthage, I tried to imagine it as the centre of the great empire that had once dominated the Mediterranean Sea. At school, I had studied Book IV of Virgil's *Aeneid* in Latin. Dido, the first queen of Carthage, falls in love with the Trojan warrior, Aeneas. Despite his love for her, Aeneas reluctantly leaves Carthage when the gods remind him of his destiny to establish Rome. Heartbroken, Dido decides to kill herself. She asks her sister to prepare a pyre under the pretence of burning all reminders of Aeneas. Seeing the Trojan fleet heading out to sea, Dido curses the

Trojans and calls for eternal hostility between them and her people. She climbs onto the pyre, lies down on the bed she had once shared with Aeneas and impales herself on his sword.

When I first read the story of Dido and Aeneas, what resonated was Aeneas's commitment to following his calling. He had wanted to stay with Dido, but his sense of duty to a higher mission compelled him to leave. I admired his dedication to leading a life of purpose.

*

Greta and I spent our last afternoon together in Sidi Bou Said, about twelve miles east of Tunis. It is a town of artists, and their wares were on display everywhere. We poked our heads into different stores, and after much browsing decided to buy cotton beach towels.

After taking photos of each other with a hawk on our heads, we found a café and sat drinking almond tea while looking out to sea over the whitewashed walls and blue windows. As Greta puffed away on her clove cigarette, we discussed Tunisia's prospects. The country had a challenging period ahead. It would have to elect an assembly, draft a new constitution and choose its new government – all while wrestling with the economic impact of the war in Libya, the drop in tourism and rising unemployment. And yet there was every reason to be optimistic about the transition. All the necessary ingredients seemed to be present. It was a country of manageable size, with a small population of around 11 million, good infrastructure, a strong middle class, a well-educated and literate population, and an established civil society. And, most importantly, it seemed to have politicians willing to compromise.

As Tunisians are a relatively homogenous population, politicians could not use sect or ethnicity to mobilize people. Instead, they would have to put forward agendas and platforms to win support. The secularists and the Islamists had both expressed their commitment to establishing democratic institutions, ensuring free and fair elections, and upholding freedom of speech and association. And the Tunisian army was small, professional and had always stayed out of politics. It had not played much of a role in the struggle for independence, nor had it been caught up in the Arab–Israeli wars.

Greta loved listening to people in the Middle East describe the sort of society they wished to build – and exploring ways in which the United States could help improve a country's higher education, media and rule of law through exchanges, partnerships, training and expertise. This was the traditional way in which the US operated; Iraq and Afghanistan – with their large-scale military occupations – were anomalies.

Tunisia really did feel very different from other Middle Eastern countries – much more moderate, much more European, much more open to the West and much more progressive in terms of women's rights.

Suddenly, our conversation was interrupted by a bunch of young men with long beards and short thobes striding through the market. 'Who are they?' I asked a shopkeeper, pointing at them.

'Answering the call,' he responded somewhat cryptically. We had no idea whether these were the non-political 'quietist'

Salafis – or jihadi ones with a cause to fight and die for. Whoever they were, they certainly walked with a sense of purpose.

But the shopkeeper did not seem concerned. 'We are a moderate people,' he said, pointing out towards the sea. 'Look, we wear shorts and go to the beach.'

'Where will you go next?' Greta asked me in the car back to Tunis.

'Damascus,' I responded. I had read an article arguing that if we had not overthrown Saddam, he would have been swept out by the Arab Spring. And the regime that most resembled Saddam's was that of Assad. I wanted to see how the Syrian government was responding to the protests that had spread there. The media reports were already concerning.

CHAPTER 3

'Assad – or we burn the country'

Syria

July 2011

The first image to greet me on arrival at Damascus Airport was a poster of President Bashar al-Assad with an Arabic slogan proclaiming: 'Leader of the youth, hope of the youth.'

I was lucky to have got here. The travel advice issued by both the US and UK governments was to stay away from Syria. And the Syrian regime, wary of interfering foreigners, was denying most requests to visit. When I'd submitted my application for a visa to the Syrian embassy in London's Belgrave Square, I had been taken to a small back office for an interview with an official who was polite but not warm. He asked me why I wanted to visit Syria at this time. I responded that I was fascinated by archaeology and was between jobs. I had been to Syria twelve years before, loved it, and wanted to make a return trip. He quizzed me on current events in Syria to test whether I was a Western journalist intent on writing negative stories about the regime. I feigned little interest, and brought the conversation back to Syria's famous archaeological sites. Satisfied by my responses, the official issued me a visa.

I jumped in a taxi outside the airport, and as we drove I asked the driver about the situation in Syria. 'Things are fine,' he assured me. 'There has been some trouble around the country, but things are OK in Damascus.' With one hand on the wheel, he waved the other hand in various directions as he pointed out where different communities lived. Druze to the left, Palestinian refugees to the right, Iraqi refugees over to the side. Alawite (a Shia offshoot) villages over there, Christian villages over here; Kurds lived in the north. Sunnis were around 65 per cent of the population, he told me.

I asked him how he knew who somebody was or whether they were Sunni or Shia. 'I don't know,' he said, 'and I'm not even interested in knowing. There is no sectarianism here in Syria.' I could not tell whether he genuinely believed this or if he was just trying to give a foreign visitor a positive impression of his country. While recognition of religious or ethnic difference might once merely have been a social distinction, it had certainly become more politicized in recent years.

We passed Damascus University. Outside, there were lots of flags and pictures of Bashar and his deceased father, Hafez, the former president. As we drove through al-Umawiyeen Square, I saw young men and women gathering, holding Syrian flags. 'It is not a demonstration,' the driver told me, 'it is a celebration – a celebration of the government.' Later, I watched the event on television; it had made the international news. Pop singers and fireworks had entertained the tens of thousands of Syrians who had come out to the square to show their support for the president. This surprised me. Most of the media coverage I had seen before my arrival shone the spotlight on opposition supporters – typically young and secular – who were demanding jobs and transparent government.

*

The next day, I walked through the 600-metre-long covered market of Souq al-Hamidiyya inside the old walled city of Damascus. It was buzzing with life. Store owners sat outside their shops, trying to entice potential customers to buy clothes, textiles, rugs, antiques, copper, spices, perfumes and sweets. Judging by the customers at the counter, Bakdash, Syria's oldest ice cream parlour, was doing fine trade.

I emerged from the market in front of the Umayyad Mosque. I entered the ticket office and paid the entrance fee for foreigners. A female attendant passed me a hooded grey abaya to cover myself. The cloak stank, and I wondered when it had last been washed and how many women had worn it in the sweltering summer heat. I put it on over my clothes nevertheless, pulling up the pointed hood to ensure my hair was covered. Then I removed my shoes and entered the mosque.

It was built on what was once the site of a Roman temple dedicated to Jupiter. When Christianity became the official religion of the Roman Empire, the temple was transformed into a Byzantine cathedral, later dedicated to John the Baptist. After Damascus became the capital of the Umayyad Caliphate, the church was demolished and replaced in 715 with the Umayyad Mosque, one of the oldest and most magnificent in the Muslim world.

In the prayer hall, Muslims are segregated by gender but not by sect. It is a splendid structure, with three aisles and columns holding up the roof. Some of the original eighth-century mosaics are still visible. In the middle is a domed shrine, believed to contain the head of John the Baptist – known as the prophet Yahya to Muslims. Mandaeans, followers of an ancient gnostic religion with dualist worldviews, press their heads up against the metal grille of the shrine during their annual pilgrimage. Even Pope John Paul II had visited.

Crossing into the courtyard, I noticed a group on their knees. One man was weeping as he repeated the invocation '*Ya Hussein*'. The others followed suit, tears flowing, looking quite distraught.

A man in a turban was addressing a group of Iranian pilgrims in Farsi. While there were few Western visitors, Shia religious tourism appeared to be thriving.

I passed three women sitting cross-legged on the ground in their black abayas. One made a rather facetious comment about my cloak. She was stunned when I spoke back to her in Arabic.

'Where are you from?' she asked me.

'London, Britain,' I responded. 'Where are you from?'

'Babil, Iraq,' she replied, telling me her group was visiting the shrines in Syria. She pointed to the shrine of Hussein, which is believed to house the head of the grandson of the Prophet Mohamad who was killed by the Umayyads at Karbala in Iraq in 680. The women and children of the Prophet's family had apparently walked here following the Battle of Karbala, and were imprisoned in the mosque for sixty days.

I exited the mosque, relieved to return the borrowed abaya. Before long, I was striding down Straight Street, passing Roman colonnades, shops selling antiques and a Christian liquor store with a picture of Assad prominently displayed. It was on the 'street which is called Straight' that the disciple Ananias met Paul, restored his sight and baptized him – or so the biblical story of Paul's conversion to Christianity is recorded in the Acts of the Apostles.

And it was at a café off this street, as a tourist twelve years before this trip, that I had by chance struck up conversation with a Syrian named Ammar. We had hung out together for a couple of days. He showed me around Damascus and took me out to the Christian village of Maaloula, where Aramaic, the language of Jesus, is still spoken. Ammar was a writer. He told me he was one of the 0.1 per cent who had not voted for Hafez al-Assad in the presidential elections. He had never met any others. No one back then had dared speak out against the regime.

How times had changed. Tens of thousands of Syrians around the country were openly calling for reforms and jobs. I wondered where Ammar was now.

Turning onto a narrow, cobbled street, I passed two seated men drinking tea. One turned to the other: 'Who says there are no tourists in Syria? There's one!' I turned around and replied, 'I am the last tourist in Syria!'

They invited me to join them, fetching me a chair and some tea. One was a hotel owner. He had recently converted an old Arab house into a boutique hotel. The previous year, he had rented rooms for $400 a night. Now he had reduced the rate to $100. But like all other hotels in town, his was down to zero occupancy.

The other man was a tourist guide. He was deeply frustrated. 'We need change,' he told me. It became clear that these two friends, one of whom was Christian and the other a Sunni, held different opinions.

The hotel owner stated, 'Bashar is a very good man. He is educated. He is decent. The problem is with the circle of advisers around him.' He pointed to his friend, the tourist guide, describing him as one of the people who wanted change. 'What do they want? Freedom? What do they mean by freedom? Who is better than Bashar? If he is removed, the country could descend into chaos like Iraq. Look, there are hardly any Christians living in Iraq now.'

The tourist guide, however, insisted that two-thirds of the people in Syria wanted change. And he would continue to support the growing movement of opposition to the regime.

Two thousand Syrians had died since the unrest ignited four months earlier in March 2011, after some schoolchildren in Dera'a – a city seventy miles south of Damascus – wrote on a wall the revolutionary chant heard on the streets of Tunis and Cairo: 'Ash-sha'b yurid isqat an-nizam [The people want the fall of the regime]'. When the children were detained by the local security chief, their families and supporters marched to the governor's house to demand that they be set free. Some were killed when security forces opened fire. Funerals turned into rallies, and more people were killed. When the children were released two weeks later, having been beaten and with rumours that their fingernails had been pulled out, protests spread around the country. The Syrian revolution had begun.

*

My phone rang. '*Salaam aleikum... Shlonij?*' the man asked.

'*Ilhamdillah,*' I responded, knowing he was an Iraqi by the dialect but not recognizing the voice.

He went on: 'Miss Emma, I am so pleased that you contact me when you are in trouble. Of course I will send you money.'

It took me a moment to realize I was speaking with Sheikh Abdullah from Mosul. I had no idea what he was going on about, but it was nice to hear from him. We chatted for a while and I caught up on his news. An hour later, a Palestinian friend called to check that I was OK. Why, I wondered, did people think I was not OK? This was odd.

It was hard to find Internet access, but in the evening when I managed to open my email, I discovered that my Yahoo account had been hacked. I could see that a scammer had logged on from Nigeria and had written to everyone in my address book telling them that I was in Spain, had been robbed and needed money sent to a specific bank account. I immediately changed my password, then emailed a friend in Liverpool and asked her to inform the police of the scammer's bank details so they could track him down. She phoned the Merseyside Police and reported back that they said I should contact the police in Syria. I shook my head in disbelief. The police in Syria?! Was no one watching the news? Did people not know what was happening?

While my friend was trying to get the police to notify the bank of the dodgy account, her husband, not recognizing the ruse, transferred $1,000 to it. Who else, I wondered, out of the kind, generous people that I knew around the world, was sending funds to this person thinking I was in trouble? I set about responding to the dozens of concerned emails I had received.

*

I did not immediately recognize Colonel Raad. We hadn't seen each other in two years, and he had put on weight and was not dressed in his habitual military uniform. We greeted each other warmly. He could not believe that I'd tracked him down in Damascus and seemed really touched. We'd first met back in 2007 in Baghdad, when he brought together a group of Sunni men in Ghazaliya to fight against al-Qaeda. He'd stood out, as he was so professional.

Colonel Raad had been a special forces officer in the old Iraqi army. Working closely with the US military during the 2007 troop surge, he had brought peace to his neighbourhood. But even so, in 2009 he was arrested in Baghdad on what appeared to be trumped-up charges, by those seeking to undermine the *Sahwa* (the Sunni Awakening). He was released after ten days, but the incident made him nervous. Fearful that at any stage false allegations could be brought against him, he had sought refuge in Syria.

We sat in a café in the Old City chatting about the past. He reminded me of the time I had called him a hero for saving so many lives — Iraqi and American. Then he spoke about how he once went to Bahrain with the US military and met with General Petraeus and Admiral Fallon; and how Ambassador Khalilzad had once asked his advice on how to set up a *Sahwa* in Afghanistan to fight the Taliban. Officers in the new Iraqi army, established after the fall of Saddam Hussein's regime in 2003, had said to him: 'Just wait. The Americans will treat you like they did the Red Indians. They will discard you like a used match.'

'How did you expect it would end?' I asked him. He told me that he had hoped the relationship would be a long one and that the *Sahwa* and Americans would work together to combat Iranian influence.

'But I was wrong,' he said sadly. 'And those officers in the new Iraqi army were right.'

We took a taxi together to Sayyidah Zainab, in south-east Damascus. The mosque contained the grave of Zainab, daughter of Ali and Fatimah — and granddaughter of the Prophet. It had become a centre of Shia pilgrimage, and this was the neighbourhood to which many Iraqi refugees had gravitated. Markets had sprung up around the mosque. Restaurants were barbequing *masgouf,* with fish from the Euphrates that they brought live in buckets. There was a large, bustling bus station, with offices selling tickets to Karbala, Najaf and Baghdad, as well as other Iraqi destinations.

The Syrian government had claimed that there were 1.2 million Iraqis living in Syria. International organizations, however, believed that the numbers had decreased to around 300,000 (60 per cent Sunni, 20 per cent Shia and 20 per cent Christian). With the increasing unrest in Syria, some Iraqis had decided to try their luck back home. I'd heard that one community had sent back six families to see how they got on. But when one person was murdered, it had deterred others from returning.

According to Colonel Raad, Syrians had been very good to Iraqis of all different ethnicities and sects, and the Iraqis lived peacefully together, grateful to Assad for giving them sanctuary. However, the troubles in Syria were starting to negatively impact relations among Iraqis. There were also some reports of Iraqis being beaten up by Palestinians taking revenge for being expelled from Kuwait in 1991, when Yasser Arafat expressed support for Saddam's invasion of that country.

Colonel Raad told me he had applied for a visa to the United States. A US battalion commander, with whom he had worked closely, had written a glowing letter of recommendation. But it had been over a year, and Raad was still waiting for a response. I advised him not to put his life on hold waiting for the visa.

But, he told me, he could not work legally in Syria, and he was afraid to return to Iraq. Where could he go? Many of the Awakening leaders had been thrown in jail, killed or, like him, had fled the country.

Raad believed that if it were up to the US military, he would get a visa to the United States. But he knew the decision was in the hands of others. I assured him that the bonds he had with those American soldiers were genuine. US soldiers who served in Iraq frequently asked after the Awakening leaders they had worked with, deeply troubled at their abandonment.

'I know,' he responded. He was still in email contact with them. 'We are brothers.'

*

Robert Ford, the US ambassador to Syria, invited me for dinner one evening at his residence in Damascus. We sat out in the garden, under an awning, catching up on each other's lives. We had become good friends in Iraq, where he had served three tours. Like me, he had been against the war, but he had volunteered to go help rebuild the country. His first exposure to the Arab world had been as a Peace Corps volunteer in Morocco. Since then, he had spent his whole State Department career working on the Middle East and was fluent in Arabic.

Robert was being openly harassed by the Syrian regime. Things had escalated after he visited Hama, Syria's fourth-largest city, on 7 July 2011, just before my visit. He had not received instructions from Washington to go to Hama. Nor had he sought permission. Instead, he had shot off an email to the State Department informing them of the trip before he headed out. He wanted to witness the stand-off between the Syrian army and local residents, hoping that the spotlight from the international community would ensure violence did not break out. Video footage showed local residents greeting Robert's arrival and draping his SUV with roses and olive branches.

But the Syrian government was furious. They viewed it as evidence of US interference in internal affairs, and accused the United States of seeking to destabilize the country. A few days after his visit to Hama, protesters breached his residence in Damascus, as well as the embassy compound. They hurled rocks, eggs and tomatoes, and replaced the American flags with Syrian ones. Robert showed me around his home, pointing out the damage that had been done.

Hama, with its giant water wheels, would be forever associated with the brutal crushing of the Muslim Brotherhood insurrection by Rifaat al-Assad, brother of Hafez al-Assad, in 1982. Over 20,000 residents had been killed in a matter of three weeks. The Assads would have expected there to one day be a reckoning – and had no doubt prepared themselves for that eventuality.

Syria had experienced countless coups from the time of its independence from France in 1946 until Hafez al-Assad became the president in 1971. An Alawite from a humble background, Hafez had become a pilot in the air force and risen up through the ranks of the Baath Party, an Arab socialist movement in Syria and Iraq. As president, he amended the constitution to recognize the Baath Party as the 'leader of the state and society'. The party reserved senior public-sector positions for its members, it indoctrinated children at schools and it monitored the security forces. Over time, real power became concentrated in the hands of Assad, his family and his close advisers. He groomed Bassel, his eldest son, as his successor. But when Bassel was killed in a car crash near the airport, Bashar, the younger son, became heir to the family business of ruling Syria.

When Hafez died in 2000, there were hopes that Bashar would be a reformer who would lead Syria out of isolation. Bashar, after all, was a London-trained ophthalmologist and a computer geek. And he was married to Asma, a Syrian Sunni born and bred in Britain, educated at King's College London, who had worked as an investment banker for J.P. Morgan.

However, after eleven years of Bashar's rule, hopes for reform had long faded.

Robert was deeply disgusted by what was going on – and was not going to remain silent when presented with evidence of people being randomly tortured and killed by their government. Slight, short and bespectacled, Robert hardly presented a menacing figure, but I observed a new steely confidence about him. He refused to be cowed, and was standing up for what he believed in. He described how the Assad regime was as bad as – if not worse than – Saddam's. Security services tortured dissenters, intimidated the population and cultivated a network of informants. There was no trust. And there was no willingness on the part of the regime to compromise.

Looks could be misleading, Robert told me. He had met Bashar in person. He had been struck by how out of touch the president was with ordinary Syrians, by his lack of concern about human rights abuses and by his ruthlessness. The man was a mafia boss, through and through. And people like that didn't change.

Two months before I arrived in Syria, Obama had given a speech in which he said, 'The Syrian people have shown their courage in demanding a transition to democracy. President Assad now has a choice: he can lead that transition, or get out of the way.' I told Robert I had heard a number of Syrians express their belief that the United States was going to intervene – just as it was doing in Libya. This belief was giving them hope, and leading more people to mobilize in opposition to the regime.

'Isn't there anything the international community can do to prevent the situation in Syria escalating to a full-scale civil war?' I asked Robert. 'Can't someone bring the different parties together to mediate some solution before it's too late?' He told me he had been trying. But his efforts didn't seem to be getting traction.

Robert explained that Assad had assumed he would not be affected by the Arab Spring because he was young, relatively new in power, and Syria was part of the axis of resistance to the US. But Assad had badly misjudged the situation. Young people were not protesting against America – they were calling for jobs and an end to corruption. Assad could have sacked the official responsible for locking up and mistreating the children in Dera'a, which might have deflected the protests or quickly taken the wind out of them. He could have shown a measure of understanding for the demands of the young, secular Syrians for transparency, better government and jobs – and implemented some reforms. But, instead, Assad had chosen to go on the attack, accusing the young protestors of being terrorists and sending gangs of Alawite thugs to beat them up. He had also released jihadists from jail, knowing that their presence among the opposition would undermine the image of the secular activists.

Towards the end of the evening, Robert told me that he expected to be withdrawn from Syria in the not-too-distant future. It would only be a matter of time. Until then, he was determined to serve as a witness to the behaviour of the regime, in the hope that his presence might deter worse human rights abuses.

*

A few days later, I jumped into a taxi to go to the Harasta station, three miles north-east of the city centre, to take a bus to Palmyra. The taxi driver was a smiling Damascene in his twenties, whose ancestral origins, he told me, were Turkish. He had graduated from university with a degree in economics and trade, but there was no work so he was having to earn a living as a taxi driver. 'It is not right,' he said. 'There have to be reforms.' He saw the difficult economic situation in Syria as part of a global trend. He pointed out that protests about the economy and unemployment were taking place in Spain, Portugal and Greece, too. Young people everywhere were increasingly frustrated at the lack of opportunities.

We talked about events in the region. 'Gaddafi is mentally ill,' he said. 'He thinks he is the king of kings. *Zenga zenga.*' He laughed as he imitated the Libyan leader.

The driver noted that Ben Ali and Mubarak had only lasted days before they gave up power. 'As for Syria, the regime will not give up power peacefully. No chance. It's Assad – or we burn the country,' he said, quoting the slogan used by Assad's supporters.

When we arrived at the station, we discovered that buses to Palmyra now departed from the Pullman station due to 'current events', so the taxi driver took me there. He pointed to the cost of the journey on the meter. I insisted on paying him double as he had been so kind and helpful. He refused. I insisted. 'God be with you,' he said, as he waved me farewell.

To get into the bus station, I was surprised to find I had to put my bag through an X-ray machine and walk through a scanner. However, there was no indication that the machines were working, as no one seemed to be paying much attention and no beeps or lights went off. Once through the entrance, I discovered a multitude of offices selling tickets to the same destinations. I was immediately approached by touts trying to get me to buy from their office and offering me special VIP treatment. I shrugged them off. I had not a clue which company to choose.

I approached a man and asked him how I should decide which bus to take to Palmyra. He took me through to the back, to where the buses were lined up. Some were large, modern, air-conditioned ones. Others were much less luxurious. He pointed to a bus run by the Ayman company, and recommended I took one of theirs. It was 250 Syrian pounds ($5) for the 150-mile trip. He then directed me to the police station 'next to the picture of the president'. Inside, an officer asked to see my passport. Then he stamped my ticket. In front of a few other Syrians he said to me: 'Next time you must give me a cell phone as a present.'

'I am the only tourist at the moment in Syria,' I replied, 'and next time you should give me a present.' Everyone laughed, including the officer.

I spent the next forty-five minutes sitting on a bench watching people go by. Young guys in jeans looking quite Western. Older men in dishdasha and keffiyeh. Young women wearing tight-fitting jeans, shirts and colourful headscarves. Others wearing more traditional abayas or long fashionable trench coats (in the summer's heat) which covered most of their contours. A woman smiled at me as she passed. A man offered to sell me a lottery ticket before he realized I was a foreigner, then he grinned. No one stared. Everyone was friendly.

On the bus, the conductor gave each of us a plastic cup for water, a black plastic bag for our rubbish and a sweet. Then he taped newspaper across the top of the windscreen to protect the driver from the glare of the sun. First, we listened to a recital of passages from the Quran, and then an Egyptian movie was put on the TV.

Before we left the station, a policeman came onto the bus to check everyone's identity papers. On the outskirts of Damascus, a makeshift military checkpoint was stopping vehicles coming into town. There were long lines of cars waiting to get through.

As we drove, I stared out the window at the neglected villages. In recent years, drought had driven more and more Syrians from the countryside to the cities, where they had not really integrated and where there were not enough jobs.

A couple of hours later, we were stopped on the outskirts of Palmyra. A man came on board to check identity cards. He barely looked at my passport, but he examined the IDs of the Syrian passengers closely. He wore a deep blue jumpsuit, with green webbing stuffed with ammunition. I looked out the window. Two men in jeans, with rifles slung over their shoulders, were stopping cars and asking to see papers. Through the front window of the bus, I saw a third man sitting under a canopy beside a pickup truck with a weapon on the back. Initially, I thought they were militia. It was only when the man in the blue jumpsuit walked past me to get off the bus that I noticed the white initials 'CTU' on his back. I assumed that stood for 'counter-terrorism unit'. I turned to the passenger next to me and whispered, 'Are they with the regime?' He nodded nervously.

After the bus dropped me off in Palmyra, I made my way to my hotel, checked into my room and took an afternoon siesta.

Later, I headed out to visit the ancient ruins. I went first to the Temple of Baal, where the caretaker seemed surprised to see me and offered me a cup of tea. He told me that prior to the beginning of the unrest they had received lots of tourists each day. Now there were none.

I paid the 500 Syrian pound ($10) entrance fee, and set out to see the sights. I walked among the ruins for three hours. No one else was there – just me. I marvelled at the size of the pillars. Some had been brought centuries ago from Aswan in southern Egypt. How on earth had they transported them? I was taken back through the centuries to the time of the Emperor Hadrian, to Queen Zenobia's rebellion against the Roman Empire. I imagined people walking along the colonnade, chatting as they went about their daily affairs. I pictured the discussions held in the theatre, the feasts in the banqueting hall. I continued up to Diocletian's camp, where the Roman emperor's army was once based. I sat on a rock watching the sun set, lost in my thoughts.

The temperature dropped quickly and I strolled back to my hotel. I ate dinner on my own, but later in the evening I sat outside on the hotel balcony and chatted with a Syrian businessman, the only other guest, over a bottle of Lebanese wine while the wind howled around us.

We discussed relations between the West and the Muslim world. 'When people in the West think of Muslims they think of bin Laden,' the Syrian lamented, shaking his head sadly. 'But this is wrong. Muslims are peaceful people. Bin Laden and George W. Bush are two sides of the same coin. We should not judge Muslims and Christians by them.'

We considered what might happen next in Syria. Would Assad be able to reach a compromise with the protesters, agreeing to significant reforms and free elections, without the Alawites deposing him? Or would the regime try to violently crush the protests and risk the country being plunged into a bloody civil war?

There was one thing of which the businessman was absolutely sure: Assad would not give up easily. He had seen what had happened to Mubarak and Ben Ali. He was going to follow Gaddafi's example and fight back. Western leaders had called for Assad to step down, but were totally misjudging his determination to stay in power.

The businessman had met Assad a number of times and thought he was a decent man. He opined that the problem was that those around him prevented change. He noted that, in Syria's history, it had always been the business class that determined who ruled. If they withdrew their support from the regime, then it would fall. So far, the business people – Alawite, Christian and Sunni – were staying with Assad.

The businessman told me that although every Syrian claimed there was no sectarianism, tensions in the country were rising. There were real problems between Sunnis and Alawites. Many Syrians were waiting to see what direction things appeared to be heading in before they committed to the government or the opposition. He said that the Al Jazeera Arabic network consistently ran stories about people being killed by the Syrian regime. This had incited the youth in Palmyra to take to the streets and protest.

When I climbed into bed, I switched on the television and surfed back and forth between channels. Footage from Homs and Hama showed tens of thousands had taken to the streets, chanting '*Irhal, Irhal ya Bashar* [Go, go Bashar]'. The government television channel told people not to believe the propaganda that members of the military were deserting. Everything was under control, it claimed. It blamed Islamist terrorists, criminals and gangs for the unrest – and accused Al Jazeera of spreading lies and sedition and pushing foreign agendas.

*

My return journey to Damascus was without incident.

At the bus station, I jumped into a taxi. I tried to strike up a conversation with the driver, who told me he was a Palestinian and that he supported the regime. He asked me where I was from. When I told him I was British, he responded coldly: 'You gave away my country.' The conversation was not off to a good start.

'Sorry,' I responded.

'I don't mean *you* personally. I mean *you*, the British.'

As a Brit, I had been accused many times of causing all the problems in the Middle East. Every child in the region knew about the 1917 Balfour Declaration, in which the British foreign secretary called for the establishment of a national home for the Jews in Palestine. In fact, Britain had made contradictory promises over who would be in charge of the former Ottoman domains. In a series of correspondence written in 1915 and 1916 between the British High Commissioner in Egypt, Sir

Henry McMahon, and the Sharif of Mecca, Hussein ibn Ali, it was agreed that Arab forces would revolt against Ottoman rule in return for a future independent Arab kingdom that would include the Arab Peninsula, Syria, Iraq and Palestine. But, at the same time, Sir Mark Sykes of the British Foreign Office and François Georges-Picot of the French foreign ministry negotiated a secret 1916 agreement to demarcate separate spheres of influence for Britain and France by a line drawn in the sand 'from the "e" in Acre to the last "k" in Kirkuk', as Sykes put it, with the Holy Land coming under an international administration.

In the dying days of the Ottoman Empire, Britain was especially interested in the fate of the Middle East for a number of reasons: controlling the region's oil fields (Churchill took the historic decision, on the eve of World War I, to shift fuel for the Royal Navy from coal to oil); supporting Jewish aspirations in Palestine in order to protect the eastern flank of the Suez Canal and to encourage American Jews to pressure the US into entering the war in support of the Allies; and safeguarding sea and land routes to India. Part of the reason that people in the region were so willing to believe conspiracy theories was because they learned from a young age of the scheming of the great powers.

In the end, Arabs had gained independence – but divided into a number of nation states rather than the dream of Arab nationalists for a single territory bound by language, history and culture. And the establishment of Israel in Palestine was viewed by many as a colonial imposition to keep Arabs divided.

The taxi driver was clearly in a bad mood – and had taken an immediate dislike to me. I sank into silence. I did not know what else to say. It was a complicated history.

When the taxi pulled up at a crossroads, I suddenly noticed a hundred or so men, to our right, dressed scruffily in dark grey clothes and carrying large batons. They looked menacing, and my pulse started to race. I had not built up any rapport with the driver and did not trust him at all. I doubted he would protect me if the gang noticed me and tried to drag me out of the car.

A policeman in the vehicle in front got out and shouted directions to the gang.

'Who are these people?' I asked the taxi driver.

'They are with the government,' he said approvingly. 'They are going over to the mosque to make sure there are no demonstrations after Friday prayers.'

So these were the feared *shabiha*. I had read about ghostly groups of thugs – believed to be gangs of young Alawite men – beating up demonstrators and intimidating people. They acted with impunity, sometimes alongside the Syrian army, sometimes independently. Videos had been posted on line of *shabiha* beating and stabbing protestors, and burning the cars and homes of activists. The regime denied any knowledge of the *shabiha* – while outsourcing to them much of the crackdown on opposition.

My driver was clearly pro-Assad and was not in the slightest bit perturbed. I sank lower in my seat. Fortunately, the traffic started to move again and we drove past without my attracting any attention.

*

A few days later, on my last weekend in Syria, I met up with Robert Ford again. He had invited me to join him and a few of his embassy colleagues on a visit to some of his favourite haunts in Damascus.

Our first stop was a furniture workshop. I watched entranced as two young men shaped small pieces of mother of pearl using a filing machine. Any lapse of concentration would have sent their fingers flying through the air. Then they inserted the different fragments they had so carefully sculpted into a block of wood. Stacked against the walls behind them were beautiful boxes, tables and chests of drawers displaying the mosaic of wood, mother of pearl and stone for which Damascus is famed.

Then we went to an art gallery, where Robert was warmly greeted by the Syrian Christian owner. He walked us around the displays hung on the walls of the beautiful Damascene house. I stopped in front of a couple of paintings by a well-known Syrian artist. He had painted heads – heads without mouths and ears.

After the tour, we sat in the courtyard drinking tea. Before long the conversation turned to the situation facing the country.

By now everyone in Syria had heard about Robert's trip to Hama – and had an opinion on it. I had heard differing views from various Syrians. Some claimed that the Americans were deliberately stoking up sectarian tensions and causing the problems in Hama; others believed that the visit had prevented more people being killed, by showing that the international community was watching. One had told me that the Americans were supporting the regime – why else would the regime have allowed the visit to go ahead?

'Next time you feel like visiting Hama, Mr Ambassador,' the gallery owner said with a smile, 'don't! Come have tea with me in my gallery instead.'

*

In the courtyard of Beit Jabri restaurant, in the Old City, I ate my last plate of *fuul*. The beautiful boutique hotels, established in restored Arab houses, lay empty. The rug stores and galleries had no customers. There were no visitors to the castles and archaeological sites.

I felt sick to my stomach. Ben Ali and Mubarak had both given up power when the security forces were unwilling to use violence to crush the popular protests. But in Syria, things were different. Assad was deliberately stoking sectarianism. He had ensured that key components of the security forces – in particular Alawites – believed their own fate was tied to his survival. They were therefore prepared to fight for him.

Before my eyes, I could see the shattering of the beautiful mosaic of Syria's different communities. Descending on this land was a horror that few seemed willing to recognize, let alone try to forestall. I had witnessed civil war before. In Iraq.

CHAPTER 4

They are all thieves

Iraq

June 2011

The sky was full of sand and visibility was poor. But out of the aeroplane window I could make out the Euphrates below. Land of the two rivers. I was coming back.

It had been nine months since General Odierno had given up command of US forces in Iraq, and I, his political adviser, had left the country with him. I convinced myself that I was returning to see how the Arab Spring was influencing Iraq. But in truth, not a day went by without me thinking about Iraq. I missed it so much. I missed the people; I missed the sense of purpose I had felt there, the feeling that I could make a difference.

I did not have an Iraqi visa. Visas issued in Iraqi embassies abroad were not recognized by Baghdad Airport. But what I did have was a letter from an Iraqi general in the Ministry of Interior, complete with a signature and stamp. At the airport, I presented my passport and letter, filled out a form, paid $80 and received a visa within fifteen minutes. I collected my bag. I was through.

I immediately spotted Aqil. We grinned at each other as we shook hands. Soon we were in his car speeding down the airport road – dubbed 'Route Irish' by the US military – towards the heavily protected Green Zone in the centre of Baghdad. I could not see any Americans. Not on the roads, not at the checkpoints. The US forces had nearly all withdrawn. What was new? I asked Aqil. What had changed?

'The situation is not good,' he told me. 'The government is bad. Too many assassinations.'

Aqil, a fixer who used to 'smuggle' me out of the heavily fortified Green Zone when I worked there and was supposed to only travel with official US security, was now 'smuggling' me back in as a tourist. 'Leave it to me,' he said, smiling and patting his heart with his right hand. Before long, we were through the checkpoints.

I was soon sitting with General Nasier Abadi in his home. He was a fighter pilot and the vice chief of staff of the Iraqi joint forces. I caught up on the news of his immediate and extended family, many of whom I had met at parties at his house. His grandfather, a former Iraqi prime minister, had married off his three daughters to a Sunni, a Shia and a Turkmen respectively, so Nasier had relatives of all persuasions.

I took a dip in Nasier's pool for respite from the forty-degree heat. The brown of the sand-filled sky was broken by flashes of grey, white and yellow lightning. Later in the evening, the rolls of thunder were replaced by the thuds of mortars targeting the US embassy down the road.

*

The next day, General Nasier instructed two young Iraqi army officers to drive me south to his farm on the Euphrates. I sat in the back seat wearing an abaya and a hijab, chatting to the two officers in the front. The young men told me they were both from Baghdad and were Shia. In the 2010 national elections, the year before, one had voted for Nuri al-Maliki to remain prime minister, but the other had voted for Ayad Allawi as he wanted a secular man to lead Iraq.

The officers both agreed that life had been better under Saddam: there had been more security, people could travel anywhere safely, petrol was cheaper, salaries went further, and there was no Sunni/Shia differentiation. They told me that people were very upset with poor public services, especially electricity, but were too scared to demonstrate. No one liked living under occupation – but people were also worried that the situation might deteriorate if and when all the Americans left.

We drove south for an hour, passing numerous checkpoints. No one checked my papers; my Islamic dress made me invisible. It was late, so the roads were not busy. Finally, we turned off the main road, down a track, through an orchard, and arrived at the house by the Euphrates. There I was met by Nasier's son, Saad, and he introduced me to his companions. Tables were arranged, and big trays of *fattoush* salad and *maqluba* (chicken and rice) were brought out from the house.

As we ate, Saad spoke about his experiences working with the US military. 'They have big hearts,' he told me, 'but they are naive. They don't know how to do contracting. They spent lots of money, but so much was wasted. They did not know who was good and who was bad. Many projects were not implemented well. Others were not sustainable. The Brits last century left us with railways, roads and bridges. What have the Americans left us?'

I asked Saad's friends about themselves. I discovered that one woman was a Kurd who was born and bred in Baghdad, two were Sunnis and the others were Shia, and all had relatives of different sects. 'We are Iraqis,' they told me firmly, one after the other. They had known each other for years.

It was midnight. I lay back on the large swing chair on the bank of the river, wrapped myself up in a blanket and fell asleep. But my peace was rudely interrupted around 2 a.m. by a massive explosion which shook the ground. For a moment, I wondered if we were being attacked. Then I speculated that perhaps there were still some Americans on a nearby base. I did not move, and quickly fell back to sleep.

I awoke again around 5 a.m. when the sun rose, and placed a shirt over my eyes. I dozed until the heat of the sun became too much. The caretaker brought me tea. He told me he had also slept outside, guarding me through the night, making sure I was safe and keeping away the dogs – which looked like wolves. I thanked him.

He squatted down beside me to chat. 'The Americans had bases here,' he said. 'Our people attacked them. Gangs. The Americans did not know who was good and who bad.' He told me how, one time, he had been up a palm tree picking dates when Americans shot at him. He giggled as he recounted how he had fallen out of the tree. Another time, he had approached an American checkpoint and they demanded he take off his top, then his trousers, then his underwear. They made him walk stark naked. On another occasion, he thought a gang was breaking into the plantation so he opened fire. In fact, it was a group of American soldiers and he wounded one. The Americans arrested him and sent him to Bucca prison camp, near Basra.

I asked the caretaker how his life was these days. He told me he only had a few hours of electricity a day at home – it came on for one hour and then went off for four hours. During the hour that it was on, he ran the air conditioner to make his room as cold as possible. It was very difficult for people, he said. They slept out on the roofs. He spoke about the 'time of the British', the 'time of Saddam', and the 'time of the Americans'. He had already consigned the American period to history.

Later, wearing a T-shirt and shorts, I climbed up on the jet ski that belonged to Saad and sped up the Euphrates. Normally, I would never go on a jet ski. They were noisy beasts that disturbed any sense of tranquillity. But this time I made an exception. I had never seen jet skis in Iraq before and it seemed too good an opportunity to miss. The dust of the previous day had cleared and the sky was a brilliant blue.

I waved to people on the banks and they waved back. I passed the Iskandriya power station that had once served as a US base. Further up on the left was Jurf al-Sakhar. The Americans used to call this area the 'triangle of death' because of the levels of violence. I remembered landing by helicopter on numerous occasions on visits to the troops, receiving briefings about insurgents moving down the river and about the efforts to clear the area. Now it was just me on the river. The insurgents had been defeated and the US bases had gone.

I jumped off the jet ski into the water and swam alongside it back down the river, floating with the current. These days, there were no dead bodies bobbing in the water, there was no stench of death. I could not wait to describe all of this to my friends in the US military.

Out the back of the house, surrounded by sheep and chickens, the caretaker was busy barbequing a fish that a fisherman brought for us that morning. Saad had gutted it earlier, washing it in the river and then butterflying it to put under the grill. One of the women placed the *masgouf* on a tray and brought it out to the table on the riverbank. We ate standing up, pulling off bits of the fish with our fingers and scooping up salads with freshly baked bread. It was delicious.

*

Back in Baghdad, Krikor Derhagopian, an adviser to Vice President Tareq al-Hashimi, invited me to his home for lunch. His family lived in a part of Baghdad that used to be a Jewish area. The 1917 census put the Jewish population of Baghdad at 40 per cent. But the position of this established community, which contributed considerably to the economic and cultural life of the country, deteriorated rapidly following the establishment of the state of Israel. Around 118,000 Jews left Iraq in the 1950s, with just 6,000 choosing to stay. Today, only a handful remain of a community that can trace its origins back to the destruction of the First Temple in Jerusalem in 587 BC.

Krikor's Armenian family had bought the house in 1954. The tapestries, rifles and photos on the walls were mementos of the bygone era of the monarchy. Krikor's great-grandfather had been such a supporter of the royal family that when he heard they had all been brutally murdered in 1958, he fell down the stairs to his death.

Against a long wall, shelves were crammed with books. Krikor lived here with his wife and son and his parents. His mother, an elegant, well-dressed woman, told me of how the Armenians escaped to Iraq as refugees from the genocide in Turkey. Many Armenians were taken in by Arab tribes around Mosul. 'The Arabs were so kind and generous to us, bringing up orphans as their own children. We will always remember how good they were to us.' Then she added: 'But we will never forgive Turkey.'

Christians have been living in Iraq since the first century, but their numbers started to decline under sanctions in the 1990s. At the outbreak of the 2003 war, the number of Christians (Chaldean, Assyrian, Syriac and Armenian; Orthodox, Catholic and Protestant) was estimated at 1.5 million. Membership of the myriad Christian communities had since gone down to under 450,000.

Krikor's mother lamented that Iraq was on the way to losing all its Christians. So many were leaving for the US. 'What will they find there? Life might be easier, but here in Iraq is where we have our families, our history, our culture.' She sighed, and told me that everyone had had such high hopes after the fall of the regime. No one had expected it to turn out this way. But even in her most depressed moments, she never wished Saddam back.

Krikor's wife had cooked a feast of Armenian foods and I sampled every plate. As I departed, she gave me a bag of leftovers that would feed Nasier's family for days.

As Krikor drove me back across town, we heard on the radio of an attack on the provincial council in Diyala that had left eight killed and over twenty wounded; an Iraqi general had also been assassinated in Baghdad.

*

One evening, Safa al-Sheikh, the deputy national security adviser, took me on a tour of Baghdad. He was an old friend who had taught me much about the country over the years. Erudite and learned, he had become religious as a young man, had joined the underground Shia Islamic Dawa Party, and while serving in the air force had also been a member of the Baath Party. Iraqis were skilled at hedging their bets. He had two wives: one Sunni, one Shia.

Baghdad had once flourished as the cultural capital of the Islamic world. It was here that Caliph Harun al-Rashid established the House of Wisdom, which served as a library, a translation institute and an academy, bringing together scholars from across the Muslim world. For five hundred years, the city was the centre of the Abbasid Caliphate (the third caliphate to succeed the Prophet Mohamad). But all that was destroyed in the thirteenth century, when Mongol hordes sacked the city. Led by Hulagu Khan, the grandson of Genghis Khan, they attacked Baghdad in 1258. Up to a million of its residents were massacred, and the caliph was murdered. Great architecture – built over centuries – was razed to the ground. Ancient systems of irrigation were demolished.

Baghdad's libraries, the repository of knowledge from the Islamic golden age, were destroyed. The waters of the Tigris were said to have run black with the ink from all the books.

British general Sir Stanley Maude, when he marched into Baghdad in 1917, proclaimed to the inhabitants that 'our armies do not come to your cities and lands as conquerors or enemies, but as liberators.' He noted that since the time of Hulagu 'your city and your lands have been subject to the tyranny of strangers, your palaces have fallen into ruins, your gardens have sunk in desolation.' Under the monarchy, which the British introduced and mentored, Iraq's fortunes improved for a while. But the royals were murdered in the 1950s. And, since then, the city had been subjected to years of wars and sanctions.

When the Americans invaded Iraq in 2003, President George W. Bush promised a new era of freedom and democracy. What followed were years of anarchy and occupation. The country descended into civil war; and hundreds of thousands were killed before it was brought under control.

Safa and I visited the neighbourhoods where fighting had once consumed the city and ethnic cleansing had shattered a previously cosmopolitan society. These were familiar haunts. I could clearly observe the changes that had taken place over the last year. The local economy had improved. The private sector was taking off. More shops were open. New cars were on the roads. People were busy going about their everyday affairs. Many of the high concrete walls, which had separated communities from each other, had been removed.

But despite the relative calm, Safa was concerned about 'the direction of the political process, corruption and assassinations'. In methodical fashion, we discussed the different trajectories Iraq might take: dictatorship under Maliki, who as well as being prime minister also served as Minister of Defence, Interior and National Security; a Russian-style oligarchy, with the kleptocratic political class living in comfort in the Green Zone, dividing up the country's oil revenues between them while the general population still lacked basic services; a war between the haves and have nots, with armed groups fighting the State for a share of the country's oil resources, as in Nigeria; or a return to sectarian conflict. Although the parliament was growing in capacity, and there were different media channels, the sectarian construct of the political system, the structure of the economy, and corruption hindered progress towards democracy, he said.

I asked Safa whether he believed US forces would remain in Iraq after the security agreement expired at the end of 2011. The Obama administration had spoken of keeping a small contingent – 5,000 or so – but did not appear to be doing the heavy lifting required to gain a new agreement. I had heard a couple of US officials claim that Maliki had assured them he intended to keep some US soldiers in Iraq.

Safa gave me a wry smile. Was this what Maliki had actually told the Americans, he asked, or what they wanted to believe? We both suspected it might be the latter. In 2010, to gain Iranian and Sadrist support for a second term as prime minister after he had failed to win the most seats in the elections, Maliki had committed to not extending the presence of US forces after 2011. He wanted to take credit for the departure of all

American troops. His party, Dawa, had recently put out a statement reiterating its 'firm stand toward the withdrawal of all the US forces from the Iraqi land, waters, and airspace at the set time, which is the end of this year'.

Our discussion went on for hours in the car as we drove around Baghdad.

Just like in the old days.

*

Dr Basima Jadiri and I met up in a café in the Green Zone. It was a grotty place – but there was limited choice. We reminisced about 2007 and how we had worked together closely to help bring down the violence that ravaged the country – she as the military adviser to Prime Minister Maliki, and me as the political adviser to General Odierno, the operational commander of US forces in Iraq. It seemed such a long time ago.

We discussed the problems facing the country today. How much longer would the patience of Iraqis continue, I asked her. She told me that people were tired. 'They want electricity and jobs. They want to eat and sleep. They want normal lives.' She went on: 'There is injustice. The country is rich, but the people do not see the benefits. The Iraqi people have been so oppressed for years that we are like sheep. Iraq today is so far away from the vision that people had after the fall of Saddam.'

I described to Basima my trips to Egypt and Tunisia, and how people felt empowered because they had removed the regimes themselves and with little bloodshed. They were debating their constitutions, and new politicians were coming to the fore to compete in elections.

Basima told me that, in Iraq, people did not feel that same sense of empowerment. They had not removed Saddam themselves. It was America who had put the current crop of politicians in power – many of whom were Islamists who had returned from exile abroad and were different from Iraqis who had remained in the country under Saddam. There had been no public debate in Iraq over the constitution. Many blamed the Americans for introducing sectarian and ethnic quotas – *muhasasa* – throughout the system of government in Iraq. And while Iraqi politicians claimed they did not want *muhasasa,* they maintained the quota system – and most political parties were sectarian or ethnic-based.

Iraq's political leaders were not helping the country heal. They had not come to a consensus on the nature of the state. They did little to promote reconciliation or an inclusive national identity to which all Iraqis could relate. Instead, they stirred fear of the 'other', instrumentalizing sects to mobilize support for themselves. And elections had not brought about change – instead they had kept the same politicians and the same dysfunctional system in place.

Iraq was evidence that the removal of an authoritarian regime did not necessarily lead to better governance. The gap between the political elite and the Iraqi people seemed to be growing even wider. Iraq's politicians were frequently derided as corrupt. Basima, who had lived her whole life in Iraq, quoted a common Iraqi refrain: 'Before we had one Saddam; now we have hundreds.' Without pausing, she concluded: 'They are all thieves.'

*

One Friday afternoon, I watched the government TV channel. It showed the Cabinet discussing progress in their ministries, development projects across the country, beautiful scenery and happy members of the public out shopping. I switched to Al Sharqiya. It criticized the government for lack of progress, highlighted electricity shortages across the country and the paltry number of hours received daily from the national grid, and provided details of the brutality of Iraqi security forces. I went back to the government channel and watched coverage of Iraqis gathering to demonstrate in Baghdad's Tahrir Square. I was initially confused, as the demonstrations looked nothing like those I had seen elsewhere in the region. The protestors carried placards with a red 'X' through a photo of Ayad Allawi, the leader of the party that had won the most seats in the 2010 elections but which had been blocked from trying to form the government. Sheikhs were shown demanding the death penalty for terrorists.

That evening, over dinner in a restaurant in Karrada in downtown Baghdad, some Western journalists told me they had been in the square that afternoon. They explained that the demonstrators had been 'pro-government' supporters bused in from Karbala, as well as Green Zone security guards who had been sent there to express their support for Maliki. The journalists had witnessed a small group of 'pro-democracy' protestors demanding more freedoms, an end to corruption and better public services. Government officials had accused them of being Baathists and terrorists. They were beaten up by plain-clothed men with batons – while the security forces stood by watching. And two, one of whom was a woman, were stabbed.

As we ate pizza and drank wine, an Iraqi singer entertained us with Bee Gees songs. The man sang with such passion, making the songs his own. When he finished, I invited him over to join us at our table. He sat down, and as he spoke, the talented, confident performer transformed into a fragile, damaged man. What was the trauma he was struggling with?

He told us that he had visited the United States for a short period in the seventies when he was a young boy, accompanying his father who had been wounded fighting on the Syria–Israel border and had needed plastic surgery. In 2003, the singer had got a job with the US military, but quit three months later after he was injured by a roadside bomb. I remembered the wonderful Iraqis who had worked with the coalition back in 2003, dreaming of building a new democratic society – many were killed by insurgents for collaborating with the occupying authorities, and many others had fled the country.

The singer brought out a pouch of tobacco. 'I dip,' he explained.

'Disgusting habit to pick up from American soldiers!' I scolded him. Why did Iraqis adopt the worst aspects of US culture?

He laughed. 'Things are slowly getting better in Iraq,' he assured me. 'Iraqis just want to live normal lives. But it is going to take a long time – a very long time.'

Iraq

January 2012

I had planned to celebrate New Year's Eve in Iraqi Kurdistan, but the fates conspired against me. My flight was delayed leaving London, so I missed my connection in Istanbul. Along with dozens of other passengers flying on to Middle Eastern destinations, I approached the Turkish Airlines desk seeking a hotel room. Only one person was on duty, so it was not long before the queue disintegrated into mayhem, with everyone yelling.

A Syrian man pointed at me and shouted at the man at the desk: 'She is pregnant and sick – she urgently needs a hotel room.'

Another Syrian, standing behind me, piped up: 'Yes! And I am the father of the baby!' The Iranian and the Turk beside us burst out laughing, bonding over the outrageous ruse of the Syrians.

Thus it was that my 'family' – formed around the pretence of my being pregnant – was given priority in the assignment of a hotel. As we were being driven there, the first Syrian told me that he was heading back to his country to participate in the demonstrations, after receiving treatment in a hospital in Vienna for recent injuries. I told him about my travels in his country the previous summer. I was worried about the increasing violence. He assured me that the Syrian people would overthrow the regime and bring about democracy in the country – even it if took 'a hundred thousand lives'.

He went on: 'Millions died in Europe to bring about democracy. We will also have to fight – and die – for democracy.'

After a day in Istanbul, I arrived in Erbil on 1 January 2012. On the news, I saw that the Iraqi government was celebrating 'fulfilment day'. Prime Minister Maliki was claiming credit for ensuring the withdrawal of all US troops from the country, in accordance with the security agreement negotiated by him and the Bush administration – and approved by the Iraqi parliament – three years earlier. The Obama administration's half-hearted attempts to reach an agreement to keep a residual force in Iraq post-2011 had failed.

Armed Shia groups called it 'Victory over America Day', claiming that their attacks on US soldiers had driven America out.

While waiting in the lounge for my flight to Baghdad, I recognized two prominent Sunni Arabs. They told me they had been visiting Kurdistan to discuss the current political crisis in the country, brought on by Maliki sacking deputy prime minister Saleh al-Mutlaq for calling him a dictator, and accusing vice president Tareq al-Hashimi of terrorism, forcing him to flee to Kurdistan. Tanks, they informed me, were parked outside the houses of leading Sunnis in Baghdad. Relations between the leaders of different communities – which Americans had painstakingly nurtured and brokered – were rapidly unravelling.

One of the Sunnis, Omar al-Jabouri, was an Islamist who in 2007 had been influential in persuading Sunni insurgents to switch sides and form the so-called Awakening, working alongside the US military to fight al-Qaeda. The other, Abdullah al-Jabouri, was a secular nationalist and the former governor of Diyala Province – and before that a dentist in Manchester. They were not fully convinced when I explained that I was in Iraq on holiday. They inquired, somewhat hopefully, whether the US military was in fact still around and had only pretended to leave! The former governor informed me that the situation in Diyala was very unstable. 'Before, we could tell all our problems to the Americans. Now we have no one to tell our problems to. Could I take your new phone number?'

Safa al-Sheikh picked me up in Baghdad and we drove southwards, passing under the archway which proclaimed the Iraqi capital *Madinat as-Salaam* (City of Peace), the epithet bestowed on it during the Abbasid Caliphate when the city was the cultural capital of the region.

Our destination was the Mesopotamian Marshes. Following the routing of Iraqi troops from Kuwait and the call by President George H.W. Bush for Iraqis to overthrow the regime, the south rose up in the 1991 Shaaban Intifada. In retaliation, Saddam ordered the killing of tens of thousands of Shia – and drained the marshes to prevent rebels from hiding there. However, following the 2003 overthrow of the regime, the new Iraqi government – as well as the United Nations, and US agencies and NGOs – had been working to restore the marshes. Safa and I wanted to take a look.

The terrain was flat and featureless, with drab desert as far as the eye could see. We drove for hours through this lacklustre landscape. Occasionally, we passed through neglected villages that lacked basic services. Pools of sewage stewed by the sides of the road.

In the car, I told Safa that since I'd seen him in the summer, I had begun teaching about Iraq in the War Studies department at King's College London. I had taken Sir Lawrence Freedman up on his offer. And just before the start of term, I was asked to teach a second course on the international politics of the Middle East, following the resignation of Professor Yezid Sayigh, an old friend I had worked with in Palestine during the nineties.

I had also been appointed a fellow of the Changing Character of War Programme in Oxford. I found teaching suited me. I had students to mentor and motivate, long holidays in which to travel – and a professional reason to follow events in the Middle East closely.

We overtook a line of Shia pilgrims making the long walk to Karbala for Arbaeen, the religious observation that commemorates the martyrdom of Imam Hussein. Men were carrying Shia flags; women, dressed in black abayas, had children walking alongside them. For some, the journey would be hundreds of miles. Tents at the side of the road provided them with food and beds. Thousands were making the pilgrimage. It had been forbidden in Saddam's time.

After a couple of hours' driving, we pulled off the main road and stopped alongside a rudimentary workshop. Safa had received information of a new discovery, and wished to see it with his own eyes. I watched, mesmerized, as a technician confidently demonstrated how he was able to increase the power generated by a motor through the use of a hydraulic system. Back in the car, we expressed amazement that a poor engineer, living in the middle of nowhere, had come up with such an invention. How successful Iraq might be if it could find ways to encourage and harness the initiative and creativity of its citizens.

Five hours after leaving Baghdad, we passed Nasiriyah and entered the marshes. The villagers had placed reeds across the roads so that cars would crush them when they drove over them, flattening them into mats. Out the car window, we could see men – and sometimes young girls – propelling the traditional *mashuf* boats with long poles, just as punters and gondoliers do in Oxford and Venice.

Finally, we came to a stop at a prearranged place. We climbed into a *mashuf* with a couple of guards and local sheikhs and set off, passing floating *mudhif* houses built out of reeds as we made our way through narrow channels between the bulrushes in the marshes flooded by the Euphrates. We saw *jamoos* (water buffalo) on the banks, and on one occasion they swam in front of us, much to our delight. I spotted ducks, herons, egrets, lapwings and sandpipers. Birds of prey hovered above us.

One of our guides explained how fighters from Dawa (prime minister Maliki's formerly outlawed party) had once hidden in these areas and fought against Saddam. 'Where is Jaysh al-Mahdi?' I asked, inquiring after the militia of the Shia cleric Muqtada al-Sadr.

One of my companions put up his hand. 'I am Jaysh al-Mahdi! And the man behind me is Asaib Ahl al-Haq, and the boatman is Kataib Hezbollah.' Everyone roared with laughter as the names of Shia militias that had once caused such problems in Iraq were bandied around. Now, the Iraqi security forces controlled the country, and the militias were dormant – if not disbanded.

After a couple of hours on the water, we moored on a bank. A large plastic mat was placed on the ground, and out of nowhere appeared dishes of food – *masgouf*, loads of flatbread and some pickles. We removed our shoes and sat down cross-legged. '*Bismillah*,' the Iraqis said, before tucking into the feast with their fingers. They were quick to direct me towards the fleshiest and least bony parts of the fish. It was the best *masgouf* I had ever tasted. As we were packing up to leave, a poet arrived unannounced to serenade 'the guests from Baghdad', waving an arm in the air as he danced on the spot.

The next day, Safa and I visited Thi Qar University in Nasiriyah and arrived to find big banners, with our names on, welcoming us. But it was slightly disconcerting to discover that I was being described as an Oxford University professor who was an expert on the marshes. Numerous men got up and delivered long speeches before I was finally invited up onto the podium.

I stood up and said, 'I will give a short speech – only for one hour!' I spoke about how, when I was a student at Oxford, I had once met Wilfred Thesiger, the British explorer who had lived in the marshes in the 1950s and written about the wonderful culture of the Marsh Arabs. I had always dreamed of visiting the marshes. And now this dream had become a reality. What an honour it was to visit the site of the Garden of Eden and the cradle of civilization. I then described the wonderful time I had spent the previous day on the boat and eating *masgouf.* And I told them that beforehand I had been scared to visit as I was worried that Shia militias might kidnap me. That received many laughs. I then sat down.

One sheikh shouted out: 'That was only five minutes; you promised to speak for an hour!'

While fear of public speaking is second in the West only to fear of death, the same is certainly not true in Iraq. They could set Guinness World Records for their ability to talk at great length without notes.

*

After finishing up at the university, we went to a marsh flooded by the Tigris. It was deeper, and the channels were broader than the marsh we had visited the previous day. One of my companions passed me his 9mm pistol so he could take a photo of me pretending to shoot fish. I put the photo up on Facebook. An American friend immediately commented on the photo, asking why I was not using dynamite. The Iraqis all roared with laughter when I read out his message, impressed by the American's knowledge of Iraqi fishing practices.

We parked up on a bank for lunch. The large mat was again rolled out, and *masgouf* and freshly baked bread set out before us. The weather was colder than the previous day, and there was a sharp wind. Seeing that I was shivering, one of the sheikhs took off his large brown cloak and placed it over my shoulders.

'You are my new husband,' I told him, much to everyone's amusement.

When we came to part an hour or so later, I handed him back his cloak. 'My new wife,' he exclaimed as he kissed me on the cheek. The others shrieked with laughter and requested to take a photo of us together.

'No, no, no,' he warned them, shaking his finger. 'That will get me into serious trouble with my wife!'

While we were in the marshes, news reached us that a suicide bomber had attacked pilgrims in Nasiriyah. There were reports of forty-five killed and over eighty injured. I suggested to Safa that we visit the hospital, as the wounded and the medical staff would appreciate a senior government official showing concern.

On our arrival at Nasiriyah hospital, we discovered that the injured took up two floors of the building. Some were badly burned; some had bomb fragments in their heads. One child could not speak as he was still in shock.

One of the wounded told us that he knew the army officer who had tackled the suicide bomber. He described how Lieutenant Uthman, a Sunni from Kirkuk, had grabbed the terrorist and tried to drag him from the crowd, putting his whole body around him. The officer died in the explosion, along with many others, but more pilgrims would certainly have been killed if not for his actions.

Another bandaged pilgrim described the heroic act of this officer. 'He is a Muslim from another sect. A true Muslim. Please do something for his family.'

Safa texted a message to the prime minister. We later heard that Maliki posthumously promoted Uthman two ranks so that his family would receive extra compensation.

Safa then told the wounded: 'This is not about Sunni and Shia. This is about terrorists who have no respect for human life or Islam.'

I was astonished by the way in which the injured reacted to the attack. A number of them spoke about their faith and how suffering was part of their Shia tradition. No one spoke about revenge. I did not hear anyone spew hatred of Sunnis.

Many Western officials and commentators attribute the violence in the Middle East to 'ancient hatreds' between Sunni and Shia. This is a simplistic explanation which assumes that the conflicts are 'in the blood' or primordial, and hence

Camel market, Omdurman, Sudan

Meroe Pyramids, Sudan

Young woman leads chants in Cairo's Tahrir Square, Egypt

Poster in Cairo's Tahrir Square depicts Mubarak's cabinet with vampire teeth

Mubarak's National Democratic Party headquarters in Tahrir Square gutted by fire

Avenue Habib Bourguiba, Tunis

A woman walking down a street in Kairouan, Tunisia

Great Mosque of Kairouan, Tunisia

Umayyad Mosque, Damascus, Syria

Palmyra, Syria

Sky visiting Mosque of Sayyidah Zainab, in south-east Damascus, Syria.
(Photo by Colonel Raad)

President Bashar al-Assad speaks with US Ambassador Robert Ford, following his presentation of his credentials in January 2011
(Photo by the office of the Syrian presidency)

US Ambassador Robert Ford, Sky and US Public Affairs Officer Bryce Isham drinking tea in an art gallery in the old city of Damascus

Sky and Dr Basima Jadiri in a café in the Green Zone, Baghdad

Sky pretending to shoot fish with a 9mm pistol in the Mesopotamian Marshes, Iraq
(Photo by Safa al-Sheikh)

The Mesopotamian Marshes, Iraq

Deera Square, Riyadh

Masmak Fort, Riyadh

Sky in Diriyah, an old
neighbourhood of Riyadh

McDonalds in
Panorama Mall,
Riyadh

beyond political solutions – it also conveniently excuses Western powers of any responsibility in creating the conflict or in helping to resolve it.

The schism in Islam stems from disagreement over the succession to the Prophet Mohamad and whether it should be through kin or competence – the bloodline or the person most suitable to rule. Yet Sunni and Shia lived together mostly peacefully in this land for centuries upon centuries. Many of the tribes who migrated to the south converted from Sunni to Shia Islam in the late eighteenth century to avoid conscription and paying taxes to the Ottomans.

Since the creation of the modern nation state of Iraq, there have been struggles over its political orientation. The main ideological tension was between Iraqi first identity (emphasizing territorial nationalism) and Arab nationalism (Iraq as part of the Arab nation). It was the 1979 Islamic Revolution in Iran that politicized religion across the region; and the 2003 US-led invasion of Iraq that unleashed sectarian conflict on a mass scale.

Yet despite all the violence, individual identities remained fluid and complex; and communal identities still continued to coexist with an Iraqi national identity. Lieutenant Uthman's sacrifice of his own life to save the pilgrims – regardless of them being from a different sect – was evidence of the desire of many ordinary people to live together peacefully as Iraqis.

*

The next day, Safa and I – along with our guards – set off for Ur, an important city-state in Sumerian times. On arrival, we came across an international archaeological team. Elizabeth

Stone, an American professor in her sixties from Stony Brook University in New York, told us she had just returned to dig in Iraq after a twenty-year absence.

She described the Sumerians who had inhabited the area. 'Here is where civilization began,' she said. 'The first settlements, the first writing, the first law.' Pointing in various directions, she conjured up images of different eras, their ways of life, their social patterns. The rich history of Mesopotamia, the pre-Islamic past – the heritage of every Iraqi.

I raced up the steps of the Great Ziggurat, which had originally been built in the twenty-first century BC as a shrine to the moon god Nanna – and restored in the sixth century BC. The massive step pyramid measures 210 feet in length, 150 feet in width and 100 feet in height. From the top, I could see for miles across the barren desert. On one side was Tallil Air Base, which had served as the US Army's Camp Adder until it was handed back to the Iraqi Air Force.

I remembered reading about Ur of the Chaldees in Bible Studies at school. Having visited Abraham's tomb in Hebron in the 1990s, I was now visiting his birthplace. Saddam had ordered the site to be restored, hoping to entice a visit from Pope John Paul II to the place where God first spoke to Abraham. The Pope had determined to mark the millennium by praying at important biblical sites. But, in the end, politics had intervened and the Pope had not come.

On the way back to Baghdad, we stopped off at the shrine of Ahmad al-Rifai, the founder of a Sufi order. It was looked after by a Sunni family – Sufis themselves – living among Shia. We were welcomed into the reception room, and sat cross-legged on the floor on cushions. The sheikh told us he was a hundred years old and had gone through eleven wives in his life. He still looked fit and active!

As we walked over to look at the shrine, I took one of the Sufis aside and asked him in a whisper: 'Do you whirl?' Yes, he responded excitedly, telling me that last summer, up to 5,000 Sufis had descended on the shrine and all whirled together. We both stretched our arms out parallel to the ground, and spun around on the spot. I told him that I had visited Sudan last year and gone to see the Sufis in Omdurman.

'Next summer, when all the Sufis come to us to whirl, we will call you,' he promised me.

'Thank you,' I replied. 'I will come.'

*

It was gone midnight by the time we reached Baghdad, and I was tired. We went through the checkpoint into the Green Zone. I had wanted to stay with my friend General Nasier Abadi but he had been forced to retire from the military, suspected of being too close to the Americans, and his house had been assigned to another official.

Rafi al-Issawi – the finance minister and a senior Sunni leader – had invited me to stay with him. But when we arrived we found a tank blocking the road, and its gun turret was pointed straight towards Rafi's house. The tank commander would not let us pass. I was furious.

Safa offered to let me sleep at his place but I declined. I had been texting back and forth with Rafi on the journey. He had dinner waiting for me.

Safa managed to get through to a senior official in the prime minister's office and explained the situation. He then passed his phone to the tank commander, who was given orders to let us through.

Safa deposited me at Rafi's door before driving back to his own home. Rafi and his adviser, Jaber al-Jaberi, welcomed me warmly. We sat in the kitchen eating stone-cold kebab. Rafi and Jaber told me that Maliki was pushing the Sunnis to breaking point with threats against their leaders, arrests of so-called Baathists, and the dismissal or 'retirement' of army officers. They warned that Sunni politicians would not be able to control the streets for much longer. They feared that Maliki's policies were pushing Iraq towards civil war again, and they blamed the US for failing to uphold the 2010 election results, thus providing an opening for Iran to broker the deal to keep Maliki as prime minister.

Jaber asked me: 'Why did America give Iraq to Iran? Everything in Iraq is now controlled by Iran.'

I did not know how to respond. The Iran–Iraq war in the 1980s had been devastating and continued to shape the world view of the leaders of the Islamic Republic. Iran was now exacting revenge. It wanted to make sure that Iraq remained weak – and never able to threaten it again.

Rafi shook his head. 'How could America leave Iraq in such a state?'

However, the Obama administration did not appear in the slightest concerned. It was more interested in taking credit for keeping good its campaign promise to bring all US troops home. In a ceremony in Baghdad the previous month to mark the withdrawal of all US forces from the country, Vice President Joe Biden had noted, 'There were those who charged that America was abandoning Iraq and that one of two outcomes would result... either Iraq would slide back into ethnic or sectarian war, or that other countries in the region would unwelcomingly fill the vacuum. In my view, in the President's view, those arguments not only misunderstand the Iraqi politics, but they underestimate the Iraqi people.'

He went on: 'You raised an army that all of Iraq and the world can be proud of, so that you can keep your people safe. And even more remarkable, you've forged a political culture based on free elections and the rule of law.'

CHAPTER 5

Zero neighbours without problems

Turkey

October 2012

I sat in the lounge of a newly opened hotel in Istanbul's Taksim Square, reading up on what was happening in Syria.

Robert Ford, the US ambassador who I had visited in Damascus the previous year, had since been withdrawn from the country. He had recently put out a statement which read: 'Assad's brutal dictatorship will come to an end... After the regime falls, it will take hard work by Syrians to rebuild their state and their country... As Syrians work to unite behind a common vision and transition plan, and to rebuild and recover from 40 years of brutal Assad dictatorship, the United States and the international community will be there to support them.'

Yet despite harsh statements from American and European officials, Assad showed no signs of stepping down. And the international community could not reach agreement in the

UN Security Council on how to stop the bloodshed. The UN Charter states: 'All Members shall refrain in their international relations from the threat or use of force against the territorial integrity or political independence of any state.' (Chapter I: Article 2 (4)). The only legal exceptions to that article are through UN Security Council authorization, self-defence under Article 51 of the UN Charter, or the consent of the government of the country in question.

China and Russia were clear that they would veto any UN resolution on Syria that could be used as a pretext for regime change. They had abstained from voting on the UN resolution to approve a no-fly zone over Libya and 'all necessary measures to protect civilians'. Later, they complained that it had been stretched beyond its original mandate and was used to get rid of Gaddafi.

On Syria, it was hard to make an argument for self-defence, as Assad was not threatening other countries. And Assad was not going to consent to Western intervention which might overthrow his regime.

Kofi Annan, the UN's special envoy for Syria – and a former Nobel Peace Prize winner and former secretary-general of the UN – had spent six months pushing a peace plan. On 30 June 2012, the Secretaries-General of the United Nations and the League of Arab States, foreign ministers from China, France, Russia, the United Kingdom, the United States, Turkey, Iraq, Kuwait and Qatar, and the High Representative of the European Union for Foreign and Security Policy met at the United Nations Office in Geneva as the Action Group for Syria. This group then issued the Geneva Communiqué, calling for the establishment of a transitional governing body that would exercise 'full executive powers' and 'could include members of the present Government and the opposition and other groups and shall be formed on the basis of mutual consent'. The communiqué set out a six-point plan to stop the violence and move towards a political agreement, with a national unity government to oversee the drafting of a new constitution and general elections.

Kofi Annan had warned the Action Group that 'an international crisis of grave severity now looms'. He described the threat of regional spillover, international terrorism, increased radicalization and extremism, and further sectarian conflict. 'No one should be in any doubt as to the extreme dangers posed by the conflict – to Syrians, to the region and to the world.'

Yet while it was acknowledged that primary responsibility for resolving the conflict lay with Syrians, neither the Syrian government nor the Syrian opposition were represented in the talks. Iran and Saudi Arabia – two of the biggest funders and equippers of opposing armed groups on the ground in Syria – were also not included.

In August 2012, Kofi Annan had resigned from his role as the UN special envoy, citing the intransigence of the Syrian government, the growing militancy of Syrian rebels and the disarray of the international community.

My reading about these events was interrupted by the arrival, on schedule, of the Turkish diplomat Murat Özçelik. Murat had served as Turkey's ambassador to Iraq during my time there. He still looked the same, with his shock of white hair and signature bushy white moustache.

Murat had a terrible cold. He blamed it on having recently given up smoking. (His coughing had got so bad that his doctor had told him to quit or die.) And even though it was only mid-afternoon, he ordered whisky for 'medicinal purposes'. I ordered white wine for 'jet lag'.

We had much to catch up on. I had recently moved to the United States. It had all come about rather unexpectedly. General Stan McChrystal, the storied commander of the Joint Special Operations Command, was teaching at Yale, after retiring early from the military due to comments that his team were alleged to have made about senior US officials, including Vice President Joe Biden. McChrystal had pulled in his old brother-in-arms, General Graeme Lamb. Lambo had asked me to come talk to their students, and on the basis of the two lectures I had given, I was offered a contract as a senior fellow at the Jackson Institute for Global Affairs. It was now October break, and I wanted to see what was going on in the north of Syria. The only way to get in was via Turkey.

Every time Murat sneezed or coughed, he poured himself another whisky. And with a laugh that shook his whole body, he raised his glass. I raised mine. 'For medicinal purposes!' we chimed in unison.

Murat was extremely agitated by the situation in Iraq. He had tried hard in 2010 to prevent Maliki from serving a second term as prime minister. But he had failed. The Iranians had outmanoeuvred him – helped by the US. Now Maliki was accusing Sunni politicians of terrorism, forcing them out of the political process. In retaliation for Turkey's support for his rivals, the Iraqi prime minster was blocking contracts with Turkish companies.

'Iran benefited the most from the Iraq War,' Murat declared, shaking his head in disbelief. Why had the US given in to the Iranian schemes?

Murat feared Iraq was headed in an ominous direction. 'After all that investment in blood and treasure, why did the US act against its own national interests?' Murat asked. It made no sense to him. He was angry; I was angry. We drank more.

After we had exhausted conversation on Iraq, we moved on to Turkey. Murat was a Kemalist – an admirer of Mustafa Kemal Atatürk, who had founded the modern state of Turkey in 1923 out of the remnants of the Ottoman Empire. And Murat was concerned at what he perceived to be the growing authoritarianism of Turkey's prime minister, Recep Tayyip Erdoğan.

Erdoğan was an interesting character. He had grown up in a working-class area of Istanbul, attended an Islamic school and become a professional football player. He was elected mayor of Istanbul in 1994. In 1999, he served a four-month jail sentence for religious incitement after reading out a poem which included the lines: 'The mosques are our barracks, the domes our helmets, the minarets our bayonets and the faithful our soldiers...' He helped found the Justice and Development Party (AKP), which was, in essence, the Turkish version of the Muslim Brotherhood. The AKP won elections in 2002 and has been in power ever since, appealing to those Turks who are working class, from rural areas and religiously conservative.

The AKP was reorienting its outlook towards the Middle East, expanding regional commerce and forging free trade agreements. It trumpeted a foreign policy of 'zero problems' with its neighbours.

Erdoğan had visited Egypt, Libya and Tunisia in September 2011, confident that the new leaders in these countries would be Islamists ideologically aligned with the AKP. He touted the 'Turkish model' of democratic Islamist politics and free market economics as an example for the region to emulate.

But a lot had changed in a year. Egyptians had already begun protesting against the poorly performing Muslim Brotherhood government that had been democratically elected in the summer. Libya had descended into chaos after the brutal killing of Gaddafi. Only Tunisia seemed to be moving forward in a positive direction. Turkey had also fallen out badly with Israel over the killing by Israeli commandos of ten Turkish activists on board an aid flotilla that was attempting to break the blockade of Gaza.

When the protests had broken out in Syria the previous year, Erdoğan had tried to persuade Assad to choose reform over repression. Even after Obama explicitly announced in August 2011 that the Syrian president had to go, Erdoğan continued reaching out to Bashar. But Assad ignored him and Erdoğan changed his tune, calling for him to step down, believing that the US was going to intervene as it had done in Libya.

Turkey was getting sucked deeper into its neighbour's civil war, and Syrians were flooding across the border in search of safety. Erdoğan was allowing Syrian opposition groups to operate out of Turkey – and for weapons and foreign fighters to pass through. According to polls, three-quarters of Turks were opposed to Turkish intervention in Syria. Their country was suffering economically because of the crisis.

Murat told me that things had heated up further in recent days. A mortar attack on the border town of Akçakale had killed five Turkish civilians. Turkey had blamed the Syrian regime and shelled military outposts in Syria in retaliation. This came on the back of the Syrian military shooting down a Turkish warplane over the Mediterranean, killing the two crew members. NATO, of which Turkey was a member, called an emergency meeting to discuss the situation, fearing that the civil war in Syria could escalate into regional conflagration.

Iran and Russia proposed that Assad oversee elections, in which the Syrian people would determine who they wanted as their leader. Turkey, in contrast, wanted Assad to step down immediately, then for Syria to implement a transition phase. Erdoğan felt that he was following the US lead – but he had become increasingly frustrated that Obama was not doing more to push Assad out.

'Turkey now has zero neighbours without problems,' Murat noted. He began coughing. I patted him on the back. He laughed and poured himself another whisky, and me more wine. We raised our glasses once more.

'It's so bizarre,' I noted. 'The US is partnered with Iraq, which is supported by Iran, which is propping up the Assad regime, which the US is trying to topple.'

Not to be outdone, Murat responded: 'And the US is partnered with Qatar, which supports the Muslim Brotherhood – and Hamas. And the US is partnered with Saudi, who are Salafis… So much for supporting democracy!'

Obama wanted to be on the right side of history. But traditional US allies in the region are countries whose values the United

States does not necessarily share, and whose interests are not always aligned with America. And these countries were sensing opportunities to advance their own pawns among the chaos.

As ambassador to Iraq, Murat had broken new territory in developing close relations between Turkey and Iraq's Kurds. But Murat was having less success in his new role dealing with the Kurdistan Workers' Party (known by its Kurdish acronym, PKK), a Turkish Kurdish militant group.

In 2005, the AKP reached out to the PKK, offering what it referred to as a 'democratic opening' to end the conflict that had caused the deaths of 40,000 people in Turkey. In 2011, the PKK officially announced that its goal was to seek 'democratic autonomy' within Turkey – not independence. But the government's outreach had since broken down. The PKK was becoming more active again, seeing in Syria an opportunity to exploit the vacuum in the north through its affiliate, the People's Protection Units (YPG).

The afternoon turned to evening, and then to the early hours of the next day. Over the eight hours Murat and I talked, I lost count of the number of bottles of whisky and white wine that we drank our way through. We had long stopped being coherent by the time we bade each other farewell.

I woke up at noon the next day with a shocking hangover, gasping for water. I recalled that at some stage during our drinking session we had solved all the problems of the Middle East. But I could not remember what our proposed solutions were. My head was throbbing.

I turned on the television. In my sorry state, I lay in bed watching Al Jazeera footage of the suffering of Syrian civilians at the hands of the regime. There were 30,000 now dead. Clips of protests, fighting, bombings – often recorded on iPhones and put up on YouTube – were being beamed across the region. It was devastating to watch. It would be hard to stop what was now set in motion. The civil war was gaining momentum.

I managed to drag myself out of bed and grabbed some kebab in a cheap restaurant, then took a ferry ride on the Bosphorus. I looked out onto Hagia Sophia and the Topkapi Palace, marvelling at this truly majestic city. The salty wind revived me.

In a glitzy hotel that evening, I sat for an hour or so with a Muslim Brotherhood member of the Syrian National Council (SNC).

'Why is the US not doing more to help?' he asked me. 'We need full US military intervention in Syria. American soldiers will be welcomed by the Syrian people. I promise you, there will be peace with Israel.' I stared at him blankly.

The man asked for stinger missiles and a no-fly zone. He urged for all financial support to the Syrian opposition to go through one funnel, the Syrian National Council (SNC), in order to consolidate its leadership of the groups fighting against Assad. Things were becoming more complicated, he told me, because the Saudis and Qataris were arming different Syrian groups. He acknowledged that the SNC was dominated by Sunni exiles who had left the country years ago. However, he claimed that the SNC would meet the following month in Doha, Qatar, to expand membership to include more Syrians still based in-country.

Lamenting his disappointment in the US response, he confided in me that he believed there was a secret agreement between the United States and Russia to maintain the status quo in Syria. Why, I asked him, would the US have such an agreement? He leaned closer to me and said conspiratorially: 'To ensure that Syria remains weak so that it will not be a threat to Israel.'

*

I took a domestic flight down to Hatay in the south-east of Turkey. The province, which borders Syria, is home to diverse communities: Alawites, Christians and Sunnis. Following the collapse of the Ottoman Empire, it had become a province of Turkey in 1939 after a disputed referendum. While communal relations were usually peaceful, tensions in Hatay had come into the open the previous month, when hundreds of protestors – mostly Turkish Alawites – demonstrated against Turkey's policy on Syria.

Looking around me at my fellow passengers on the plane, it was hard not to notice that perhaps a quarter of the men were travelling without women and had beards – big bushy ones. Fighters from all over the world who were seeking to go to Syria mostly took this route, as it was easy to fly to southern Turkey and then walk across the border. Some were idealists, inspired to protect fellow Muslims from the brutality of the Assad regime, or seeking purpose in life, a sense of belonging, adventure. Similar factors in the 1930s had enticed 2,500 Brits, including George Orwell, to go and fight the fascists in Spain's civil war. Others were hardcore Salafi jihadis.

We landed in Antakya, which had become one of the hubs for foreign fighters travelling to Syria. I imagined this was what Peshawar must have been like back in the 1980s, when Arabs turned up looking to go into Afghanistan to fight the Russians.

I wandered through the streets of the city, famed for its churches and ruins and a museum that boasts the second-largest collection of Roman mosaics in the world.

Antioch (as Antakya was once known), was founded in 300 BC by one of Alexander the Great's generals and became a key trading city on the Silk Road. After annexing it, the Romans made it the capital of their province of Syria. It was one of the earliest centres of Christianity, where the followers of Christ were first called Christians and where St Paul the Apostle was once based.

The market was buzzing and doing thriving business; I heard Turkish and Arabic being spoken. There were lots of restaurants with enticing menus – the town was renowned for its cuisine. I passed cafés selling *simit* rolls and ice cream. Sitting at a juice bar, I ordered freshly squeezed orange, and drank it while Dido sang out from the radio.

One evening in the city, I hung out with a European journalist, a Syrian rebel and an Iraqi cameraman, all of whom made regular trips back and forth over the border. They discussed what was happening in Syria.

The expectations of a ceasefire for the Muslim Eid festival were low. Both sides had a number of conditions, and there was no way of monitoring compliance. The head of the opposition's military council was suspicious of the regime's motives in consenting to a break in fighting. He did not believe it was possible to hold peace talks until the regime had fallen

– otherwise all the loss of life would have been for nothing.

The Syrian rebel claimed that the opposition had had the momentum until a few months earlier, when the situation reached a stalemate. Fighting had been intense in the north. The regime was focusing on retaking border towns. It was transporting its soldiers around by helicopter. Regular army units called in air power to bomb the rebels. Crude bombs, made by filling barrels with explosives and adding a detonator, were being rolled out the doors of helicopters onto population centres below, causing massive casualties. The rebels were having difficulty holding territory.

I asked about the Free Syrian Army (FSA), which had been founded back in July 2011 by officers who had defected from the regime. The FSA now seemed to be an umbrella name for many of the different components of the opposition. It was a complex picture, the Syrian agreed. He went on to say that Jabhat al-Nusra and the Farouq Brigades were the most militarily capable. They were receiving funding and supplies from Qatar. He told me that rebel fighters were angry and disappointed that the US was not helping more. They wanted American weapons but not US troops on the ground.

'We are all Muslims, but some of us are more religious than others,' the Syrian rebel explained. He referred to the jihadis with great respect, describing them as fearless and experienced. Some referred to themselves as *ghuraba* (strangers). 'One jihadi is worth twenty ordinary fighters,' he told me.

An FSA unit, which included jihadi elements, had taken Aleppo. The regime had retaliated. This had brought destruction on the city – and disaster for its civilian population.

The Syrian rebel regarded the FSA in Homs as quite disciplined. Many of them were former Syrian army. They planned properly and gave briefings. They even provided escorts for journalists. The Muslim Brotherhood were stronger there.

He said that the FSA groups around Latakia were apparently managing to hold ground. The regime was focused on protecting the Alawite villages and shelling rebels. A new front could open up in Raqqa, he added. But there was no clear FSA plan as yet.

I went to bed with my head spinning with all this information. It was not clear what the overall strategy of the Syrian opposition was. The FSA did not seem to have any recognizable command and control. And I did not know who were the *ghuraba* – or whether there were many of them.

The next day, by chance, I bumped into Yezid Sayigh, the professor whose course I had taken over teaching at King's College London after he resigned and moved to Beirut. I explained to Yezid that I had finished the academic year at King's and had just started at Yale. Somehow, I was not surprised to find him here on the Turkey/Syria border – nor he me.

Over dinner, Yezid shared with me what he had learned since arriving in Antakya. The Syrian opposition did not appear to have a strategy – nor a coordinated leadership. They were neither focused on winning over the population nor on decreasing support for the regime. Nor were they even trying to degrade regime capabilities by cutting off supply lines and destroying airfields.

Those who had defected from the Syrian army tended to fight like regular soldiers – but they were up against the more capable military of the regime. Jihadi fighters focused on propaganda of the deed, launching terrorist attacks to undermine the government. They did not seem to care about protecting civilians. They fought from within built-up areas, knowing full well that there would be a violent response from the regime. And in many places, civilian committees had been taken over by armed groups.

The FSA was not a cohesive structure and there was not a unified command. Colonel Riad al-Assad, the supposed commander of the FSA, was unable to direct the different groups, and was criticized for being based in Turkey rather than Syria. Anyone who took up arms claimed to be part of the FSA. There was a plethora of groups competing against each other for control of different geographical locations. The only thing that appeared to unite them was the desire to remove Assad.

Yezid described the competition between armed groups to attract funding and weapons from donors. While many in the opposition bemoaned the lack of a single mechanism for funding, it was also difficult to create because there was intense rivalry over who should be the funnel.

And there were significant obstacles to developing a coherent political strategy, too. There were so many different opposition groups, with competing leaderships and with no common vision of what a post-Assad future might look like. The secular moderates spoke of elections and inclusive institutions. The jihadists wanted an Islamic state. Kurds sought to secure an autonomous region.

The way the insurgency was being waged did not bode well for the future.

*

I took a taxi along the border. We drove to Apaydin, which housed officers who had defected from the Syrian army. I could not get in as the camp was tightly controlled by Turkish authorities. There were still reports of Syrians deserting the regular army, but the numbers had declined over the previous few months, due to rumours that some had been tortured by the FSA to see if they were infiltrators and others had been killed. And the Syrian regime was apparently threatening families of potential defectors in order to dissuade them.

We continued driving, passing refugee tent camps, supplied by the Red Crescent and funded by the Turkish government. Over a hundred thousand Syrians had fled into Turkey.

I had intended to cross the border into Syria, and it was easy to find a smuggler who would take me. But then I questioned my own motives. Why did I want to go? I was not an official. I was not a journalist. How would I forgive myself if something happened to those who were taking me in? And, unlike in Iraq, I did not have trusted friends there to show me around.

In the end, I decided not to go over the border. I stood at the Bab al-Hawa crossing between Syria and Turkey, watching the trucks smuggling who knows what in and observing wounded Syrians coming out. I struck up conversation with a couple of Syrians milling around, who told me that they were worried about remaining in tents in Turkey during the winter. They hoped that the international community would create a safe haven in the north of Syria, allowing them to go back to their homes.

With my plans to go to Syria aborted, I took a taxi to the Monastery of St Simeon Stylites the Younger, south-west of Antakya. I walked among the ruins of three churches until I reached the octagonal space where the base section of a pillar still remained. It was on top of this pillar that Simeon the Younger had lived for years in the sixth century, the Christian version of an oracle.

I stood for several minutes in silence, imagining this as a pilgrimage site in former times. The location was so isolated. In the distance, I could see the hills of Latakia inside Syria.

Over a decade before, I had visited Aleppo and gone to see the remains of the pillar on which a fifth-century ascetic Syriac saint, Simeon the Elder, had sat for almost forty years. From his perch, he had preached to those who came from far and wide to hear him speak.

I had always been fascinated by the stylite saints. I could not sit still for a minute, and was always on the move. They, in contrast, had sat on top of pillars in contemplation for years and years, enduring heat, cold and lightning. What truths had they learned from their lives of piety? What wisdom about life had they shared?

What drove one pious person to asceticism – and another to violent fanaticism? This region had seen such a spectrum of fundamentalists: from the quietist Salafis and monks to jihadis and crusaders.

*

On the plane back to Istanbul, I sat next to an American doctor who told me he lived in California but was of Syrian origin. He had spent the last two weeks volunteering to treat the wounded in makeshift hospitals on the Syrian border. He was surprised to find the majority of those he was treating were 'mujahideen' and 'brainwashed'. He reckoned most were aged between eighteen and twenty-two. Many were paralysed by their injuries. 'They told me,' he said, shaking his head in disbelief, 'that their only regret was being unable to go back to fight so that they could die as martyrs.' They had taken so many painkillers that they were addicted. Many suffered from post-traumatic stress disorder.

The doctor's family had come up from Idlib in northwest Syria to visit him in southern Turkey. His brother described to him how his house had been ransacked by the FSA and all his property stolen. He claimed that the FSA blew up people's cars so that they could blame it on the regime in the media.

The doctor told me he desperately wanted to see change in Syria. It was the crimes of the regime that had driven him into exile in the US. But he was adamant that armed struggle was not the right way. 'It will bring disaster,' he declared.

*

The Arab Spring was rapidly descending into a winter that threatened to be long and bitter. It was so depressing. Syria was now mired in civil war, with tens of thousands dead. Yemen was a mess. Politics in Iraq had broken down and violence was increasing.

For every step forward, the region seemed to take two steps back. I decided my next trip would be to Saudi Arabia. It had used its petrodollars to spread its version of Islam far and wide. Perhaps in Riyadh I would find more clues to understanding why the Middle East was proving so resistant to reform.

CHAPTER 6

Better sixty years of tyranny than one night of anarchy

Saudi Arabia

December 2012

'Here is Chop Chop Square.' As we exited the museum in Riyadh's Masmak fort, my Bangladeshi escort pointed towards the ochre-coloured Deera Square.

It was mid-morning. The square was almost empty. Beheadings, if any, took place at 9 a.m. I looked around, envisaging the executioner with his sword, the terrified blindfolded prisoner with his hands tied behind his back, the expectant crowds. The clamouring, the hush, the wailing. In 2012, seventy-nine executions were reported. The decapitated heads were sewn back onto the bodies before they were buried in unmarked graves. Only one country in the region carried out more executions than Saudi Arabia this year. And that was Iran, with 314.

I checked the buttons on my abaya to ensure I was fully covered. I did not want to get into any trouble with the *mutawwa*, the religious police for the promotion of virtue and prevention of vice.

I had purchased the abaya the previous month in New York, with the help of my old friend, Mike Juaidi, who had served as a translator to the US military in Iraq. Mike took me to a shop in Brooklyn. The shop owner proudly showed me the latest fashions in abayas, embroidered with glitz and bling. I insisted that I was only looking for a functional garment.

'I am going to Saudi,' I told him. 'I just need a black cloak to throw over my clothes.'

Disappointed, he took me to the back room to view the cheap abayas. I tried one on. 'It looks beautiful on you,' he insisted. 'We can take it in at the sides to show your figure more.'

I told him that wouldn't be necessary. 'For goodness' sake, I'm not going to Saudi in search of a husband!'

An old Arab woman, seated in the corner of the store and dressed in full Muslim garb, laughed out loud at that.

*

I had never previously visited Saudi Arabia – nor had I desired to, frankly. My earliest image of the country had been formed from watching *Death of a Princess*, a 1980 docudrama about a Saudi royal who had been executed for adultery. The broadcasting of the film on ITV in the UK had been met by strong protests from the Saudis and the expulsion of the British ambassador.

Newly appointed as the current British ambassador to the Kingdom of Saudi Arabia was John Jenkins, who had previously served as ambassador to Iraq and Syria, envoy to Libya, and consul-general in Jerusalem. JJ had sent me the letter of invitation that I needed in order to apply for a Saudi visa.

JJ kindly offered to host me at his residence in Riyadh. It was comfortable and spacious, but not particularly lavish. I was assigned the guest quarters. Over the years, a stream of distinguished British officials from royals to prime ministers had slept in that bed.

During my stay, I had breakfast each morning with JJ and his wife, Nancy. JJ would read *The Times* on his iPad and Nancy the *Guardian*. And I, the *New York Times*. We would interrupt each other constantly to share titbits of information, to comment on articles and to argue. JJ was a grammar school boy from Birmingham. He and Nancy had met at Cambridge, while JJ was working on his PhD in Classics.

After breakfast, we each went our separate ways: JJ to the embassy, Nancy to the American International School where she was the principal, and I to explore the city with JJ's Bangladeshi driver.

As a woman, I was not permitted to drive, nor to venture out on my own. I was supposed to always be accompanied by a husband or male relative. However, for reasons that I did not want to fathom, Asian men were allowed to escort foreign women. The country was awash with Asian workers, brought in to do the jobs that Saudis regarded as beneath them.

I was expecting Riyadh to be like Dubai, and was surprised that the city did not appear more modern. The public spaces were not well cared for and the roads were not in great condition. And yet over the tall walls I could glimpse mansions of opulence – there was considerable wealth in the private space. GDP per capita in Saudi stood at $24,000 – but that figure gave no sense of the gulf between rich and poor.

One morning, I visited Diriyah, an old neighbourhood of Riyadh, in which the houses were made out of mud. The area was being restored, but the Saudi foreman allowed me to wander through the dusty streets. I took photos with my brand-new iPad mini, which I showed to the foreman, expecting to impress him with the latest technology. The foreman took out his iPhone 5, grinning at me. All the latest Apple products were already available. Saudi Arabia, I learned, had one of the highest per-capita usages of social media in the world.

I returned to the residence in the afternoon to find JJ sitting in shorts and a T-shirt, beating away at his drum kit, muscles flexing and the veins in his shaven head pulsating. He was passionate about music, and had once played in a band.

We dined together in the evening and discussed our respective days. JJ and Nancy lived in different Saudis. He operated in the official circles of men. Nancy moved in the hidden world of women – a world she wanted to introduce me to.

One afternoon, Nancy invited me along to a Saudi 'ladies' tea', and I had a glimpse of life behind closed doors. I hung my abaya alongside the other ones, which were, I noted, rather different to my own. They were luxurious, fine woollen, embroidered cloaks, which must have cost a thousand dollars apiece. Soon my eyes were bulging at the apparel of my fellow guests: cleavage-revealing tops, Prada handbags and three-inch-heeled Christian Louboutin red-soled shoes. I was wearing Diesel jeans and Birkenstocks. In order that we should all mingle, the host proposed 'speed-dating'. So I found myself moving from sofa to sofa, while grabbing mouthfuls of food and drinking tea.

A divorced woman revealed to me that her husband had prevented her and their children travelling outside the country. 'He received a text from the airport when I tried to fly out of Riyadh with the children.' I asked her why Saudi women put up with all these restrictions on their lives.

'King Abdullah is a modernizer,' she explained, 'but he is pushing against traditional forces which are very resistant to change.' Women were not so much scared of the *mutawwa* (the religious police), she told me, but feared being ostracized by their families. The alternative to the monarchy was religious conservatives – and that would make the position of women even worse.

The Saudi state was based on an eighteenth-century pact between Mohamed Ibn Saud and Mohamed Ibn Abd al-Wahhab. The latter's followers, the Wahhabis, had strict interpretations of Sharia law, enforced by *mutawwa*.

'Our society was not so strict when I was growing up,' the divorcée told me. However, things changed after several hundred Islamist extremists seized the Grand Mosque in Mecca during the annual Hajj pilgrimage in 1979, taking hostage around 50,000 people.

The leader of the attack declared his brother-in-law to be the Mahdi. He proclaimed that the house of Saud had lost legitimacy because it was corrupt and a puppet of the West.

Rumours circulated that America was behind the mosque attack. Anti-American demonstrations broke out around the world. The US embassy in Islamabad was burnt to the ground, killing two Americans and two Pakistani employees.

The US accused Ayatollah Khomeini of inspiring the attack. Earlier in 1979, he had returned to Iran from fourteen years in exile (mostly in the Iraqi city of Najaf) after the Western-backed shah, Mohamad Reza Pahlavi, fled the country in the wake of popular protests at inequality, corruption and state oppression. Fearful that the US was going to reinstall the shah, some Iranian students took American diplomats hostage at the embassy. Iran's Islamic Revolution politicized religion to a new level, electrifying the whole region.

Saudi forces were initially reluctant to respond to the siege as it was forbidden to bear arms in the sacred Grand Mosque. The al-Sauds had to get a fatwa from the *ulema*, the religious establishment, to authorize a military response. The Saudi forces counterattacked, using tanks and artillery – and the help of French special forces. The two-week battle left over 250 dead.

But a deal had been made. In return for its approval of the use of force against the Islamist militants, the *ulema* was granted the ability to enforce stricter Islamic codes over personal behaviour. Women had to cover themselves in cloaks and were not allowed to appear in photographs or on television; longer hours of religious studies were introduced in schools; and the religious police became more rigorous.

In response to the challenges it perceived to its legitimacy at home and abroad, the Saudi monarchy began using its petrodollars from the oil boom to shore up its Wahhabi base at home and to promulgate Wahhabism overseas.

An elegant young woman told me she was convinced that change was coming to Saudi Arabia. There had been a few protests in Saudi but they were not widespread. The monarchy had increased stipends to citizens to discourage dissent. Nevertheless, she was insistent that the country could not withstand the influence of the Arab Spring.

She asked me whether I thought a country that is rich in oil could ever move towards democracy.

I was impressed by her question. It was something I had been reflecting on a lot myself. An oil-rich country did not support itself from the taxes raised from its citizens. Instead, it lived off oil 'rents' paid by foreigners. Hence, it was independent from society and unaccountable.

Democracy requires the possibility of the transfer of power, belief in the fairness of the system and the opportunity for different groups to win elections. As far as I could make out, the legitimacy of the Saudi monarchy came from the family's history of conquest, its deal with the Wahhabis – and the fear of the alternative. The regime had been able to maintain itself through oil-based patronage and a strong internal intelligence system that monitored opposition. For its external defence, Saudi was dependent on the US.

However, Saudi's oil would run out in twenty years at the existing levels of poor management and high domestic consumption. The monarchy had limited time to diversify the economy away from oil and create jobs for the country's youth, who were increasingly connected to the rest of the world via the Internet and iPhones.

It was a fascinating afternoon. During my travels in the Middle East I had nearly always interacted with men. In Riyadh,

I was forced to wrap myself up in an abaya and forbidden from travelling around on my own. I was surprised to meet such interesting and intelligent women. While they were not at all representative of women in Saudi Arabia as a whole, I was learning there was much here that did not meet the eye. These women wanted change to come to their country. But they believed that more rights and freedoms for women would come by evolution rather than revolution.

A couple of days later, Nancy and I were invited by two of our new Saudi friends to visit one of their homes. We sat smoking shisha together in the yard. It felt terribly rebellious. Everything felt naughty in Saudi Arabia. It was like being back at school.

They told us that women were calling for more rights. They had tried to register for municipal elections. They had made headlines with their right-to-drive campaign.

One of the women was an artist. She took us inside her home to see the portraits she had painted. They hung on her own walls as she could not display them in galleries, because it was forbidden to depict heads and faces in art.

The other was a teacher. 'One year at school, the students made models of Snow White and the Seven Dwarves,' she related. 'The *mutawwa* came and chopped off all the heads.'

It took a while for this to sink in.

Seeing my dismay, the teacher went on: 'The Wahhabis even destroyed the shrines of the Prophet's descendants in Mecca.' They had perceived such sites to be symbols of idolatry. It was this same reasoning that had led the Taliban to blow up the Buddhas of Bamiyan in Afghanistan.

The teacher explained that the education system in Saudi Arabia was awful, despite the country's great wealth. The king was sending tens of thousands of Saudis overseas to study. This was bound to have an impact on society one way or another when they returned.

The two women described how people were much freer in the port city of Jeddah. And in other parts of the kingdom, different peoples – Shia, Zaidis, Sufis – continued to pursue their way of life.

'You must come on a camping trip with us in the spring,' the teacher proposed. It was an invitation that would almost make it worth returning to Saudi. Almost.

*

One evening, I went over to one of the international compounds to visit Clarisse Pásztory, a European diplomat who had previously served in Iraq. We sat in the café compound, where a sign said it was forbidden to wear an abaya. The intent was apparently to prevent a rule enforcing such clothing – but it irked me to constantly be told what I could and could not wear.

Clarisse explained to me how the Saudi version of Salafism was 'quietist', as in non-political, and how Saudis tended to support the maintenance of the status quo. The monarchy was hostile to the Ikhwan, viewing it as a shadowy underground movement that aimed to upend the existing state of affairs across the Middle East, including in Saudi Arabia. 'Better sixty years of tyranny than one night of anarchy' is the oft-quoted Arabic adage, attributed to the medieval writer Ibn Taymiyyah.

Clarisse described how oil had brought about the close

relationship between Saudi Arabia and the United States. In 1933, the Saudi monarchy had granted a concession to the US company Standard Oil – later to be called Aramco – to drill. But it was not until 1938 that it struck oil and Saudi Arabia was discovered to have massive reserves. President Roosevelt declared that the defence of the kingdom was of vital interest to the US.

In February 1945, on his way back from Yalta, where he had discussed with Churchill and Stalin the future of post-war Europe, President Roosevelt met up with Abdul Aziz ibn Saud, the first monarch and founder of Saudi Arabia, on the USS *Quincy* in the Suez Canal. It was the first time Ibn Saud had left his country. Roosevelt did not have long to live, but he wanted to cement a personal relationship with the Saudi ruler, recognizing the strategic importance of the country. In return for a steady flow of oil, the US guaranteed Saudi Arabia's security.

That guarantee was put to the test when Saddam invaded Kuwait in 1990 and threatened Saudi Arabia. The United States led a coalition to evict him and to ensure that he would not gain control of the region's energy reserves. The number of US troops in the Gulf increased from hundreds to tens of thousands.

But since 9/11, relations between the two countries had become more complicated. Back in the 1980s, the US had regarded Saudi Arabia's increased religious outreach as a check against communist expansion – and both countries had supported the mujahideen in Afghanistan to counter the Soviet invaders. But Osama bin Laden, a Saudi citizen and a so-called Afghan Arab veteran of that war, had turned against the United States, attacking the symbols of US power in 2001: the Twin Towers and the Pentagon. Fifteen out of the nineteen hijackers were Saudi citizens. This raised concerns about the form of Islam practised in Saudi Arabia.

The two countries no longer saw eye to eye on current events in the region. Much to Saudi Arabia's dismay, the Obama administration seemed to applaud the overthrow of Mubarak in Egypt. If the US was prepared to so quickly abandon a long-term partner such as Mubarak, how reliable was it as an ally? The Saudis wanted Assad removed, but the US remained hesitant about intervening in Syria.

With technological advances, including fracking, increasing US shale production, the United States was weaning itself off its dependence on Saudi oil. Meanwhile Saudi Arabia was strengthening its trade links with China by meeting Beijing's soaring demand for oil while importing cheap Chinese goods.

Not only were its relations with the United States under strain, but Saudi Arabia also felt itself challenged within the region. The custodian of the two holiest mosques in Islam – the Great Mosque of Mecca and the Prophet's Mosque in Medina – was competing not only for leadership of the Muslim world but also for the role Islam should play in political life. The young people who came out across the region to protest in the Arab Spring were in essence questioning the political legitimacy of ruling elites.

'The Saudis view the Arab Spring as a conspiracy – backed by the West – to bring the *Ikhwan* to power,' Clarisse explained.

In the recent parliamentary elections in Egypt, the Muslim Brotherhood and al-Nour Party (a Salafi group) had won 70 per cent of the vote between them; and the presidential election had been won by the Muslim Brotherhood's Mohamad Morsi – even though the Ikhwan had initially pledged they would not put forward a candidate. In the elections in Tunisia for a new constituent assembly, the Islamist party Ennahda won a plurality. Saudi viewed democratic Islamist parties as a threat to its leadership of the Sunni Muslim world.

In addition, Qatar was playing an outsize role on the global stage, using its wealth to gain influence far beyond that which might be expected from a country of 300,000 people with limited military strength. It shared the North Dome gas field with Iran and was the world's leading exporter of liquefied natural gas. Qatar had become a major backer of the Ikhwan across the region – as well as of Islamist fighters. The Doha-based Al Jazeera broadcaster extensively covered the protests against regimes, shaping perceptions across the region and beyond with its footage from the front lines – an effective instrument for promoting Qatar's partisan position.

Turkey also saw opportunities to increase its role in the region, with Erdoğan holding up his country's political system as an example for others to emulate. Libya had become the major battleground for models of governance in the Sunni world, with Middle Eastern countries providing support to different factions. All this was pushing apart former allies – and bringing closer former competitors such as Saudi Arabia and the United Arab Emirates.

Despite all the limitations on day-to-day life, Clarisse seemed to be enjoying her posting in Saudi , watching geopolitical shifts up close. There was no domestic politics as such to analyse, but there was court gossip. Lots of it. Ibn Saud had fathered forty-five sons, and all the kings of Saudi have come from this pool. But which of the grandsons would lead the country once all of the sons had died? There was much speculation over the succession.

*

During my visit, JJ hosted a dinner at the ambassador's residence, inviting a number of diplomats from different countries. Classical music played in the background as the guests mingled before taking their seats.

Next to me was an Arab diplomat who gave me further insights into Saudi Arabia. He observed that Saudi Arabia, has a different outlook from other Arab countries, because it was never colonized.

'Saudi Arabia is obsessed with Iran's projection of power – and this defines how it views the Middle East,' he noted. He went on to outline how the Iraq War had kindled a new Cold War between Saudi Arabia and Iran. And Saudi Arabia did not feel it was doing well in this contest. It had accused the US, he said, of 'handing Iraq to Iran on a silver platter'.

Iraq, which had previously been the major buffer to Iran, had turned into a battlefield. Saudi Arabia's King Abdullah was hostile towards Iraq's prime minister, because Maliki had not fulfilled a promise he had made to work towards reconciliation with Sunnis – and because he regarded Maliki as a puppet of Iran. Yet the king had great respect for the 'quietist' Shia cleric, Ayatollah Sistani, an Iranian based in

Najaf. Previously, the Saudi monarchy had supported certain Shia parties against Saddam.

'The king,' the Arab diplomat said, 'is fearful of Iran and its ambitions.' Iran even portrayed the toppling of the regimes in Cairo and Tunis as a continuation of the Islamic Revolution of 1979. 'The king believes Iran is trying to destabilize the Saudi regime through its Shia population.'

Saudi Arabia's Shia, who constitute around 10 per cent of the country's population, were concentrated in the oil-rich Eastern Province. When some of them joined in the Arab Spring protests in 2011, calling for equal rights, the king suspected an Iranian hand.

Saudi Arabia had intervened militarily in Bahrain in March 2011, invited by the monarchy to help restore order following weeks of demonstrations. Saudi Arabia suspected that Iran was supporting Shia protests in Bahrain's capital, Manama, in an attempt to overthrow the Sunni monarchy. The US called for restraint – its navy's Fifth Fleet was based in Bahrain and the US had close ties to Bahrain's royal family.

'Syria has now turned into the key battleground between Saudi and Iran,' the Arab diplomat explained. The late Syrian president Hafez al-Assad had maintained cordial relations with King Abdullah, and before he died in 2000 he had even asked the Saudi monarch to look out for his son, Bashar. However, the king had turned against Bashar al-Assad for Syria's alleged involvement in the 2005 assassination of a key Saudi ally, Lebanon's former prime minister Rafic Hariri; and for maintaining close ties to Iran. The political alliance between the Islamic revolutionary regime in Tehran and the secular

Baathist regime in Damascus had initially been forged over mutual hostility towards Saddam and Israel – and resistance against the West. Now the Iranian-Syrian alliance was against Saudi Arabia.

Saudi Arabia and Iran sought to prevent the expansion of each other's influence not through direct military conflict but through proxies.

Assad's violent response to the protests in Syria was driving his country into civil war, leading different groups to seek external support in their domestic conflict. Iran deployed some of its own military advisers to bolster the Assad regime, as well as Shia militias from Lebanon, Iraq and Afghanistan. Foremost among these was Hezbollah, the Party of God, which Iran's Revolutionary Guards had helped Lebanon's downtrodden Shia establish in the early 1980s to resist Israel.

Saudi Arabia had initially provided funding and weapons to the more secular Free Syrian Army before turning to Salafi groups it deemed 'acceptable' – while steering clear of the more extreme ones. But Sunni fighters were frequently switching groups, gravitating to whichever one seemed the most successful at any given time and competing against each other.

'Saudi strategy in Syria is not going at all well,' the Arab diplomat acknowledged.

*

'No trip to Riyadh is complete without a visit to the mall,' Nancy announced as she instructed the Bangladeshi driver to take us to Panorama Mall. It was quite a bizarre experience. As we wandered through, I noted that all the stores were

Western – Marks and Spencer, Zara, Karen Millen. But the McDonald's and Baskin Robbins food counters and seating areas were segregated by gender; the mannequins had all been decapitated in deference to Wahhabi sensibilities; and there were no changing rooms in the stores for women.

Nancy, who was quite the fashion queen – with her short peroxided blonde hair, bright red lipstick and gold-embroidered abaya – took me to Desigual and helped me choose a tight-fitting low-cut dress, covered in a bright print of women's heads.

Over dinner on my last evening in Riyadh, I spoke to JJ about the contradictions I had seen. 'Modernity for many Saudis,' he suggested, 'is a commodity that you can buy. It is Baskin Robbins, it is the iPhone. Modernity for us Europeans, at least, is Descartes, Hobbes, Hume… the French Revolution. We are cognitively modern but we ache for a past of certainty. They take an unchanging divine revelation as their foundational text but ache for a future of change.'

I went to bed wondering whether he was right. Weren't the Internet and smartphones disrupting everything?

I had gained a more nuanced view of Saudi Arabia during my visit, but there was so much I would never understand even if I spent years here – which I had no intention of doing. Everything was hidden behind walls and abayas. So much did not make sense. Why, for God's sake, would anyone cut off the heads of Snow White and the Seven Dwarves?

CHAPTER 7

… to the hill of frankincense

Oman

December 2012

Although the sultanate of Oman borders Saudi Arabia, it seemed a world away. I did not have to wear an abaya and could travel around on my own. I felt free.

One morning, I took a taxi to Muttrah. Its *souq* is one of the oldest in the Arab world. I was soon lost in the labyrinth of market stalls, eying up a silver *khanjar* (traditional dagger) and the multicoloured spices, inhaling the smouldering frankincense, and poking my head into treasure troves that opened up magical and mysterious worlds.

Emerging from the *souq*, I strolled along the corniche. I was sprayed by the waves crashing against the harbour wall. I looked out at the old wooden fishing dhows bobbing on the water and the huge tankers in the distance. About a fifth of the world's petroleum passes through the Strait of Hormuz, the waterway between the Persian Gulf and the Gulf of Oman. Although Oman's oil reserves are smaller than other Gulf countries (with the exception of Bahrain), it still has 5.5 billion barrels and 80 per cent of its revenues come from oil and gas.

I entered the vegetable market. 'Where are you from?' an old man asked me when he saw me admiring his produce. From Britain, I responded. 'It is good there,' he said, nodding. 'There is no chaos. Do you have rain?'

'Yes,' I told him, 'we have plenty of rain – too much rain in fact.'

I told him it was my first visit to Oman and that the country was beautiful.

'We have security here,' he responded. 'It is safe. The sultan is a good man.'

I followed my nose towards the fish market by the harbour. Set out on slabs were sardines, swordfish and prawns. Trade was brisk. And no one paid any attention to me as I walked up and down.

*

The next day, Greta Holtz, newly appointed as the US ambassador to Oman, invited me to attend a lunch at her residence with Omani leaders and influencers. I was seated next to a young journalist, who told me increasing numbers of Omanis were discussing political issues online, many on the web forum *Sablat Oman*.

The journalist was Baluch – and spoke Baluchi at home with his parents. There were apparently 200,000 Omanis of Baluchi descent – making it the largest non-Arab ethnic group in Oman.

Omanis, he informed me, were a diverse people – the legacy of a seafaring nation with a vast trading empire that had once extended as far south as Zanzibar. There were thousands who had returned from Africa and still spoke Swahili.

We discussed the Arab Spring. In Oman, demonstrations had begun in February 2011, influenced by events in the region. The journalist told me he had been involved in the protests. 'We called for better governance and an end to corruption,' he said. 'We demanded reforms – not the overthrow of the regime.' A petition was presented to Sultan Qaboos bin Said, with requests including an increase in salaries and the creation of more jobs.

The journalist believed that the protests had had an impact. 'Sultan Qaboos replaced twelve ministers,' he told me. 'Thousands of new jobs were created. This calmed things down.' The sultan also raised the minimum wage and introduced unemployment benefits. He abolished the Ministry of Economy, which was widely regarded as corrupt. And he sacked the police chief for being heavy-handed towards the protestors – a handful had been killed in clashes with the security forces in Sohar, a port city 125 miles north-west of Muscat. Qaboos also announced that the *Majlis al-Shura* (the parliament) would be given certain legislative and regulatory powers.

The demonstrations in Oman had ended in May 2011 after the release of a hundred or so protestors who had been detained. Sultan Qaboos – the longest-serving ruler in the Middle East – had listened to his people's demands and addressed them.

*

In order to explore Oman's interior, I hired a guide who owned a 4 × 4 car. Abdullah was in his late forties, and like most

Omanis wore a white dishdasha with a *kumma*, an embroidered cap that originated in East Africa but had long since been appropriated as Omani national dress.

On our first day out, we headed westwards towards Jebel Akhdar, the Green Mountain. Abdullah showed me the irrigation system – the *aflaj* – the origins of which dated back to 500 AD and which must have been among the most sophisticated in the world at the time. We left the car to head off on foot to the remote villages built out of mud on the edge of the rocks. The air was clean, the views stunning. We reached the oasis of Niswa, where we ate fish and biryani rice for lunch before exploring the fort.

Every village, no matter how remote, had electricity around the clock. Abdullah pointed to places where the sultan had camped out in order to hear the needs of the people. As I was to discover during my stay in Oman, Sultan Qaboos was extremely popular.

Abdullah talked to me about his country. 'Oman is the first country in the Arab world on which the sun rises each day,' he proclaimed. 'We are mostly Ibadis – not Sunni or Shia.' Oman is the only country with an Ibadi majority.

I asked Abdullah how Ibadis differed from other Muslims. He was not really able to answer the question, but simply said, 'We are very moderate and tolerant. We have good relations with everyone. We are the only Arab country to have good relations with Iran.'

In the local papers that morning I had read how Oman had helped secure the release of an Iranian who had been detained a few years previously in the UK as part of an American sting operation. Oman seemed to act as an intermediary between

Iran and the West. It was Oman that had helped facilitate the 2011 release of three Americans detained while hiking in Iraqi Kurdistan along the Iranian border.

Abdullah told me that he travelled abroad a fair amount. He enjoyed visiting Dubai on a regular basis. With its booming economy, skyscrapers and endless ambition, it was a magnet for people in the region.

'It is good to change the place from time to time, to breathe different air,' he said. 'Omanis want jobs and money to buy material goods. They are not so interested in political freedoms and democracy.'

Back in the car, Abdullah put on some music. He sang along to the songs. I did not know the words so was on percussion, keeping the rhythm by clapping my hands and drumming on the dashboard.

The roads were of very high quality, so it was easy to drive fast. Abdullah had downloaded a satnav app on his Samsung 3 smartphone, which tracked our route. 'She's a good girl,' he said, decreasing speed once again when the female voice warned him of speed cameras. 'Women are usually expensive. This one has saved me a lot of money!'

*

A few days later, I flew down south to Salalah, close to the border with Yemen. The climate was tropical, and not like anything I had ever experienced in the Middle East. I walked through a banana and coconut plantation, declining the invitation of the workers to join them for lunch. I emerged at al-Husn Souq but the market was closed. It was Friday, and most were at the mosque for prayers. The sound of the ocean drew me towards the beach. Stretched out in front of me was miles of fine, pale yellow sand. I sat alone with the birds. This was paradise.

The next day, I walked around the ruins of the port of Sumhuram, also known as Khor Rori. It had once been an important hub of the frankincense market. Used for religious ceremonies, embalming, medical remedies and as an insect repellent, frankincense had been in high demand from Europe across to Asia and valued like gold. Oman had been integrated into the global economy, with its merchants trading to the Mediterranean, India and the Silk Road.

At the Sumhuram museum, I watched a video that showed the great strides that Oman had made over the preceding four decades, earning it recognition from the United Nations as the country that had made the most progress in terms of development.

What was not mentioned was that Sultan Qaboos had come to power in 1970 by deposing his father in a coup that was aided by the British. Said bin Taimur had kept the sultanate isolated, personally approving all entry visas and restricting exit visas; he had not used oil revenues to modernize the country – there had only been three schools and six miles of paved roads; and he had forbidden people from smoking in public, playing football and wearing jeans or sunglasses. He was sent into exile at the Dorchester Hotel in London.

When Sultan Qaboos came to power, aged twenty-nine, the sultanate was beset by insurgency. The young sultan delivered a speech saying that Oman had once been at the forefront of

the Arab world – and would become great again. I watched
old footage that showed him touring the country, spending
weeks sleeping out in a large tent so that Omanis could come
to him to express their concerns and needs.

Qaboos had attended the Royal Military Academy Sandhurst
and served as an officer in the British Army. SAS troops trained
his bodyguards and helped his forces fight the adoo (enemy) in
Dhofar. With British advice and support, the sultan launched a
successful counter-insurgency operation. He won the hearts and
minds of the local population by addressing their grievances.
He offered the rebels amnesty and the chance to switch sides
to fight on his behalf.

At the museum, I struck up conversation with a well-travelled
American couple in their late sixties who were from Seattle. I
told them how Salalah brought back memories of a trip I had
made a quarter of a century before, when I had hitchhiked
alone from Morocco across the Algerian Sahara, in an effort
to reach Timbuktu. I had not been able to get into Mali due
to fighting, so instead I had continued south through Benin
until I reached the coast. There, I walked for miles through a
coconut plantation, comforted by the assurances of a Béninois
who told me that one of the laws of nature was that coconuts
never fall on the heads of humans. I found a beautiful spot
on the beach, unrolled my mat and spent the night there.

'Where are you staying in Salalah?' the American man asked.

I squirmed, looking down at my feet. 'The Hilton,' I
admitted. 'But I got a good rate,' I added, trying to somehow
negate the sense of guilt I felt about my metamorphosis from
backpacker to tourist.

'You know,' he told me, 'I made it to Timbuktu in the seventies. Do you want to shake my hand?' I grabbed it. They had seen so much of the world, and had once followed the hippie trail.

'George W. Bush destroyed the hope of the new century,' the woman declared. 'Now Americans are frightened of the world and don't travel so much.'

*

My guide in Salalah was Asi, an Indian from Kerala, who wore jeans and shades. I had been expecting an Omani guide. 'Omanis,' Asi informed me, 'are never on time. And that is why I am your guide.' He exuded confidence. As Oman's connections to India dated back centuries, I did not dare complain.

Asi told me that Kerala was just like Salalah, with the same climate and with coconut plantations everywhere. 'It is an amazing law of nature,' I told him, 'that coconuts never fall on people's heads.'

'What do you mean?' he responded, looking at me as if I were stupid. 'We always hear of people being killed by falling coconuts in Kerala!' I went quiet. For twenty-five years, I had believed that coconuts never landed on human heads, and had walked through plantations without fear.

As we drove, I listened to Asi's tales of life in India: of black magic, mischievous spirits, and an elephant who had once chased him up a tree. Suddenly, as we were going downhill, Asi stopped the car, put it in neutral without the handbrake on and turned off the engine. The vehicle began reversing up the hill of its own accord.

'You know why this is?' Asi asked. I shook my head and waited for him to tell me that the car was possessed by a *jinn*.

'It is because of the magnetic field,' he proudly announced. With no other explanation, he put the car into drive and we continued up to Jebel Samhan, the highest point in the Dhofar mountain range, avoiding the camels and cattle that continually crossed the road.

Asi told me had previously worked in Qatar. The money there was better, but Asians were treated more like slaves. He liked Oman. People here were poorer but regarded Asians with greater respect.

The next morning, Asi announced that we were going to see the tomb of the Prophet Job. I was surprised to hear that it was here, not least because I had once visited his tomb in Turkey.

When we arrived at the mausoleum, I was struck by the length of it. 'People were much taller in those days,' Asi assured me. I looked at him, and could not tell whether he was joking.

We drove westwards, along the beautiful, jagged coastline, before ascending up Jebel Qamar, the Mountain of the Moon. Frankincense trees grew among the ragged rocks. In a few weeks' time, incisions would be made into the bark to collect the resin, which would then be dried and hardened.

Beyond lay the Empty Quarter – an expanse of endless desert that stretches into Saudi and Yemen and that once attracted intrepid travellers such as the British explorer and travel writer Wilfred Thesiger, who had also spent years living in Iraq's marshes. It had been over a decade since I had visited Yemen. Protests the previous year had pushed Ali Abdullah Saleh out of power after serving as the president of Yemen

since its unification in 1990 – and before that as president
of North Yemen from 1978. His deputy Abdrabbuh Mansur
Hadi had been elected as president in February 2012, running
unopposed. But things in Yemen were not looking good. There
was insurgency in the north, secessionist struggle in the south,
and a jihadi group named al-Qaeda in the Arabian Peninsula
(AQAP) had established itself there.

Asi used his smartphone to snap photos of the scenery,
which he immediately sent to his wife in Kerala. He told me
that they were newlyweds, and that it had been an arranged
marriage. His family had sent him photos of his future bride,
he liked the look of her, had agreed to the union and had
married her. He was going to bring her to live in Salalah once
he found a suitable place to rent.

'What happens if you find out that you don't like each
other?' I asked.

Asi turned to me, saying sharply, 'That is not our culture.
We are not like in the West. We have different expectations.
The marriage will of course work.'

Asi quickly moved the discussion on to new technological
developments such as driverless cars and the possibility of trips
to the moon. He told me how his father had lived a similar life
to his grandfather – but now, thanks to modern technology,
his own life was very different to theirs.

Before I flew back to Muscat, Asi made me promise to return
to Salalah during the *khareef* (monsoon) season between July
and September, when warm rains would turn the landscape
emerald green.

*

On Christmas Day, I drove out with Abdullah, the guide with the four-wheel drive, to Wadi Shaab, a gorge about two hours south of Muscat. A small boat ferried us across the lagoon. From there we hiked through the spectacular valley, over boulders and along irrigation channels, before reaching the turquoise pools. I left my daypack with Abdullah and, in my shorts and T-shirt, swam across the clear blue water.

An Omani man appeared out of nowhere. 'Hello, my name is Juma,' he told me. 'Follow me, it is this way.' Abdullah had told me that I might come across Juma. He was often in the *wadi*, and knew it like the back of his hand.

I swam behind Juma. 'Watch the rock here, be careful there,' he instructed. He spoke with such certainty that I followed his orders. We soon came to the narrow entrance to a cave. 'Now, turn your head to the side, hold on to the rock and pass through the keyhole.' I was worried that my head might get stuck, but Juma went ahead of me and showed it was possible. The two of us swam around the covered cave, surrounded by glistening rocks. At one end, a waterfall cascaded down.

'You want to climb up?' I did not know whether Juma was asking or instructing me. Against my better judgement, I found myself following him, using a rope to help ascend the side of the waterfall. It was incredibly slippery but Juma appeared to be half-man and half-fish, and he advised me where to put my feet. Somehow, I emerged at the top of the waterfall to discover more stunning views of the *wadi*. I sat savouring the scene for about ten minutes, spotting kingfishers and herons, before jumping into the water below.

I swam back to where I had left Abdullah. On the walk back to the car, my clothes dried off. We drove to a nearby village where we ate fish and biryani, waving off the flies that hovered over our plates. After we had washed down lunch with a couple of cups of tea, we drove to Wadi Tiwi, parked the car and explored on foot. As the sun set and the moon rose, the rocks turned to pink-and-green marble.

The next day, Abdullah and I set out for Jebel Shams, the Mountain of the Sun. We drove for a couple of hours before the paved road gave way to a dusty track, then parked the car and set out on foot. The 'balcony' walk took us along the rim of Jebel Shams, passing goats foraging in juniper trees. The path was narrow, with no handrails or fences to the sides – just a steep drop of more than half a mile down to the ground.

We made our way along the winding edge of the cliffs for about an hour before reaching the village of As Sab, which was abandoned about forty years ago. We could see how the former inhabitants had built stone houses into the rocks, kept livestock and planted crops on the terraces.

We sat by the waterfall with a panoramic view of the 'Grand Canyon' of Oman. Vultures hovered overhead. Around us was a huge natural amphitheatre.

'Western women are great,' Abdullah announced. 'You would never get an Omani woman to do such a walk.'

*

I was sad that my time in Oman was coming to an end. It was quite the most beautiful country that I had ever visited in the Middle

East. It was clean, there was no hassle, it was safe. It respected women's rights. And it had frankincense.

This was the country that Sultan Qaboos had developed. He seemed genuinely concerned for the well-being of all of his country's diverse peoples, whether they lived in the mountains, on the coast or in the desert. He had kept the country out of regional conflicts. Yes, there were limitations on political participation, freedom of speech and assembly – and opposition was not tolerated. But this seemed a price that Omanis were willing to pay in return for stability – at least as long as Qaboos was alive.

But the issue with benevolent dictators is who will replace them when they die? It was not clear who would succeed the sultan as he did not have any children. The Basic Law – the Omani constitution – stipulated that after the sultan's death, a family council should meet to decide the successor. If the family could not agree within three days, then a letter written by the sultan would be opened to reveal his choice of successor.

On my last evening, Greta took me to see *The Nutcracker* performed by a Russian ballet company at the Royal Opera House in Muscat. The stunning building, with its white marble façade, reflects Islamic as well as contemporary Omani architecture. It is set in landscaped gardens, as part of a complex that includes a concert theatre, auditorium and restaurants. Spanish tenor Plácido Domingo conducted the inaugural opera, Puccini's *Turandot*. The opera house had opened in October 2011, a few months after the protests for jobs and wage increases had ended. Its cost was never made public.

Before the performance, we stood in the foyer. A number of people, Omani and foreign, came over to greet Greta. Seeing me staring at the interior design, a man came over and expressed his admiration for the wooden panelling and ornate stuccos. He informed me that the ceiling was made from Burmese teak and the marble came from Italy. He looked to be in his late sixties, and by his accent I could tell he was British. I asked him what had brought him to Oman. He told me he was a retired army officer and had served in Oman for years on loan to the sultan's armed forces. He loved Oman so much that he had bought a house and retired out here.

Our conversation was cut short, as the performance was about to begin. As we were ushered to our seats, I told Greta about the retired British officer. 'Could you imagine anyone who served in Iraq retiring there?' I asked her.

I reflected a moment and then answered my own question. There was one place in Iraq where veterans would be welcome: Kurdistan.

CHAPTER 8

We have no friends but the mountains

Kurdistan

July 2013

If there was one group that had benefited unequivocally from the overthrow of Saddam, it was the Kurds. Investors were flocking in from the US, Europe, Middle East and Asia – landing in northern Iraq at Erbil International Airport, with its new sixteen-gate facility and one of the world's longest runways.

Kurdistan was booming – and investors sensed it. This was the land of opportunity. It had the feel of a gold rush.

And Kurds could not be more welcoming to foreigners. Retired American and British officers – some of whom had helped the Kurds in the first Gulf War in 1991, and others in the more recent one – were regular visitors. The Kurds also hosted Gold Star families (relatives of fallen US soldiers) to thank them for their sacrifices, which had served to liberate the Kurds from Saddam's dictatorship.

The Kurds had long dreamed of a state of their own. Their hopes had been raised by the dismembering of the Ottoman

Empire in the 1920 Treaty of Sèvres and then thwarted in the 1923 Treaty of Lausanne, which saw them living as minorities within new nation states. In the century since, the Kurds have continued to struggle for their rights.

After the overthrow of Saddam in 2003, the Kurds, who constitute around 15 per cent of Iraq's population, agreed to remain part of Iraq on condition that their region would be allowed to consolidate its autonomy. Still, the relationship between the Kurdistan Regional Government and the central government in Baghdad remained rocky, with differing interpretations of federalism, and each side accusing the other of violating Iraq's constitution.

Kurds had their hearts set on independence. But they did not have international support like South Sudan (and even with that support, the world's newest country, which had gained its independence in 2011, was not faring well). Nor was there agreement on the border between Kurdistan and the rest of Iraq. Masoud Barzani, the president of the Kurdistan Regional Government, viewed the annexation of the disputed territory of Kirkuk as essential for achieving independence. But no Iraqi prime minister could afford to lose Kirkuk and its oil fields. While Kurds constituted its majority, the city also had significant communities of Arabs and Turkmen, mostly Sunni but also Shia. And many of them had made it known that they did not want to be part of an independent Kurdistan.

Back in 2010, Barzani asked me: 'When the fighting breaks out between Arabs and Kurds whose side will the Americans be on?' He had never forgotten how the United States had let down his father in his moment of need in 1975, after the Shah of Iran suddenly cut support to the Kurds in return for Saddam Hussein's recognition of Iran's territorial demands as part of the Algiers Agreement. Mullah Mustafa Barzani had turned to America for aid, but the request was rejected – and Kurdish resistance to Saddam Hussein had collapsed.

*

On 3 July 2013, I was sitting in a wicker chair in Barham Salih's garden in Erbil – the city referred to as 'Hawler' by the Kurds – as we drank tea and chatted about Iraqi politics. Barham was a senior official in the Patriotic Union of Kurdistan (PUK) party, and had previously served as the deputy prime minister of Iraq as well as the prime minister of Kurdistan. Before that, he had spent years living in exile in the UK, where he had been involved in left-wing politics and had participated in demonstrations, chanting, as he enjoyed telling me: 'Maggie, Maggie, Maggie, out, out, out!' As a University of Liverpool-trained engineer, he had also been involved in building sections of the M25 ring road around London.

On the large screen that Barham had erected in the garden, Al Jazeera English was reporting from Egypt. In the preceding days, millions of Egyptians had protested against Mohamad Morsi – who had been sworn in as president the previous summer – expressing their anger that the Muslim Brotherhood had hijacked Egypt's revolution. An Egyptian grassroots movement, Tamarod, had collected millions of signatures calling for early elections. The Egyptian military had issued Morsi with an ultimatum to respond to the protestors'

demands – or else. But Morsi had remained defiant, insisting
he would sooner die than give up power.

Barham switched the channel to BBC Arabic. The defence
minister General Abdul Fatah al-Sisi was reading out a statement
live announcing that Morsi was no longer president, that he
was freezing the Egyptian constitution and that there would
be new elections.

As we watched, a ticker at the bottom of the screen displayed
the latest headlines:

> *Egyptian army: Military is committed to its role in*
> *country's democracy.*
> *Egyptian army says it will step in only to ensure peace*
> *and stability in Egypt.*
> *Egyptian army tanks have been sent to the pro-Morsi*
> *protest rallies.*
> *Egyptian army blocking off roads in Nasr City where*
> *pro-Morsi protesters are.*
> *Egyptian presidency is accusing military of planning a*
> *coup d'état to take power.*

Barham and I turned to each other and said in unison: 'A coup!'

Within two hours of the announcement, Saudi Arabia's
King Abdullah issued a public statement praising the Egyptian
army for saving the country. Cairo had boomeranged back
into Saudi's orbit – and away from Qatar's.

It was hard to get my head around how, within two and a
half years, Egyptians who had chanted for dignity and rights
were now welcoming the return of military rule, calling Sisi
the saviour and worshipping him as a 'new Nasser'. It was true

that Morsi had been a terrible leader. The Ikhwan had failed to govern effectively and had monopolized power. But surely it would have been preferable to replace a poorly performing democratically elected government through the ballot box rather than in a military coup.

The United States avoided calling the intervention a 'coup' so as not to jeopardize the annual $1.3 billion military assistance that the US gives Egypt (to underwrite its peace treaty with Israel and secure access to the Suez Canal).

In the weeks ahead, the Ikhwan would be branded as terrorists; and Morsi and his colleagues would be arrested and a thousand or so Ikhwan would be killed in demonstrations against the overthrow of the elected government.

However, I did not remain in Erbil as these events were unfolding. I had other plans in mind. But first I needed to get to Sulaymaniyah.

*

I took a taxi along the back road from Erbil to Sulaymaniyah. It had less traffic these days, as the new Kirkuk bypass road was much quicker. Once out of Erbil, I observed that the villages had seemed to change little over the past decade. I saw old men in baggy pants and waistcoats with keffiyehs – those iconic black-and-white checked scarves – wrapped around their heads, their life experiences etched on their faces. And I saw women, some in black abayas, others in colourful dresses, going about their daily lives.

I asked the taxi to divert to Taqtaq. The town had grown. But the countryside was how I remembered it: the Zab River,

the pastoral idyll, and the road that the paratroopers of
the 173rd Airborne Brigade took to liberate Kirkuk back
in 2003. We passed camps for employees of oil companies.
There were a number – including Exxon Mobil, Chevron
and Total – that were active in the region. And Genel Energy
had started exporting crude oil directly to world markets
through Turkey, escalating the dispute between Erbil and
Baghdad over control of Kurdistan's estimated 45 billion
barrels of oil. Kurdish leaders believed they would soon
be able to generate more income from the direct sale of
Kurdistan's oil and gas than from the existing arrangement,
whereby Baghdad controlled sales and allocated 17 per cent
of Iraq's total budget to Erbil.

The taxi driver, who looked to be in his sixties, spoke good
Arabic. He told me about his years in Basra, and his time as
an Iraqi soldier during the Iran–Iraq War of 1980–88. It was
during this war that Saddam had launched his Anfal (Spoils
of War) campaign to crush the Kurdish rebellion in the north,
which at the time was being supported by Iran. An estimated
100,000 Kurds were killed in bombardments; and 5,000 were
killed on a single day – 16 March 1988 – in a chemical gas
attack on the city of Halabja.

After Kuwait was liberated by the US-led coalition at the
end of February 1991 and the Iraqi army was driven out,
the Kurds rose up again in response to the call by President
George H.W. Bush to overthrow Saddam. This was when my
driver had moved to Kurdistan and switched from being an
Iraqi soldier to being a Kurdish Peshmerga (literally 'Those
who face death'). But Saddam's forces pushed back. And the

driver, along with millions of Kurds, fled to the Turkish border, fearing retribution by chemicals once again.

The driver had come down from the mountains two months later when the US and UK imposed a no-fly zone over northern Iraq, above the 36th parallel, to protect the Kurds. Safe in their haven, the Kurds built up an autonomous region. But the rivalry between Masoud Barzani, whose father Mustafa Barzani had founded the Kurdish separatist movement, and Jalal Talabani, who split from the movement in 1975 to establish the leftist Patriotic Union of Kurdistan, was very much a feature of Kurdish politics. It spilled over into civil war in the 1990s, with both sides prepared to do deals with Baghdad, Tehran and Ankara against each other. The US managed to broker a peace deal which Barzani and Talabani signed in Washington in 1998.

Following the end of Saddam Hussein's regime in 2003, the two Kurdish leaders buried the hatchet and worked together, with Masoud Barzani becoming president of Kurdistan and Jalal Talabani becoming president of Iraq. The taxi driver was thankful that the Kurdish parties seemed to have set aside their differences.

I smiled at hearing this. When I had been based in Kirkuk after the invasion, one of the coalition's greatest challenges was managing the competition between the two main Kurdish parties: the PUK and the Kurdistan Democratic Party (KDP), who each had their own Peshmerga forces.

The driver admitted he could not read or write. But his children had received government scholarships to study abroad. He was proud of their achievements – and of the overall progress in Kurdistan. The Kurds had only had a short period of self-government but they were doing much better than the Arabs, he told me.

He rushed to drop me off at my hotel as he wanted to be home in time to watch his favourite TV series, a Korean soap opera. One of the legacies of the South Korean troop deployment to Kurdistan (its contribution to the US-led coalition) was the introduction of some of their TV programmes. Dubbed into Kurdish, the tales of plotting and intrigue in Korea 300 years ago resonated in Kurdistan and were hugely popular.

The taxi driver waved goodbye and wished me all the best. There were no grumpy old men in Kurdistan. The older generation were thrilled that life had turned out so well for them and their families.

*

In Sulaymaniyah, I met up with my old friend Aram Yarwaessi and his brothers Allan and Amanj. Aram and I had worked together in Baghdad from 2007 to 2010 while he was serving as an adviser to President Talabani. The Yarwaessi family had escaped Saddam's Iraq to Iran, before finding sanctuary in Britain. After Saddam's fall, the brothers had returned from London to Iraqi Kurdistan.

The brothers took me on a tour of Sulaymaniyah to show me what had changed. I saw new houses everywhere, painted in crazy bright colours that shouted out: 'We are here; we are alive.' Everywhere I looked there was construction, bright lights – and often alcohol.

We visited the American University of Iraq. Last time I had seen it, it had been a skeleton. Now it looked exactly like the mocked-up computer images its founder, Barham Salih, had once shown me on his laptop. I walked round the state-of-the-art campus, which was built on an expansive 418 acres, before touring the classrooms, the computer lab and the library. Already, around 500 students were studying business management, international studies, information systems, computer technology and engineering. Their numbers would continue to grow.

We drove out to the foot of the mountains behind Sulaymaniyah, to Hawary Shar Park. Looking across the valley, I could understand how Jalal Talabani had once sat for an hour at the observation point admiring the view – and no doubt contemplating how many changes he had seen in his lifetime, and the progress that the Kurds had made. When we passed Talabani's house, Aram repeated a joke that Mam Jalal, as Talabani was locally known, once told:

> One afternoon, on his way back to his house in Sulaymaniyah, Mam Jalal spotted a man sitting on his own by the side of the road drinking alcohol. Talabani told his driver to stop the car, and went over to speak to the drunk. After a brief discussion, he asked the drunk whether he recognized him. The drunk did not.
>
> 'Have you never seen my picture?' Talabani inquired. 'I am Mam Jalal, the president of Iraq!'
>
> The drunk responded: 'Have another drink – soon you will tell me I am President George Bush!'

In all his years as a Kurdish Peshmerga battling Iraqi government forces, Talabani had never imagined that he, a Kurd, would one day become president of Iraq. He proved himself adept in that role. Although the post was largely ceremonial, Talabani used his position to bring politicians together over dinners, to defuse tensions and to build bridges. He was a pragmatist, always seeking compromise.

When I served with the coalition in Iraq, Talabani had charmed us all with his chuckles and kebabs. For this reason, US officials were slow to see his closeness to Tehran – and how his family were enriching themselves.

I remembered Talabani announcing over dinner one evening, 'A Kurdish independent state is the dream of poets!' After a pause, he added: 'And I hope to be a poet one day!'

But he never achieved that aspiration. Intent on staying on as president despite his ailing health and his advanced age, he was left unable to speak following a stroke in 2012.

*

One evening, I sat with the Yarwaessi brothers and a couple of their friends in a café, smoking lemon-and-mint shisha. The conversation quickly turned to Kurdish politics. Aram was now working in the private sector and was not finding it easy. The political parties controlled everything: there was so much corruption, mismanagement and pocketing of oil wealth.

We spoke about Iran. Once it had been Iraqi Kurds who fled to Iran and sought refuge there. Now it was Iranian Kurds who were coming to Iraqi Kurdistan seeking economic opportunities and political sanctuary. The Western sanctions placed on Iran due to its illicit nuclear activities were biting.

And then discussion drifted on to Turkey. The recent protests over the urban development plan in Gezi Park in Istanbul's Taksim Square – and the violent response of the security forces – were on people's minds. Tayyip Erdoğan was clamping down on all opposition. Barzani was now closely aligned with the Turkish premier, and Turkish companies were heavily invested in Iraqi Kurdistan. Meanwhile, Abdullah Öcalan, the Turkish Kurdish leader of the Kurdistan Workers' Party (PKK), remained languishing in his Turkish island jail since his capture in 1999.

The conflict in Syria was adding further complexity to the Kurdish question. Around 10 per cent of Syria's population were Kurds, many without legal status or rights. The PKK had previously been based out of Syria, used by Damascus in power plays against Turkey and Iraq. In 1998, Turkey's threat of military action forced the PKK to relocate its headquarters to the Qandil Mountains inside Iraqi Kurdistan. When the Syrian uprising broke out in 2011, the People's Protection Units (YPG), the Syrian Kurdish offshoot of the PKK, had returned from the Qandil Mountains to Syria, where it was establishing its authority over predominantly Kurdish areas – much to Erdoğan's great concern.

I was fascinated by the Qandil Mountains. A few years back, I had attended a Kurdish film festival in London. One film was set in the mountains, with Kurdish outlaws living beyond the reach of government in the most beautiful surroundings. Since the time of the Ottoman Empire, Kurds had fled to this region seeking refuge, moving around on foot or horse. And no government had ever managed to bring the territory under control.

It seemed that now was as good a time as any to visit the Qandil Mountains, as a ceasefire was currently in place and the Turks and the Iranians were not bombing the PKK. I wanted to meet with some of the fighters to understand what motivated them.

Allan, the middle Yarwaessi brother, told me he would be interested in going with me. He could take time off work and he had a car with government number plates, which would facilitate our passage through checkpoints.

I called my friend Fazel Hawramy, and he, too, was interested in going. I had originally met Fazel in London through Amanj, the youngest of the Yarwaessi brothers, and had immediately been drawn to him. Under the strapline 'Kurdish blogger', Fazel had been taking photos and writing about any protest he came across in London. He had wild black curly hair, he was a rebel and a survivor, and he was charming. Fazel told me he had grown up in Iran, where Kurds made up around 7 per cent of the overall population and were treated as second-class citizens. He had yearned to flee to the West. His first attempt had failed, but he tried again and managed to get to Turkey. In Turkey, he paid more smugglers to get him into Europe. But they cheated him and he lost his money.

Despite this, he eventually made it to France. In Calais, he climbed under a truck and stayed there on the ferry journey over to the UK. When the truck disembarked, he waved his shirt to attract the driver's attention. The driver duly stopped. Fazel turned himself in to the authorities and claimed asylum.

Fazel had not spoken any English when he arrived in the UK. After a period of time in an immigration centre, he was sent to the north of England. There, he started work in a factory and quickly made British friends who helped him learn English, which he now spoke perfectly. He described how ordinary Brits had welcomed him into their lives and communities, and helped him become successfully absorbed into a new society. His self-confidence had grown, and he went on to study at university in London. After getting his British passport, Fazel had moved out to Iraqi Kurdistan, where he now worked as a journalist.

Fazel submitted a request to the PKK asking permission for me, a researcher, to visit them in the Qandil Mountains. They responded positively.

And so it was that the three of us set out early one morning from Sulaymaniyah, with Allan driving his Kurdistan Regional Government-issued 4 x 4.

Skirting around Lake Dukan, we drove through the town of Ranya. After four hours on the road, we passed through the last checkpoint manned by the Kurdistan Regional Government, with Allan's badge and number plates assuring us easy passage. We took photos of ourselves against the barren backdrop of the road stretching into the unknown.

The mountains began to get taller and a little greener as we headed into no man's land. There were no longer electricity pylons.

We reached the first PKK checkpoint, marked by flags. PKK guerrillas stood in front of a small shed. We presented our names and waited. I looked over at a nearby hill, on which –

etched in the brown stone, among the scattered bushes – was the face of Öcalan, the leader of the PKK.

It was at this moment that I suddenly wondered what on earth I was doing. The PKK had shortwave radios and satellite phones to stay connected. What would happen if the PKK googled me and discovered I had worked for the US military? They might think I was a spy.

What reason did I really have for visiting? Was I an adrenaline junkie who enjoyed the thrill and danger of war? Did I miss being around people prepared to kill and die for a cause? Or was I simply drawn to the remoteness of the Qandil Mountains and the romantic life of runaways and outcasts?

Whichever way I looked at it, going up to the mountains now seemed indulgent and impulsive.

But at this stage, it was really too late to be questioning my own motives. I was committed. And I trusted my two Kurdish friends to keep us all safe. We had come in good faith and we would be treated in good faith, I assured myself. And the PKK did not have a track record of taking foreigners hostage or putting them in orange jumpsuits.

The man we had given our names to returned to give us instructions. He told us to keep driving down the road until we went over a bridge, then to take the dirt track on the right until it crossed over a stream, where we would be met by PKK fighters.

We followed the directions, continuing for half an hour or so before we reached the bridge and turned onto the track. We had all gone quiet by this stage, nervous with anticipation. After crossing the stream, Fazel signalled for Allan to pull over on the left.

Getting out the car, we were greeted by half a dozen members of the PKK, including one woman, all wearing the standard uniform of baggy khaki trousers and a buttoned shirt with a gilet over the top.

After brief introductions, they invited us into a hut to join them for lunch. We sat at a long table, and one of the PKK set in front of us rice, beans and freshly baked bread which was still warm. He apologized that they only had simple fare. I was just grateful that they generously shared with us what they had.

They regretted that they were not authorized to discuss PKK strategy. That was fine with me. I was more interested in what had driven them to give up their lives in their villages in Turkey, take up arms against the Turkish government and then move to the mountains of Iraq.

To my surprise, they only spoke a little about the prejudice they had faced as Kurds in Turkey. Most of the discussion was about Marxism, economic inequalities and the discrimination against workers.

I asked them what it would look like to succeed in their struggle. I expected them to talk about a peace settlement with Ankara and returning to their villages inside Turkey. But they did not.

'Equal rights for all people around the world,' one responded.

Theirs was a class struggle. And a struggle for women's rights. The creation of a utopia. A struggle for broader humanity that went beyond their own ethnic group. They seemed to be leftovers from another era: such left-wing groups had largely disappeared the world over.

After lunch, we sat outside on the patio under the vine leaves, drinking sweet tea out of glasses. It was so peaceful: the rustle of the stream, the whistle of the wind in the trees, the craggy terrain. We were off the grid – away from consumerist trappings of modernity.

I chatted with the female guerrilla of the group, while Fazel and Allan took it in turns to translate. She wore a green scarf on her head, tied in a knot at the back and coming down the front over her left shoulder. She showed me a pink-covered photocopied book of the teachings of 'Apo', the nickname they used when they referred to Öcalan. Talking to her, it was clear that she did not allow herself to dream of a homecoming, of having children and raising a family. The PKK insisted on celibacy and she was wedded to the cause.

We thanked our guests for lunch and headed out of the mountains the way we came.

We stopped off to visit the cemetery to walk among gravestones that bore the names of hundreds of PKK fighters who had died. Fazel commented on how well-maintained each grave was, with a miniature garden of shrubs planted in front of it. The PKK honoured the memory of their dead. On the way down the mountain, we paused at a memorial dedicated to PKK fighters who had been killed by a rocket.

At a shop by the side of the road, we bought water and drank more tea. The shop owner noted that no government provided this remote area with any services. It was the PKK who extended medical care to the villagers.

It had been a short visit. But it had given me a glimpse into the lives of PKK fighters and their resilience.

*

Barham Salih invited Aram and I to join him at his place in Mergapan, near Sulaymaniyah. We headed out of town, into the beautiful valleys that lay beyond. It reminded me of Scotland.

'I lived here as a boy,' Aram told me, pointing to the left. 'I used to get on a donkey and go high into the mountains to collect snow. I would bring it back so it could serve as a fridge for a few days.'

It was hard to imagine that Aram had once lived in these mountains – and that he, his brothers and mother had spent years in jail under Saddam. Their lives today were so different.

We joined Barham in his garden, where other guests were already drinking and eating *masgouf.* The environmentalist Azzam Alwash was there, and I went over to chat with him. Azzam had grown up in the marshes of Iraq before fleeing to the US. After 2003 he had returned, and focused his energies on restoring the marshes. He had set up an NGO – Nature Iraq – and was on the board of the American University in Sulaymaniyah.

Azzam introduced me to a man called Abu Ra'id, describing him as a 'construction guy' from Kadhimiyya in Baghdad who had 'built half of Saudi'. Abu Ra'id told me he had lived all over the Middle East. He never had any clue who among his staff was Sunni or Shia. It was irrelevant to him, and he had never been interested in knowing. The whole sectarian classification disturbed him greatly. He hadn't been brought up to think that way. As far as he was concerned, he was Iraqi.

Abu Ra'id was angry that Shia Islamists had usurped the definition of what it meant to be Iraqi. He was Shia by birth, secular by choice and Iraqi nationalist by identity. He was also married to a Sunni.

Azzam told us that he and a couple of friends were going white-water rafting on the Little Zab the next day and invited us to join them. Abu Ra'id did not want to go. I accused him of being chicken. The gauntlet was laid down; he had to accept.

The next morning, we put the dinghy in the water just down from Lake Dukan. We were six in total, with Azzam, who was an experienced rafter, acting as the captain. I was seated opposite Abu Ra'id. It soon became clear that he was not willing to take orders from Azzam. He paddled so hard that the boat went around in circles.

The scenery was stunning, with the mountains as the backdrop. A few stones marked the sites of Kurdish villages that were destroyed in the Anfal campaign. We spotted wild pigs on the left bank, and goats and sheep on the right. We passed a couple of illegal refineries. It was a beautiful landscape, and unspoilt – that is, except for the gravel from the mines, the rubbish thrown into the river and the floating plastic bottles.

We could hear the rapids as we approached. Class 3 white-water rapids, Azzam told us. I wrapped up my camera in plastic and stowed it well. 'Keep the boat straight,' Azzam ordered. 'Here we go!'

Abu Ra'id was not listening. And we were still at an angle. The waves beat the boat and then broke over into it. We were drenched immediately. Having come down from the mountains, the water was freezing. We were all screaming and shouting. The boat took on more water as we frantically tried to get it straight.

And then we were through!

We sat back, high-fiving each other. We had done it! Azzam had never seen the water so high, nor the rapids so strong. The boat had taken in so much water we were lucky not to have capsized.

*

Kurds used to claim that they had no friends but the mountains. That certainly was no longer the case. Foreign businesses were doing trade. New hotels were opening. And Arabs were visiting on holiday.

However, the joy and exhilaration that I experienced in Kurdistan stood in stark contrast to my feelings about the Middle East in general. In the space of two years, the aspirations of the youth for a new future had been countered and their agency constrained by powerful forces seemingly beyond their control.

I decided that next summer I would travel beyond the region to non-Arab Muslim lands. And I would go ride some wild horses.

CHAPTER 9

… but surely we are brave, who take the Golden Road to Samarkand

The Silk Road

June 2014

I posted a message on my Facebook page asking whether anyone knew a shepherd in Kyrgyzstan with a horse. I was looking to ride through the mountains of Central Asia. Within a matter of hours, Facebook came good. A Kyrgyz shepherd had been found.

A few weeks later, in June 2014, I flew to Bishkek, the capital of Kyrgyzstan. After a stay in a Soviet-style apartment block that was not in the least homey, I set out for Lake Issyk-Kol, a stopover on the Silk Road. It was baking hot. The driver kept the car windows closed even though the air conditioning was not working. We broke down twice before reaching the southern shore of the alpine lake.

Before long, I was seated on a cushion on the floor of a yurt, eating noodles cooked by the shepherd's wife. She described to me, in broken English, the traditional way of life of Kyrgyz. There were apparently forty different Kyrgyz tribes, and one was supposed to know one's lineage seven generations back. When a Kyrgyz man married, he paid a dowry to his wife – typically nine camels or horses.

I knew next to nothing about Kyrgyzstan. But I had read a story that Kyrgyz men kidnapped women they wanted to marry. Were these stories of bride-napping to be believed? The shepherd's wife assured me that this was greatly exaggerated. In the old days, it had sometimes been used as a way to escape dowry payment or parental disapproval – but most marriages back then had been pre-arranged. It was now illegal, with a punishment for bride-napping of ten years in prison.

Kyrgyz were good fighters, she told me, but had not adapted to modern warfare. They had suffered many massacres. And thousands had fled to China.

The founding legend of the Kyrgyz was tied up with the warrior Manas. It was Manas who had unified the forty tribes against the Oirats, a Mongol tribe. This was symbolized by the forty rays of sun on the country's modern flag. The *Epic of Manas* is one of the longest of its kind in the world – about 500,000 lines – and tells the story of Manas and his descendants and their battles against their enemies.

The shepherd's wife told me that they had studied Russian history at school. They had never been taught about their own history, having to learn it themselves. She had read the work of Ella Maillart, a French-speaking Swiss woman who explored the 'Stans in the 1930s, and published books about her journeys. She accompanied the adventurer and travel writer Peter Fleming on the journey across Turkestan that formed the basis of his *News from Tartary*.

The shepherd's wife described their faith as a mixture of shamanism and Islam. 'We are nomads,' she explained. 'How can we pray five times a day? Who will look after the animals?' But more girls had started to wear the hijab. It had become a fashion item of sorts. And Saudi Arabia was pumping money into the country and building new mosques to promulgate its fundamentalist form of Islam. This was having an impact, she noted. Communism had previously provided the 'idea', the framework through which to view the world. Now it was gone. Some looked to Islam for an explanation of the meaning of life.

That night, I woke up at 1 a.m. to the sound of cars speeding past, hooting their horns. Had some Kyrgyz woman been snatched to be a bride?

*

I saddled up in the morning. The saddle was large and wide, with a big pommel, similar to Western saddles. I was given a stallion to ride, a handsome brown beast with a thick forelock that came down between his ears to below his eyes. The shepherd explained how to hold the reins in one hand. 'Say "*drrrr*" to stop the horse, and "*chu*" to make it go.' He demonstrated and the horse responded. It looked easy enough.

I rode down the lane behind the shepherd. We were going out for a few hours to see how I handled the horse. Kids on rickety bikes passed us in the opposite direction. Three old women sat on a bench, handkerchiefs wrapped around their hair, chatting intently as young children milled around. Soon we were off the road, riding through verdant pastures, bright emerald-green fields, with wide vistas ahead and snow-topped mountains in the distance. My horse stopped to eat grass, and I did not try to pull his head up. I took photos with my iPhone using one hand, while the other hand held on to the reins. The horse walked on some more and easily crossed over streams.

Then suddenly, without any warning, my docile horse transformed himself into a wild beast, charging off as I hung on for dear life, my hat flying away. I yanked on the reins and shouted '*drrrr*' over and over again. But no response.

Just as I was about to be thrown off, the shepherd appeared on his horse alongside me, grabbed my reins and brought both our beasts to a halt. I looked at him in amazement. He explained that my stallion had got excited as he had seen a mare. The shepherd told me I needed to pay more attention.

Relieved to be in one piece but somewhat humiliated, I lamely noted that the stallion did not seem to understand my accent. I had repeatedly said '*drrr*' and the horse had ignored me. But the shepherd had shown his skills and I was confident about heading out into the wilds with him.

In the evening, I sat in the yurt, downloading the news over Wi-Fi. I read with shock and confusion that the Islamic State, ISIS, had swept into Mosul and now controlled a third of Iraq. There were emails from newspaper editors asking me to write articles, journalists who wanted a quote, and US generals asking what the hell was happening. I had been closely following

Maliki's sectarian policies in Iraq and the impact they were having on Sunnis. But I was still taken by surprise at the speed with which the Iraqi army had collapsed.

*

The shepherd and I set out on horseback the next day, loaded with supplies.

It soon began to drizzle. And then pour. I put on my waterproof trousers and anorak. The rain rushed into the rivers and the paths became muddy and slippery. On a number of occasions, my horse lost his footing but managed to recover before we both went tumbling down the hill. The shepherd appeared to know every route, but I understood how Alexander the Great's men had got lost here. I had quickly become disoriented as we wound our way through the wooded sides of the mountains.

The scenery was spectacular and unspoilt. No roads. No cars. Out in the wilds, the only sound was the horses trudging along the path.

Late in the day we dismounted, took off the saddles and the bags attached to them, and tied a rope to one of the legs of each horse and then to a stake. We pitched our tents under the trees, near a glade beside the river. A dozen wild horses were gathered close by, mares with their foals at their side. They did not seem perturbed by us.

The shepherd lit a fire and cooked us dinner. We sat huddled around the fire eating fried pork sausage and pasta as the rain came down once more. It wasn't long before I was in my tent, out of my wet clothes and wrapped up in my sleeping bag.

The next day, we packed up our tents, saddled up and rode off down the side of the mountain. The rain had stopped. We passed a woman, well wrapped up, hanging washing on a line she had set up outside her yurt. Smoke was rising out of the tent through a pipe. The area was enclosed by a wooden fence and chickens ran around. The shepherd exchanged a few words with her. I smiled. She nodded back.

Our horses passed through the grassy glades, walking around the large stones that were scattered along the way. The clouds hung low.

My bottom was hurting. I wished I had worn tights. My legs also ached. And my inner thighs. And my knee joints. I was not used to sitting in this position, and especially not for eight hours a day. Whenever we alighted, I stretched my limbs and got the circulation flowing. The pain eased momentarily until I was back up on the horse. There was nothing that I could do except grin and bear it.

We stopped for lunch and built a fire to warm ourselves. An elderly Kyrgyz man rode up to us and the shepherd invited him to join us. He got off his horse, with some difficulty, and sat down with us. He was wearing a warm, long blue coat, a woollen hat and boots. I passed him some bread and sardines. Our horses lay down, seemingly exhausted. The shepherd and the old man chatted. Occasionally, the shepherd translated a few details for me in his limited English. The old man was ninety, he said. This had always been his way of life. This was his world. His children had left it behind, and one was living in Europe.

Here we were, I mused to myself, strangers without many words in common, sharing food and providing each other with company.

After we had finished eating, the shepherd helped the old man back up onto his horse. Secure in the saddle, he galloped effortlessly off into the distance, he and the stallion moving in unison. I would never have that relationship with my horse. It was clear who was in charge – and it wasn't me.

When we passed another yurt, a woman offered us *kymys*, fermented mare's milk. I took a swig and nearly choked on the sour, acidic liquid. It was quite the most disgusting thing I had ever tasted. The woman and the shepherd smiled at me encouragingly. I struggled to smile back, desperate to spit it out.

I stopped counting the hours and the days. My body began to adjust. The daily rhythm was now defined by our stops to eat and our nights sleeping under the stars.

Slowly, I was withdrawing from the modern world.

*

After we returned from our journey, I said farewell to the shepherd and took a taxi to Karakol, at the eastern end of Lake Issyk-Kol. It happened to be market day. Horses, cows and sheep were on sale, with money passing from hand to hand. A similar scene to the one I had witnessed in Khartoum. Minus the camels.

All the men I saw in Kyrgyzstan were clean-shaven. And then, among the crowd, I spotted one with a skull cap and long beard. A Salafi, I thought! Even here. The reach was long.

At the guest house I was staying at, I chatted with Azamat, the manager, who ran what he described as a 'community-based tourism' project. His parents were artists. He was educated and spoke good English. The television was on in the background, with footage of Putin strutting around on horse and on foot, in towns and in the countryside, riding high after annexing Crimea. Kyrgyzstan was fed a diet of Russian news.

'Crazy Putin!' I commented.

'Crazy Americans!' Azamat replied immediately. 'It was Americans who invented al-Qaeda; and it is Americans who are causing problems everywhere. Look at what is happening in Ukraine and Syria!' It had not taken much to provoke such a passionate response.

It was clear that Azamat was very pro-Russia. He explained that Kyrgyzstan would soon sign a customs union with Russia. After independence in 1991, the economy of Kyrgyzstan had suffered. They'd lost Soviet subsidies, which had amounted to 75 per cent of the budget. Now, the markets were flooded with cheap Chinese produce. But once the customs union was signed, everything would be Russian. Most of the tourists in Kyrgyzstan were Russians, as it was cheap and convenient for them to visit. Many had stayed on in the country after independence, although they never learned the language or intermarried with the locals.

Russia was reasserting its influence in Central Asia. It now operated four military installations in Kyrgyzstan. Earlier in 2014, President Almazbek Atambayev, who had been elected in 2011, ensured that the US vacated Manas Air Base, which it had been using since December 2001 to support military operations in Afghanistan.

Our discussion turned to religion. Azamat said that more people were becoming religious. Mosques were springing up everywhere, paid for by Arab countries. Imams were going off to Middle Eastern countries to study, and were returning to teach and preach. There were no extremists in the north of Kyrgyzstan, only in the south, where it was ethnic Uzbeks, he said, who were causing problems.

There had been a series of protests and revolutions in the country over the last decade. In the 2005 Tulip Revolution, President Askar Akayev fell from power and fled to Russia. His successor, Kurmanbek Bakiyev, fled the country in April 2010, going into exile in Belarus. In the ensuing general lawlessness, minority groups were attacked. Violence erupted in Osh between Kyrgyz and Uzbeks, claiming hundreds of lives. A hundred thousand ethnic Uzbeks fled over the border into Uzbekistan.

Azamat was into gadgets. He had a Samsung phone which was much more popular in Kyrgyzstan than the iPhone. Google, he told me, was a global platform, not just an American one.

*

About an hour outside Karakol, a bus dropped me and Dan, my Kyrgyz guide, at the start of the walk to Altyn Arashan (Golden Spa). It was ten miles uphill, through the most beautiful valley. I was lucky to have Dan to carry all the food for the trip.

The early stretch was easy enough. And as we walked, I asked Dan questions about his life. He was studying software engineering in Bishkek. He had become religious three years earlier. He had had many problems, including with his father, and it was religion that had sorted him out. His dream was to lead a good Muslim life, to get married, to have children.

Before long, we walked in silence. We did not have much to talk about. Dan's English was limited; my Kyrgyz and Russian non-existent. And I had exhausted questioning him about his life. We stopped for lunch, washing vegetables in the stream and eating sardines with bread.

The walking got harder and the tracks less easy. But the scenery was stunning: silver streams, green gorges and flocks of sheep.

After five hours or so of climbing up the valley, we reached the top and it began to level off. There were a few huts containing beds. Seeing that I was a single female, the guard kindly vacated his own room for me. There was plastic lino on the floor, cracked windows covered by flimsy curtains, and a single bed on top of which I rolled out my sleeping bag. The room was sparse. But it was shelter.

The guard also handed me a key to the 'hot spring', pointing to a hut a hundred yards away. I did not know what to expect, but my feet were killing me. I could feel the blisters. So I removed my boots, put on sandals and walked over. I unlocked the padlock. Inside was a small tiled pool. I took off my clothes and dipped one foot in the water. It was boiling hot. Gingerly I climbed in among the wafts of sulphur. I submerged my body in the water. The climb had been worth it – just for this.

I would have liked to have stayed immersed in the sulphuric water for an hour, but I wanted to see the sun set. It did not disappoint. The clouds had broken, and I walked through a meadow of blue, yellow and red daisies. In the distance, the snow-capped Palatka peak turned pink. And around me, the side of the mountain changed to orange as the sun went down.

I joined Dan in the communal area, where he had cooked up a feast. Another Kyrgyz man picked up a guitar and played songs he had learned while conscripted in the Russian army. A couple of Russians, there on holiday, applauded.

*

Due to border issues, I could not go overland to Uzbekistan, so needed to return to Bishkek. As we drove around the north of Lake Issyk-Kol, the driver asked if I wanted to go see the 'petroglyphs'.

As we drove up the road on the outskirts of the resort town of Cholpon-Ata, we had to avoid the Russian women rollerblading in bikinis. The driver, who seemed nonplussed, parked the car. I got out and walked into an open-air museum: a field of glacial boulders on which 3,000 years ago images of animals and humans had been carved. On one large boulder, I made out hunters stalking ibex with the assistance of snow leopards. A peek into a way of life from centuries ago.

*

I had a day to kill in Bishkek. There were few sights for a tourist to see in the city. I walked to Ala-Too Square and watched soldiers goose-stepping in front of the statue of the Kyrgyzstan hero Manas that had replaced the one of Lenin.

On arrival at the airport in Tashkent, I was met by Phil Kosnett, the Deputy Chief of Mission at the US embassy in Uzbekistan. I had worked with Phil in Baghdad, and he had graciously offered to host me in Tashkent. He was kind, decent and competent. And a devout Christian, which although common in the US military was rather a rarity at the State Department.

Phil took me home and introduced me to his wife, Alison, who worked on democratization and justice-sector reform in Uzbekistan for the US Agency for International Development.

I then looked down to see what was yapping at my heels. The thing was running around in circles, a bewitched bundle of black-and-brown fluff. I was not sure whether it was a rat or an electronic toy.

'Let me introduce you to Malika,' Phil said by way of explanation.

'But what is it?' I asked, bending down.

'It is an Uzbek Chihuahua,' Phil announced. For a brief moment, I was charmed by its bulging dark eyes and I reached out to stroke it. It responded with teeth and attitude, before it was off again in a mad circular frenzy.

Phil managed to grab Malika and held it under one arm, smiling at it lovingly with paternal pride. I was going to have to be careful not to trip over the thing while I stayed here. That would clearly not go down well with my hosts.

After a few days in Tashkent with the Kosnetts and Malika, I decided to follow Alison's advice and use a local tourist company for travel around the country. It would book hotels, arrange a driver and register me with the police in every location as required by law for foreigners.

Given the country's human rights record, I wanted to avoid all contact with the police. Uzbekistan was one of the most repressive and corrupt states in the world. Islam Karimov had been ruling the country since independence and had built up an effective police state, cracking down on his political opposition and driving them into exile, where they were fragmented and feuding. There was no free media or civil society to speak of. And the tentacles of the security forces went right down to the roots of society.

Karimov could not live forever, of course. But it was not clear who his successor would be. He had been grooming his daughter, Gulnara Karimova, who was a pop star, model, socialite and businesswoman. However, she had been placed under house arrest earlier in the year following allegations of money laundering and corruption in Switzerland and Sweden. Gulnara lashed out, comparing her father to Stalin and accusing her mother and sister of sorcery.

There was little sympathy for Gulnara in the country. A WikiLeaked US cable reported: 'Most Uzbeks see Karimova as a greedy, power hungry individual who uses her father to crush business people or anyone else who stands in her way… She remains the single most hated person in the country.'

Ouch.

Under Soviet rule, Uzbekistan had been cut off from the Islamic world. The only mosques that were officially allowed to operate had to be registered with the authorities and their imams approved. But with independence in 1991 came an Islamic revival which President Karimov, the former head of the Uzbek Communist Party, initially embraced before he began branding every practising Muslim as a Wahhabi.

Karimov had been an international pariah prior to 9/11, with Uzbekistan's human rights record decried by Human Rights Watch as 'atrocious' and 'abysmal'. However, the Global War on Terror rehabilitated Karimov. President Bush invited him to Washington and the US increased its aid to Uzbekistan, with the Uzbek police and intelligence services receiving $79 million despite the State Department's website noting their use of 'torture as a routine investigation technique'. In return, Uzbekistan permitted the US to open up an air base, known as K2, at Karshi-Khanabad in the south-east of the country, close to the Afghanistan border.

Craig Murray, the former British ambassador to Uzbekistan, had repeatedly accused the Karimov regime of torture – and of boiling prisoners to death. In the run-up to the Iraq War, Murray argued that Karimov's human rights abuses were worse than Saddam's. He also claimed that Uzbekistan was 'part of a global CIA torture programme'. He was dismissed from his post for 'operational' reasons, which may or may not have had something to do with his relationship with an Uzbek lap dancer.

In 2005, there had been unrest in Andijan in the Fergana Valley. Two dozen local businessmen were jailed for alleged ties to a banned Islamist group. Armed men attacked the prison and released them. Apparently inspired by the Tulip Revolution in Kyrgyzstan, protestors gathered to voice anger at government corruption, persecution of people simply for being practising Muslims, and increasing poverty. Government forces stormed the square, killing around 600 people. Karimov claimed that those killed in Andijan were members of the Islamic Movement of Uzbekistan, an organization which had declared jihad against the state and sought to create a caliphate in Central Asia. Angered at US demands for an international investigation, the Uzbek government shut down the American air base on the Afghan border and moved closer to Russia.

However, the United States reached out again to Karimov, after a souring of US relations with Pakistan made it increasingly difficult to move supplies to US troops in Afghanistan through that country. Karimov agreed to open up Uzbekistan as a supply route into Afghanistan.

Karimov justified his authoritarianism as the price of preventing Islamist militancy. And it was a price that the United States – as in the Middle East – was willing to pay. There was plenty of evidence of how authoritarian regimes across the Muslim world pushed some of their citizens towards extremism and then presented themselves as the solution. But tactical concerns over terrorism outweighed pressure for reforms.

Trade with China had increased considerably, particularly over the last decade. In 2013, the Chinese government announced its 'One Belt, One Road' initiative, seeking the revival of the ancient Silk Road routes from China to Europe. As a result, it committed to investing further in Uzbekistan's infrastructure, including railways and pipelines.

*

One early morning, I headed to the railway station in Tashkent to take the train to Samarkand.

It was not any old train, I might add, but the Afrosiyob bullet train. It had been built by a Spanish company, Talgo, with Uzbek financing. My seat was comfortable and I had a table, lamp and footrest. The breakfast was edible. And the train flew like the wind. It took two hours to make the 214-mile journey to Samarkand, travelling at speeds of up to 160 miles per hour. All for around $30.

In my youth, I had tried and failed to make it to Timbuktu. But I had reached Kathmandu. And now I was on my way to Samarkand – another one of those mystical places that adventurers through the centuries have been drawn to.

The city's name evokes a long and rich history. On conquering Samarkand in 329 BC, Alexander the Great announced that everything he had heard about the city was true, 'except that it is more beautiful than I ever imagined'.

> We are the Pilgrims, master; we shall go
> Always a little further; it may be
> Beyond that last blue mountain barred with snow,
> Across that angry or that glimmering sea.

When I got off the train at Samarkand, I quickly spotted a woman holding up a sign with my name on it. She introduced herself to me as Suzanna.

It was a blisteringly hot day, with bright blue skies. Suzanna and I walked towards the Registan, the ancient centre of the city and the main square, where people once gathered for royal proclamations, parades and executions. It was stunning. I feasted my eyes on the three madrasas that stood around the square: the portals and the minarets, the azure, turquoise and gold mosaics. I imagined students studying maths, astronomy and philosophy in the beautiful rooms inside.

Suzanna, I discovered, was an Armenian polyglot – and a walking encyclopaedia. She knew the history of Samarkand inside out, and the myths entwined within it.

We walked down the street, through the spice market, to the Bibi-Khanym Mosque. Suzanna told me that the wife of Timur

(Tamerlane, or Timur the Lame as we know him in the West) ordered the mosque to be built for him as a surprise while he was away. The architect fell in love with her and kissed her. But the kiss left a mark which Timur saw. He ordered her to be thrown from the top of the minaret. But she was saved from death by her robes, which acted as a parachute.

Suzanna was also a foodie, and blogged about her country's cuisine. 'For centuries Uzbekistan was famed for its gastronomy: Omar Khayam admired Samarkand wines, gourmets of China appreciated the sweetness of Samarkand peaches, merchants, exhausted after long, dusty trips along the Great Silk Road, enjoyed Samarkand *plov* [a meaty rice dish], lamb, *non* [flatbreads] and other specialties,' she wrote.

For lunch, Suzanna ordered for us *samsa*, puff pastry filled with minced lamb and onions. I was relieved she had not asked for fatty tail. From her blog, I learned that fatty tail was a delicacy in Central Asia, and that a mature ram's tail could carry up to twelve kilograms of the prized fat. I was quite happy to give it a miss.

After lunch we drove to the Shah-i-Zinda necropolis, then wandered on foot through the narrow streets that ran between the eleven mausoleums. This was the burial place of royals and nobles and remained an important point of pilgrimage. We were surrounded by turquoise domes, exquisite tilework, majolica, mosaics and Quranic inscriptions. The focal point was the shrine to the 'Living King' Qusam ibn-Abbas, a cousin of the Prophet Mohamad who was credited with bringing Islam to this area in the seventh century – and was beheaded by Zoroastrians. I entered one of the mausoleums and sat for a while in the cool, quiet room to reflect.

Afterwards, we drove to the tomb of the Prophet Daniel on the banks of the Siob River. I was surprised to find it here, as I had visited another tomb supposedly of Daniel in Kirkuk, Iraq. Some religious 'histories' seemed tall stories.

When I entered the five-domed building, I discovered that the sarcophagus was 18 metres long. The body apparently grows half an inch each year.

Suzanna, fashionable in her sunglasses, scarf and knee-length skirt, also knew exactly where to shop. She took me to the place that made the best rugs and *suzani,* the exquisite embroideries of Uzbekistan. Outside, the store owner explained the different dyes. We then went inside, walking past women weaving, to reach the 'showroom' at the back of the store. The owner brought me tea and then started to lay out cushion covers, bedspreads, table cloths and wall hangings. 'What colours do you like?' he asked. 'What are you looking for?'

I was not looking for anything in particular, but I made the fatal mistake of appearing interested. He got me to look at the silks, the different stitching and the natural dyes of indigo, pomegranate and sumac. He told me about the women in the villages whose work was on display. He explained the motifs associated with different parts of Uzbekistan, including the Fergana Valley and the villages around Samarkand. He had me hooked.

I could not choose between them. In the end, I bought one large wall hanging for my living room, two cushion covers for my sofa and a smaller hanging to go above my bed. I spent my entire budget for Uzbekistan in one sitting, borrowing cash from Suzanna.

*

It was impossible to visit Uzbekistan and not be reminded of the Mongol hordes, the confederation of nomadic tribes – led by Genghis Khan – who rode out from the steppes of Central Asia and bore down on the Muslim world in the thirteenth century. In 1220, they took the cities of Samarkand and Bukhara. Genghis Khan ordered the execution of everyone who had fought him in Samarkand – and pyramids formed from their severed heads.

More than a century later, Timur sought to emulate Genghis Khan. His military campaigns are estimated to have caused the deaths of 17 million people – about 5 per cent of the world's population at that time. Cities were sacked, their populations massacred and Christian churches destroyed in much of Asia. But under Timur's reign, Central Asia blossomed. In today's Uzbekistan, he is heralded as a hero, with monuments to him everywhere.

Suzanna took me to the Gur-e-Amir mausoleum, where Timur was buried alongside two sons and two grandsons. She told me that Timur had developed diplomatic relations with France and Spain, against the expansionist Ottoman Empire.

The old city of Samarkand had been restored and manicured; its traditions and crafts were being preserved. But it had long since lost its position as a major hub on the Silk Road. Its name was associated with a celebrated past – not with its present. Cut off from the rest of the world, it had lost the cosmopolitan culture for which it had once been famed.

But it had still produced Suzanna. And when I said farewell to her in Samarkand, I knew I was going to miss her company.

*

After checking in to my hotel in Bukhara, I ate a plate of *plov* at the foot of a mulberry tree that had apparently been planted in 1477. Once I had finished, I passed through the old city gates where artisans sold their pottery, calligraphy and musical instruments. I walked along the cobbled streets, drawn to the turquoise domes of the mosques and the forty-seven-metre-high Kalon Minaret, which had so impressed Genghis Khan that he spared it. I sat in its shadow, in front of the Mir-i-Arab Madrasa. What devotion had inspired such architecture? It was of such breathtaking beauty that it brought tears to my eyes.

During the age of the Samanid Empire, in the ninth and tenth centuries, Bukhara had become the intellectual centre of the Islamic world, second only to Baghdad. It was here that Rudaki and Firdausi wrote poems – the former heralded as the father of Persian poetry, the latter famed for *Shahnameh* ('Book of Kings'), the national epic of Iran.

And it was here, in the eleventh century, that Ibn Sina, known in the West as Avicenna, philosophized. He was perhaps the most influential thinker of the Islamic Golden Age, writing on logic, ethics and metaphysics. His *Canon of Medicine*, a five-volume encyclopaedia, was the authoritative medical textbook in the Muslim world and Europe for centuries.

But it all came crashing down when Genghis Khan conquered the city. By the time Ibn Battuta, the great traveller and scholar from Morocco, passed through the region in around 1333, he found it in ruins.

Bukhara's old city had long since been renovated. But its intellectual life was a shadow of its former self. Once a place that attracted great thinkers, it had become isolated. An expansive Jewish graveyard was testimony to a thriving community that once was, but most of its Jewish residents had long since departed. Only one functioning synagogue remained.

*

In the evening, I sat in the lobby of my hotel reading Peter Hopkirk's *The Great Game: On Secret Service in High Asia.* In the nineteenth century, Britain and Russian agents, in various disguises, had crossed the mountains, mapped passes and developed relations with local leaders – and spied on each other. Young men, serving their country, on dangerous and exciting missions.

The next day, I went to the Ark, a massive fortress in the north-west of the city. The photos on the walls were reminders of the unfortunate fate that had befallen previous British adventurers. It had not all been fun and games.

Colonel Charles Stoddart had arrived in Bukhara on 17 December 1838 to try to build an alliance between the British East India Company and Nasrullah Khan (the Emir of Bukhara) against the Russian Empire, which was expanding its influence south and making inroads towards India, the crown jewel of the British Empire. Britain believed that it would be welcomed by the Central Asian khanates. Colonel Stoddart, however, got off on the wrong foot. In keeping with military protocol, he saluted the emir while still seated on his horse. In Bukhara, visitors were supposed to dismount and bow. Nasrullah Khan stormed off without a word.

I went to have a look at the 'Bug Pit', the infested dungeon into which Stoddart had been thrown. He was kept there for months until given the choice between execution or conversion to Islam.

Stoddart had chosen conversion. He was brought out of the pit and placed under house arrest at the home of the chief of police. Nasrullah Khan met with Stoddart on several occasions and began to seriously consider allying with the British against the Russians.

Three years after Stoddart's arrival in Bukhara, a rescue mission finally arrived in the form of a cavalry officer, Captain Arthur Conolly, the man who coined the term 'the Great Game' in reference to the competition in Central Asia between the British and Russian Empires. Negotiations were cordial until Nasrullah Khan realized that Conolly had not brought with him a reply from Queen Victoria to the letter he had sent her. On top of that slight came the news that the Afghans had massacred the entire British Army as it retreated to India after having tried to impose a puppet regime on Afghanistan. There was only one survivor who had lived to tell the tale: Dr William Brydon.

Nasrullah lost all interest in aligning with the British, and Stoddart and Conolly were thrown in prison. They were later brought to the square in front of the Ark and ordered to dig their own graves. Before he was beheaded, Colonel Stoddart called out that the emir was a tyrant. Conolly was offered the chance to convert to Islam to save his own life. He refused and was also decapitated.

Their exploits might have been lost for posterity were it

not for Joseph Wolff, an eccentric German Jewish Christian missionary, who went looking for them in Bukhara in 1843 only to discover they had been executed the previous year. He believed he only escaped the same fate because the emir burst into fits of giggles at the full canonical garb Wolff was wearing. In 1938, British adventurer Fitzroy Maclean travelled across Central Asia to Bukhara, paying homage in the autobiographical *Eastern Approaches* to his two compatriots who were killed playing the Great Game.

*

I got up just after dawn. I had a long journey ahead across the Karakum Desert and I needed to make an early start. My driver stopped in a village along the way so that we could stretch our legs. I wandered over to the mosque. It was the beginning of the month of Ramadan, when Muslims fast from dawn to dusk. I was surprised to see lots of people gathered outside at a table, openly eating. They smiled and beckoned me over to join them. There was little sign of outward religiosity in Uzbekistan. It was, after all, punishable in very nasty ways.

We arrived in Khiva as the sun set, turning its ancient mud walls pink. I spent a couple of days exploring the city, which had been infamous in bygone times for its slave trade and ruthless emirs, whose barbaric torture methods were displayed in the Khuna Ark, a twelfth-century fortress.

During the Soviet era, all the residents had been forcibly relocated and the city turned into a museum. But since independence in 1991, some of the former residents had returned and it had been repopulated.

On my way to the Kalta Minor Minaret, remarkable because it was never completed and was instead left short and stumpy, I was distracted by the *chugirma* (sheepskin hats) on display on either side of the path. Some were dark brown, others reddish or white. Some were furry, and some curly. A *chugirma* apparently depicted a person's social status. And in the old days, those who were foreign to the city were required to wear ones which distinguished them from the locals.

Walking down a thousand-year-old street, I came to the Tosh-Hovli Palace and immersed myself in the harem. I read that the khan had been permitted four wives – and had around forty concubines. There was, unsurprisingly, lots of plotting at the palace. The khan was paranoid about being poisoned, so killed off his potential rivals. He never slept in the same room two nights in a row, for fear of being murdered. Even the khan's sons were only allowed to remain in the harem until they were ten years old.

*

Nukus is an ugly, remote city in a desolate region of north-west Uzbekistan. The only reason to stop there is to see the remarkable art collection at the Savitsky museum. Igor Savitsky, a twentieth-century Russian painter and archaeologist, had collected avant-garde works that were condemned by the Soviet authorities as 'decadent bourgeois art' for not conforming to socialist realism and idealized images of farm and factory workers.

After one night in Nukus, my driver and I headed for the Aral Sea. On the way, we passed large areas of land that the government had allocated for cotton. Soviet Russia had effectively turned the country into a cotton plantation, and Uzbekistan was still one of the top-five cotton producers in the world.

As the crop requires lots of water, the government diverted most of the country's water resources to irrigate it. During the annual harvest season, the government drafted a million people to pick cotton, praising their patriotic participation in upholding tradition while paying them a pittance. The government then traded the cotton, which it called 'white gold', in the global market, reaping huge profits.

After a few hours of travelling in silence, the driver stopped the car. I had learned the Cyrillic alphabet in order to be able to decipher signposts – and menus – but we shared no language in common. However, words were not needed to explain what I was looking at.

Stretched out in front of me were rusted fishing boats lying in a sea of sand. A cemetery for ships that served as a memorial to a bygone fishing industry. The Aral Sea, once the fourth-largest lake in the world, with twenty-four different species of fish, had turned into the Aral desert, a toxic expanse of white sand and salt laced with pesticides – one of the world's worst environmental disasters.

*

Rather than make the long journey back to Tashkent via land, I decided to take a domestic flight from Nukus. I thought the plane was never going to make it off the ground. It bounced along the runway, and when it did manage to get its nose in the air, it struggled to gain altitude. I did not think it would stay

Old men in oasis of Niswa, Oman

Women in Ibri market

Royal Opera House, Muscat

Qandil mountains,
Kurdistan

Sky discussing
the teachings
of Öcalan with
female PKK
guerrilla in the
Qandil mountains

PKK checkpoint to enter the Qandil mountains

Sky with Iraqi leaders Barham Salih and Adel
Abdul Mahdi in Mergapan, Kurdistan

Amanj Yarwaessi and Sky north
of Sulaymaniyah, Kurdistan

Sky in Fairy Tale Canyon on southern shore of Lake Issyk-Kol, Kyrgyzstan

Horse exhausted after long ride in the mountains of Kyrgyzstan

Yurt in the mountains of Kyrgyzstan

The Registan of Samarkand, Uzbekistan

Ship cemetery in the Aral Sea, Uzbekistan

Idomeni transit camp near the Greece-Macedonia border

Poster welcoming refugees in Skopje, the Former Yugoslav Republic of Macedonia

Sarajevo, Bosnia Herzegovina

Celebration of the life of murdered British Member of Parliament Jo Cox in London's Trafalgar Square on 22 June 2016

Outside the Queen Elizabeth II Conference Centre near Parliament Square in London on 6 July 2016, awaiting the publication of the findings of the Chilcot Inquiry into the Iraq War

Wild horses in the Pyrenees, France

Signpost marking the Camino de Santiago pilgrimage, Spain

airborne. Everything was creaking and shaking and I feared the plane was breaking apart. Passengers whimpered and wept.

So this is where I die, I thought. I recited prayers over and over again to stay calm. I had done a lot in my life. I could not complain. But in that moment, when I believed my time was up, the only regret I had was that I had not submitted the manuscript I had been working on. I had left no children; the only indication of my time on Earth was that book which bore witness to the Iraq War, explained what had gone wrong and why, paid tribute to those who had strived so hard, and honoured those who had lost life and limb. Now their stories would not be told – and all the learning would be lost.

Somehow, we landed safely in Tashkent. I vowed never to fly Uzbekistan Airways again. And I submitted my manuscript.

Travelling along the Silk Road had been educational and exciting, a reminder of the impact of great power competition on those caught in its wake, as well as the lasting legacy of writings, art and architecture. But even in the most remote places, I had been distracted by the reports of jihadis raising their flags across the Middle East.

The vision of the Arab Spring protestors for a more just society had been usurped by ISIS.

CHAPTER 10

The Islamic State: A caliphate in accordance with the prophetic method

Jordan

March 2015

My Iraqi friend Azzam Alwash, the environmentalist, picked me up from the Four Seasons hotel in Amman and drove me to the Jordan Valley. As we sat on the bank of the Dead Sea gazing out across the salt lake, the sun disappeared behind the rocky crags of Israel. I recounted a trip I had taken to Jordan twenty years previously, to conduct field research on Palestinian refugees. This had been part of an initiative, sponsored by the Middle East peace process, aimed at ensuring that, within a decade, nobody in the region would consider themselves a refugee.

Back then, no one had an inkling that the number of refugees in the region would increase exponentially, with millions displaced from their homes by international intervention, civil war and ISIS.

I related to Azzam my visit in 2014 to Zaatari, the refugee camp in Jordan close to the border with Syria that had become the fourth-largest city in the country. Most of the Syrian refugees lived in tents provided by the Office of the UN High Commissioner for Refugees (UNHCR). The lucky ones had trailers similar to the one I had lived in for part of my time in Iraq. But I'd had the trailer to myself – and shared a bathroom with one other woman. The refugee camp trailers each housed a family of about ten, and they had to share a toilet with 250 other people. The refugees I had spoken to were bored, had no work and wanted to go back to Syria. There was nothing for them in Jordan. They missed home, and were worried about their children growing up in such conditions. What future would they have? I'd heard that young girls were being married off, sometimes for protection, sometimes for economic reasons.

I spoke with a number of NGO workers in the camp, most of whom were Jordanians of Palestinian origin. They described how they were reminded of the stories they had heard from their grandparents, who had fled Palestine carrying their front door keys, certain that they would soon return. I asked them how long they thought it would be before the Syrian refugees went back to their homes. One responded that the best-case scenario was five years. Another responded: 'They are never going to go home. It is going to be just like the Palestinians.'

Turkey had taken in three million Syrians and Jordan a million. In Lebanon, refugees now made up a quarter of the country's population.

Back in Amman, Azzam and I went out to an Italian restaurant with a group of our Iraqi friends – Sunni and Shia, Kurd and Arab. It was a reunion of sorts; some of us had gone white-water rafting down the Little Zab river in Iraqi Kurdistan a couple of years before.

The conversation soon turned to ISIS, and one of those at dinner, a secular liberal man, claimed that the United States was behind its creation. I groaned out loud. It was a common view I'd heard expressed in the region, propagated by Sunni and Shia alike. Local media had reported on alleged US airdrops to Daesh. Some outlets even referred to the ISIS leader Abu Bakr al-Baghdadi as an Israeli-trained Mossad agent.

'What possible reason,' I asked, 'would the US have for creating Daesh?'

'The US wants to make Sunni and Shia fight each other so that the US can continue to dominate the region,' the man responded.

I pointed out that this was twisted logic. Obama was trying to disengage from the region – and to stop the US from being forever at war. The previous year he had delivered the commencement address at West Point, telling the 'long gray line' of graduating cadets that they were the first class since 9/11 who might not be sent into combat in Iraq or Afghanistan.

'OK, so where do you think Daesh came from?' he asked me.

I admitted that it was true that if there had been no Iraq War, there would be no Daesh. The war in Iraq had collapsed the state and left ungoverned spaces in which al-Qaeda in Iraq had been born. And Maliki's sectarian policies had led to Daesh rising up out of the ashes of al-Qaeda in Iraq and expanding to Syria in the chaos of the civil war there. But the US had not deliberately created Daesh – that was nonsense. It was an unintended consequence of the war.

I described how Daesh was a symptom of bad governance and poisonous politics. There was a symbiotic relationship between corrupt politicians and terrorists – they justified each other's existence, each claiming to provide protection from the other.

The Iraq War had also enabled the resurgence of Iran. And this change in the balance of power in the region had increased competition between Iran and Saudi, leading to them supporting Shia and Sunni extremists, respectively, in different countries.

Azzam then spoke out. 'Daesh are Muslims. Fundamentalist Salafi Islam is to blame for their existence.' He went on: 'The problem is the literal interpretation of the Quran, which, for example, spells out harsh criminal punishments reflective of practices of the seventh century. Other religions have moved forward and reformed because they were willing to interpret texts in the context of their own time.'

A heated argument broke out as others at the table defended Islam and accused Azzam of being brainwashed by the West.

'If we Muslim intellectuals are not self-critical, if we refuse to take responsibility and address the issues,' he responded, 'what hope is there for the Middle East?'

*

Everyone seemed transfixed by the jihadis who, dressed in black jumpsuits and masks, had planted their black flags across Syria and Iraq. Daesh now ruled over a territory the size of the UK. Up to 10 million people were believed to be living under its control. It had proclaimed that it would 'remain and expand'.

Daesh had swept into Mosul the previous summer, while I had been in Kyrgyzstan. Iraqi security forces had disintegrated in the face of its advance. On 5 July 2014, ISIS leader Abu Bakr al-Baghdadi appeared at Mosul's Great Mosque of al-Nuri, wearing a black cloak and black turban. 'Appointing a leader is an obligation on Muslims, and one that has been neglected for decades,' he said in a sermon that was beamed around the world. 'I am your leader, though I am not the best of you, so if you see that I am right, support me, and if you see that I am wrong, advise me.'

The Muslim community had been led by a caliph (literally meaning 'successor') since the death of the Prophet Mohamad. The first four caliphs to succeed the Prophet were known by Sunnis as the Rashidun (the rightly guided ones). The first caliph was Abu Bakr, followed by Umar, followed by Uthman. As with the Prophet Mohamad, they had each made their capital Medina. The fourth caliph, Ali ibn Abi Talib, moved the capital to Kufa, in present day Iraq. He was assassinated in 661 and buried in Najaf. After Ali's death, his main rival, Muawiyah, claimed the caliphate and founded the Umayyad dynasty, ruling from Damascus.

In 750, the Umayyads were overthrown by the Abbasids, who made Baghdad their capital. The city flourished as the centre of culture and trade. However, the Islamic Golden Age came to an end in 1258 with the sacking of Baghdad by the Mongols under Hulagu Khan, one of the grandsons of Genghis Khan.

Arab civilization never recovered from the Mongol invasions. It lost its libraries, its universities, its scholars, its artists, its doctors, its astronomers. Centuries of learning were erased. But, in truth, it had already begun to decline before the Mongols invaded. During the first four centuries of Islam, there had been vigorous debate over laws. However, leading Sunni jurists then declared that the essential legal questions had been answered and that there was no longer any need for *ijtihad* (independent reasoning). Although the gates of *ijtihad* never totally shut, philosophers were disparaged and translations of works from other languages trailed off. The decline of Arab civilization set in when it became less open to the rest of the world.

The Mamluk rulers of Egypt re-established the Abbasid Caliphate in Cairo in 1261 – but with the caliph's authority limited to religion. Then, in 1517, the Ottoman sultan Selim I claimed the caliphate with its capital as Constantinople. The Ottoman Empire competed with the Safavid dynasty over control of Mesopotamia, the land between the two rivers of the Tigris and the Euphrates. The Safavids' rule of Persia began in 1501, and over the next 200 years they converted the inhabitants from Sunni Islam to Shia. They established Shia Islam as the official religion of their empire, giving it a unique identity that would help mobilize people against their enemy, the Ottomans.

After the collapse of the Ottoman Empire, Mustafa Kemal Atatürk officially abolished the caliphate in 1924 as part of his reforms, separating religion from state. Ninety years after the dissolution of the caliphate, Abu Bakr al-Baghdadi was declaring its revival.

Daesh was now competing with al-Qaeda for leadership of the Salafi jihadi movement. Osama bin Laden had focused al-Qaeda on attacking the 'far enemy', the United States, which he blamed for propping up the corrupt authoritarian regimes in the Muslim world. He had been one of the 20,000 or so volunteer fighters who travelled to Afghanistan after the 1979 Soviet invasion in order to defend Muslim lands from the atheist invaders. A member of a wealthy Saudi business family, bin Laden interpreted the withdrawal of Soviet forces from Afghanistan as a triumph for Islam over one of the world's superpowers. He calculated that the 9/11 attacks on the US would cause the sole remaining superpower to crumble in the same way that the Soviet Union had.

Bin Laden's strategy was to develop popular support and drive Western infidels from Muslim lands before setting up a caliphate. Abu Bakr al-Baghdadi's approach was different. He was focused on the immediate establishment of the caliphate. For him, this was essential in order to enforce Sharia – the ethical teachings and laws that followers of Islam believed God provided to guide humanity – in the manner they had been applied in the seventh century.

Abu Bakr al-Baghdadi had been born Ibrahim Awwad Ibrahim al-Badri in Samarra, Iraq, in 1971. He claimed descent from the Prophet, had grown up deeply devout, and completed a PhD in Islamic Studies. In the 1990s, he joined the Muslim Brotherhood in Baghdad. But he left the group after gravitating to Salafi jihadism. After the US invasion of Iraq in 2003, he was arrested in Fallujah while visiting a friend who was on a wanted list. He was held for nearly a year at the US detention camp at Bucca.

Baghdadi took over the leadership of al-Qaeda in Iraq in 2010, four years after the death of its founder, Abu Musab al-Zarqawi. It was Zarqawi who had deliberately set about provoking a sectarian war in order to collapse the Iraqi state, so that it could be replaced by the caliphate. His indiscriminate killing of Shia even earned him a rebuke from bin Laden, who was worried about public opinion. When Baghdadi took over the movement in Iraq, it had almost been destroyed as the tribes turned against it and American and Iraqi special forces killed its leaders. But as US forces withdrew and Iraqi politics degenerated, Baghdadi built it back up – and attracted new recruits.

*

Across its territory, Daesh had put up flags and signs saying 'The Islamic State: A Caliphate in Accordance with the Prophetic Method' and quickly developed a sophisticated bureaucracy and procedures for governing. Below the caliph were two deputies – one responsible for Iraq and the other for Syria. It had tens of thousands of fighters, all wearing Islamic State patches on their uniforms.

Most of the fighters were Iraqis and Syrians, while around 10 per cent were believed to be foreign. The largest number of foreign fighters came from Tunisia, the only country where the Arab Spring had brought about a transition to democracy. There were also significant numbers of Saudis, Turks and Jordanians.

Jihadist groups from Asia to Africa had all pledged allegiance to the caliphate, and the proclamation of the restoration of the caliphate was reverberating around the world. Daesh's transnational message, promoted far and wide over the Internet and through social media, attracted jihadis from east and west. Some seemed rational and religious. Others appeared to be psychopaths, attracted by the sex, guns and gratuitous violence on offer. Some were seasoned fighters of different conflicts. Others were newly religious and quickly radicalized; having not received a thorough grounding in Muslim culture growing up, they had come under the sway of charismatic recruiters, been further influenced by radical preachers on YouTube, and groomed over the Internet by jihadis who lured them in by making them feel part of a wider community. Each fighter assumed a nom de guerre: Abu-something, followed by the country or town from which they came – Abu Mohamad al-Amriki, Abu Abdullah al-Tunisi.

Daesh's military council, led by former Iraqi army officers, was responsible for the defence and the expansion of territory. Revenue from taxes and tolls, and the selling of oil and antiquities, was supervised by the financial council. The Islamic State letterhead appeared on parking fines and taxation forms. Governors were appointed to ensure delivery of services in the provinces.

The Shura council ensured that directives issued by the caliph were disseminated. The Sharia council, led by religiously trained individuals, developed ISIS's interpretations of Islam, with religious police and courts ensuring adherence. Daesh was committed to purifying the world through the killing of *kuffar* (apostates). It accused all who did not accept its authority of being heretics – rather than just sinners. Shia

Islam was regarded as an innovation; hence all Shia were declared apostates.

Saudi textbooks were downloaded and distributed at schools under ISIS control. The penalties imposed for sins and crimes were the same as those in Saudi Arabia: death for blasphemy, murder, adultery and homosexuality; amputation of a hand for stealing. But unlike the Saudis, Daesh glorified, filmed and broadcast its violence.

The media council produced a wide range of propaganda videos. Some showed acts of savagery to intimidate and instil fear. Some showed victorious fighters with guns. Others portrayed the high quality of life under the caliphate, with good hospitals and welfare.

ISIS was organized and had resources. It attracted former Iraqi Baath party members, and military officers dismissed from their jobs by the US in 2003 following the invasion. It became the dominant rebel group in the region, taking control of the weapons that outside powers had provided its competitors.

At the same time as it pushed forward its state-building project, Daesh called for the armies of Islam to fight the armies of 'Rome' (the West) in Dabiq in Syria, to bring on the apocalypse.

*

In August 2014, Daesh released a video of a man clad in black clothes and desert boots, holding a knife in his left hand to the neck of American journalist James Foley, who was dressed in an orange jumpsuit like the prisoners in Guantanamo and Bucca. The masked man said the execution of Foley was in response to air strikes that Obama had ordered against ISIS in Iraq.

Former Western hostages who had been held in Raqqa in Syria had nicknamed the four jihadis who held them captive as 'The Beatles', due to their British accents. In the video that ISIS released, they recognized one of their former captors – the one they called John.

Daesh released a second video of 'Jihadi John', as the British media dubbed him, this time killing Steven Sotloff. 'I'm back, Obama, and I'm back because of your arrogant foreign policy towards the Islamic State... You, Obama, have yet again, through your actions, killed yet another American citizen.'

Americans were terrified and enraged. In response to the public outcry, Obama ordered airstrikes against Daesh in Syria.

Jihadi John's next victim was David Haines, a British aid worker, followed by Alan Henning, a British taxi driver captured while delivering humanitarian aid to the Syrian people.

Next came Peter Kassig, an American aid worker who had converted to Islam.

Then two Japanese men were executed after the Japanese prime minister publicly pledged $200 million in non-military aid to countries fighting ISIS.

Jordan, too, was not spared. Jordanian pilot Muath al-Kasasbeh had ejected from his F-16 fighter aircraft on 24 December 2014, following a bombing raid on ISIS targets. He was taken captive and later videoed, clad in an orange jumpsuit, burning to death inside a cage – symbolizing, Daesh said, the manner of death of the victims of his aerial bombings.

*

One evening, Sheikh Abdullah al-Yawar invited me to dinner with his family at his house in Amman. He was an Iraqi from Mosul who I had got to know well during my time in Iraq. From 2003 onwards, Abdullah had decided that he and his family would cooperate with coalition forces rather than fight against them. He was also the paramount sheikh of the Shammar tribe, which had around five million members in Iraq, Syria, Jordan and Saudi Arabia. Like many of Iraq's wealthier Sunni Arabs, he had relocated to Amman.

Abdullah described how, the summer before, in the wake of the Daesh takeover of Mosul, his mother and brother managed to escape just hours before their palatial twenty-seven-room house near Rabia – north-west of Mosul on the Syrian border – was blown up, his photos and carpets destroyed, and his horses scattered to the wilds. It was a house I knew well and had visited many times.

That same summer, in response to the ISIS takeover of a third of Iraq, Obama had announced the deployment of 300 US special forces. I had been travelling in Central Asia and was asked to brief some of them.

'Ma'am, do we have a real mission?' one of the soldiers asked me. 'I'm prepared to die for the mission, but I want to know we have a mission to win – not just be seen to be doing something. I worry that we're just being sent as window dressing so that the administration can claim it's doing something.'

They had all previously served in Iraq and been convinced that they had defeated al-Qaeda. Now they were being called on again – to tackle its latest incarnation.

I did my best to explain to them how Maliki's sectarian policies had created the conditions that enabled Daesh to rise up out of the ashes of al-Qaeda in Iraq and proclaim itself as the protector of Sunnis. Sunni tribes, who with US support had previously contained al-Qaeda, determined that ISIS was the lesser of two evils when compared to the Iranian-backed sectarian regime of Maliki.

The administration continued to give unconditional support to a leader whose very actions were driving people towards ISIS – and then deployed US troops to deal with the symptoms of its failing strategy.

Following my trip along the Silk Road, I had gone back to northern Iraq to try to better understand what was going on. I had learned that the Iraqi security forces in Mosul had quickly disintegrated in the face of the advance of Daesh. Although they far outnumbered the ISIS fighters and were better equipped, they were poorly led. Prime Minister Nuri al-Maliki had replaced competent officers, who he feared were too close to the Americans, with people loyal to himself. Corruption was rife. Some officers had taken the funds meant to buy food and ammunition for their soldiers. None gave orders to their forces to fight. So the soldiers took off their uniforms and deserted, leaving behind their US equipment for Daesh to capture. I had met men with large moustaches who claimed to be spokesmen for insurgent groups. They said there was a widescale Sunni uprising against Maliki – with ISIS as one of several players.

I asked Abdullah what had happened to those men. He responded that they had been all talk. Some had grown beards and joined ISIS. Others had done nothing.

Daesh did not suddenly take control of Mosul the previous summer, Abdullah told me. For years, there had been so much corruption in local government that Daesh had been able to buy influence and supporters. Government in Iraq, he said, was a business – a family business in which politicians stole millions of dollars of the country's wealth. ISIS had been able to exploit this, presenting itself as a better alternative.

The attention of Daesh had quickly turned to Iraq's minorities. Christians were forced to flee their homes on the Ninewa plains, on which they had lived for centuries – the alternative being to convert and pay taxes under pain of death. ISIS had systematically set about slaughtering and enslaving Yezidis, followers of an ancient religion which believed that God created the world and entrusted it to seven archangels, including Melek Taus (the Peacock Angel) who refused to submit to Adam, and was hence identified as Lucifer, the fallen angel. ISIS considered Yezidis devil worshippers and *mushrik* (polytheists) – not people of 'the Book'.

I had penned an op-ed for the *New York Times*, which was published on 7 August 2014, urging the US to intervene to save Iraq's minorities from certain genocide. That same evening, Obama, who had previously dismissed ISIS as the 'JV team' – al-Qaeda's junior varsity team – ordered strikes against Daesh positions in Iraq.

Major General Majid Ahmed Saadi, an Iraqi Air Force officer from Basra, was in charge of delivering supplies of food and water to Mount Sinjar and lifting off the Yezidis trapped there. He had taken leave from his job training the Iraqi air force to help. With a big bushy moustache and aviator sunglasses, he insisted on personally flying rescue missions in a Russian-made Mi-17 transport helicopter. He told my friend the *New York Times* journalist Alissa Rubin, who was covering the efforts to rescue the Yezidis from the mountain, that this was the most significant thing he had done in his whole life.

On 12 August 2014, as General Majid was taking off from Mount Sinjar with over twenty Yezidis on board, a bullet hit the rotary tail, causing the helicopter to crash and roll. A number of the passengers were wounded – including the Iraqi parliamentarian Vian Dakhil, herself a Yezidi, and Alissa, who fractured her skull. But only one person died: the pilot, General Majid.

For General Majid – a career air force officer – saving lives was a far stronger instinct than taking lives. And he was prepared to risk his own in the process – and to make the ultimate sacrifice. Following his father's death, General Majid's son, who was also a military officer, transferred to Army Aviation to become a pilot.

Sheikh Abdullah, for his part, had tried to save hundreds of Yezidi girls by offering to 'buy' them. He claimed that the KDP Peshmerga had failed to defend the Yezidis on Mount Sinjar, and that it was Syrian Kurds of the YPG who had heroically tried to rescue them – with coalition air support.

'Who are the Iraqis in Daesh?' I asked Sheikh Abdullah.

Many, he told me, came from the town of Tal Afar, where there had been bitter fighting between the Sunni and Shia populations during the civil war that followed the 2003 invasion. They were former Baathists and members of Saddam's military and intelligence services who had been dismissed from their jobs by the US-led coalition. Some became al-Qaeda, and now they were Daesh. They felt excluded and marginalized. Daesh gave them a sense of empowerment and let them present themselves as the defenders of the Sunnis against Shia, Iran and the United States.

Abdullah and his wife provided me quotation after quotation from the Quran to prove that ISIS violated the tenets of Islam. They were deeply offended by Daesh. 'These are not real Muslims,' they both repeated.

I told them that I judged people by how they behaved rather than by what they believed. 'I think of the hospitality shown to me, a foreigner, whenever I travel in the Arab world,' I said. 'Sadly, when I now tell people in the US that I am off on holiday to the Middle East, they worry that I will be kidnapped and have my head chopped off.' I had finished the vine leaves and tabbouleh salad we had been eating, and kebab and chicken were now heaped onto my plate. I told them I thought I faced a greater risk of death from overeating.

Abdullah turned serious. 'We need more help from America. Look at what Iran is doing. Iran is now in Tikrit.' Iranian military officers were highly visible as advisers to the Shia militias who were leading the efforts to retake Saddam's hometown.

'This is a huge humiliation for the Sunnis. This is not the way to destroy Daesh. It will cause a worse reaction in the future,' he concluded.

*

'No one wants the overthrow of the monarchy,' Suheil, a well-connected Jordanian, told me over dinner at a restaurant in

Amman. 'The opposition only go as far as saying they would like him to reign rather than rule.'

The instability in the region was having a profound effect on politics in Jordan. Opposition groups had eased off pushing for major reforms, fearful of creating instability that could be exploited by Daesh.

Not only was Jordan burdened by the influx of refugees but the shutting down of cross-border trade with Syria and Iraq was severely impacting an economy that was already strained, mismanaged and reliant on US aid.

Suheil admitted that King Abdullah II was facing difficulties. Abdullah had never expected to be king. King Hussein had named his own younger brother, Prince Hassan, as the crown prince in 1965. Abdullah, whose mother was British, had been educated in the UK and the US. He had graduated from Sandhurst and had been commissioned into the British Army. On his return to Amman, he joined the Royal Jordanian Army and pursued a military career, rising to command Jordan's special forces and achieving the rank of major general. However, King Hussein, a few weeks before his death in 1999, unexpectedly nominated Abdullah to be his heir – replacing Hassan.

Abdullah did not have his late father's personal connection with the people, and nor was he as adept at managing Jordan's elites. He missed the opportunity to implement reforms that would empower moderate, secular forces. Instead, he unintentionally strengthened the Muslim Brotherhood. And there were rumours of a gambling habit.

Suheil leaned towards me, conspiratorially looking from side to side. 'There is a new Sykes–Picot Agreement being planned,' he whispered, referring to the 1916 secret agreement between Britain and France. 'Sykes–Picot' had become a cypher for foreign schemes to dominate the region by keeping it divided and in conflict.

'They are seeking to create a large Sunni region in Jordan, the West Bank, western Iraq and Syria,' said Suheil.

He did not elaborate on who 'they' were.

I was reminded of Suheil's words when watching a YouTube video of an ISIS fighter proclaiming the end of 'Sykes–Picot' as he walked across the berm dividing Syria and Iraq, erasing the borders drawn up by the colonial powers. The song playing in the background proclaimed:

> *My Ummah, Dawn has appeared, so await the expected*
> *victory.*
> *The Islamic State has arisen by the blood of the righteous.*

The a cappella was hypnotic and had such a catchy tune that I found myself chanting '*dawlat al-Islam qamat*'. It was beguiling and would not leave my head.

*

Sheikh Ghassan picked me up from my hotel and took me to a restaurant that he said was owned by Christians from Baghdad. I had first met Sheikh Ghassan al-Assi of the Obeidi tribe in 2003 in Kirkuk, where I had served as the coalition's governorate coordinator. Ghassan had been highly critical of the coalition but, even so, we had become friends. He had moved to Syria when Iraq descended into civil war, returned to Iraq after the situation stabilized, then fled to Jordan in 2014 in the wake of the Daesh blitzkrieg.

When the waiter came to take our order, Ghassan, with his familiar acerbic wit, said to him: 'The Americans and British destroyed our country – but we still invite them to lunch!'

Daesh had blown up the grave of his father, the paramount sheikh of the Obeidis, and destroyed the houses of his uncles because they had collaborated with Prime Minister Maliki. He had hoped that his house would be left alone, since he had not worked with the US or the Iraqi government. But the previous week, Daesh had turned up with C-4 explosives and blown it up. He did not know why.

He took out his iPhone. 'Bastards, bastards, bastards,' he muttered as he flicked through the photos of his destroyed home.

'Who did this?' I asked him. He described how some people in Hawija, south-west of Kirkuk, had seen an opportunity to improve their status by joining ISIS and overthrowing the old social order. Tribal leaders like him had been totally undermined as a result. Many had left the country and had little influence over their tribesmen. Kurdish Peshmerga and Turkmen Shia militiamen were currently fighting Daesh in Hawija.

'Are any Sunnis fighting against Daesh?' I asked Ghassan as he picked out the best parts of the barbecued fish and put them on my plate.

'Miss Emma, how can we?' he responded. 'No one supports the Sunnis. No one gives us help to fight Daesh.'

Not only was Ghassan fearful of ISIS, he was also deeply concerned about Kurdish ambitions to annex Kirkuk. The US was supporting the Kurds to fight ISIS with weapons, intelligence and air power, as well as advisers. But it paid little attention to how the Kurds were benefiting from the conflict to expand their control over disputed territories, including Kirkuk and its oil fields.

After lunch, Ghassan took me to visit the Royal Automobile Museum. We wandered around looking at the old cars and motorbikes that King Hussein had once owned: Aston Martins, McLarens, Ferraris, even an Amphicar. There was a photo on the wall of King Hussein driving Queen Elizabeth in a Range Rover to Wadi Rum. Like the late king, Sheikh Ghassan was a motorcar enthusiast – and Daesh had destroyed his treasured Mercedes convertible.

The museum evoked nostalgia for bygone times, an era when Iraq and Jordan seemed to be on similar paths towards progress. The British had appointed the sons of Sharif Hussein of Mecca as kings of Jordan and Iraq as a reward for the Arab uprising against the Ottomans. Abdullah I ruled Jordan from 1921 until 1951, when he was shot dead by a Palestinian while he was visiting al-Aqsa Mosque in Jerusalem. His son Talal succeeded him, but abdicated after a year as he was mentally ill. Hussein became king in 1952, aged sixteen, and ruled until his death in 1999.

In Iraq, Faisal I ruled from 1921 to 1933, dying of a heart attack aged forty-eight. He was succeeded by his son Ghazi, who was killed in 1939 while driving his sports car. His son, Faisal II, was three years old at the time so his uncle served as regent. Faisal and his cousin Hussein both attended Harrow School in the UK and were close friends. Faisal came of age in 1953. But on 14 July 1958, Faisal and his whole family were murdered in a coup that marked a revolution against an entrenched elite who had refused to reform. Iraq became a republic and went on to suffer decades of instability. In Jordan, the Hashemite monarchy endured, overcoming threats to its rule and serving as an arbiter between the different groups.

Over a cup of tea, Ghassan showed me photos of one of his sons. He had a goatee, was wearing a red-and-white-checked scarf, and was posing for the camera like a male model. I was surprised; I had never expected a boy born and bred in Hawija – a rough provincial town – to turn out looking like this. Even in Hawija, it seemed, there were people who just wanted to lead normal lives, to wear the latest fashion. It was Dubai, not Daesh, that represented the sort of society they wanted to live in.

Sheikh Ghassan laughed at my astonishment. 'Miss Emma, what is life without love?'

*

'Are you married?' the taxi driver asked. How many hundreds of times had I been asked this question by complete strangers in the Middle East. I had given different responses over the years. When I replied no, I received a look of sadness: poor woman, on the shelf, no life. Sometimes I lied and claimed to be married, and would then be pushed into giving details about my imaginary family and explaining why they were not with me.

'No,' I responded this time. I debated whether to argue that there were worse things in life than being single – or whether to confide in him that I had fallen in love with the wrong men. In the end, I decided to go on the attack in the hope that it would close down the conversation. 'Men are no use,' I said.

He looked at me in the rear-view mirror, shocked. Then he asked me if I lived with my parents. I told him I was an orphan. Siblings? None.

He summoned up the courage to ask if I had a boyfriend. He told me that he had a friend who had gone to London and was able to have a girlfriend without getting married to her. This was much less stressful, much less of a burden. Was such an arrangement really permitted, he asked me. Jordanian society did not allow such a thing.

I assured him it was indeed true. In the West, we could have sex for pleasure and love, within a relationship or outside a relationship. 'We have freedom,' I told him.

I went on: 'You can even be born a boy – and then become a girl. Or vice versa. Quite a few people are doing it these days. They don't feel they were born in the right bodies.' That shut him up. The expression on his face said it all. It had changed from a look of interest into one of pure horror.

*

On my last day in Jordan, Jaber al-Jaberi, an Iraqi member of parliament from Anbar Province, drove me to Jerash, an ancient city outside Amman. Daesh had destroyed a number of Iraq's pre-Islamic archaeological sites, including Hatra, Ashur Temple, Khorsabad, Nimrud and Nabi Younis, and we both wanted to visit Jordan's.

In the car, we spoke about Syria. He, like everyone I met, was horrified by the daily carnage that the international community seemed unable or unwilling to stop. Back in 2011, Obama had said that Assad must go. He had led Syrians to believe that the US was going to help – but had subsequently done very little. The US training of moderate rebels had been an embarrassing failure. It had spent $500 million training

Syrian fighters, who had to sign a pledge that they would only fight ISIS – not Assad who was doing most of the killing. Only a few dozen agreed and signed up, and they promptly got wiped out or defected.

Every time the UN envoy brokered a ceasefire, the Syrian regime and Russia broke it and stepped up the violence, attacking the very groups that the United States and its allies were supporting. There were no repercussions. The US kept saying that there was no military solution – while Russia and Iran changed the dynamic on the ground through military support to Assad. Robert Ford, the earnest US ambassador to Syria, had resigned in February 2014, unable to continue to defend US policy. He was burdened by the knowledge that the US had provided enough support to prevent the moderate opposition from being destroyed but not enough to pressure Assad to the negotiation table – and hence was perpetuating the civil war.

Assad was still in power, Jaber claimed, because the Israelis wanted him to remain as president because he kept the border quiet.

Assad was still in power for a host of reasons, I responded, but Israel was low down on that list.

The conversation then turned to Iraq. Jaber had been forced to leave his home in Anbar amid the Daesh advance. I peppered him with questions: How had everything gone so badly wrong in Ramadi? How had Daesh been able to take over? Who were these people?

Jaber described a subculture in Ramadi of uneducated men in their twenties and thirties. Some were thieves and petty criminals. Others had developed fundamentalist thinking.

And when al-Qaeda in Iraq came into existence after the fall of the former regime, it was within that organization that they found a sense of power and identity.

However, when the Sahwa (the Awakening) turned against al-Qaeda in Iraq and aligned with US forces during the troop surge in 2007, many of these same young men were drawn away from the insurgency and swapped sides, turning themselves into local police. That was why the violence in Anbar had dramatically declined from 2007 onwards and stability had returned to the province.

The agreement that my former boss, General Odierno, the commander of US forces in Iraq, had negotiated with Iraqi prime minister Maliki was that 20 per cent of the Sahwa would be integrated into the security forces and 80 per cent into civilian jobs. But the deal had never been implemented.

Rather, as US forces withdrew, Maliki reneged on his promises to the Sahwa and arrested its leaders. He accused Sunni politicians of terrorism, driving them out of the political process. Rafi al-Issawi, the medical doctor and finance minister I had stayed with in Baghdad when he had a tank outside his home, had fled first to his native province of Anbar before leaving the country. Sunnis set up protest camps. But Maliki refused to meet their demands and sent in security forces to violently crush the demonstrations.

Jaber explained that the tribes in Anbar had lost trust in the government and refused to fight ISIS. They remembered only too clearly how the Sahwa had been betrayed. 'We could not convince them that the experience would be different from before.'

When Daesh took over Ramadi, Jaber and two of his sisters moved to Baghdad. Two of his brothers left for Amman. Another sister went to Iraqi Kurdistan, joining the majority of Ramadi's residents. Daesh had murdered a number of Jaber's relatives.

Like many of Anbar's tribes, loyalties in Jaber's family were mixed. He remained supportive of the government and the political process, whereas one of his brothers was opposed to both the government and Daesh, and a small portion of his tribe were with Daesh.

'The Sunnis of Iraq are like the Palestinians,' Jaber said. 'We've been displaced from our land.'

Sunnis had been cleansed from Diyala Province and the Baghdad Belts by Shia militias that had mobilized after the collapse of the Iraqi army. Many more Sunnis had fled from the provinces of Anbar, Ninewa and Salah al-Din because of Daesh. Jaber estimated that over 80 per cent of Iraq's Sunnis had been displaced from their homes.

The Sunnis, he said, had no real leaders. And the Shia militias were more powerful than the Iraqi security forces. Maliki had finally been replaced as Prime Minister. But the damage was done.

'Iraq is finished,' he lamented. 'There is no state left. It is a state of militias.'

I told Jaber that terrorists could not erase Iraq's past. 'Iraq's history survives in archives, in exhibits in the British Museum, on the walls of art galleries in Amman, in poems recited around the world. Iraq is the land where humans first experimented with settled agriculture, where King Hammurabi enacted the first written laws, where Jews wrote the Talmud.'

Jaber, I saw, had tears in his eyes.

'Nothing can take this away, Jaber,' I told him. 'Nothing. Not these terrible terrorists, not these militias, not these awful politicians. A new generation will come one day that can build on this. The hope is the youth who just want to live their lives.'

'*Inshallah,*' Jaber responded.

But Jaber's attention was very much fixed on the present, trying to get food and water to his displaced tribesmen, many of whom were living in terrible conditions in makeshift accommodation in the desert. While the better-off were able to rent places in neighbouring countries or Kurdistan, others lived in tents in camps, relying on family and friends to make ends meet. And some were trying to reach Europe.

CHAPTER 11

What happens in the Middle East does not stay in the Middle East

The Balkans

January 2016

In 2015, a million migrants – three-quarters of them Syrians, Afghans and Iraqis – crossed the Mediterranean Sea on flimsy dinghies and rickety fishing boats, seeking refuge in Europe.

Coastguards and fishermen kept pulling people out of the water. But despite their efforts, 3,771 were recorded as drowned in the Mediterranean that year. Among them was Alan Kurdi, a three-year-old Syrian boy. He and his family had set out on a small boat from an isolated beach near Bodrum on 2 September 2015, trying to reach the Greek island of Kos. Crammed with passengers to double its capacity, the boat quickly overturned. A photo of Alan Kurdi's prostrate body lying on a Turkish beach went viral.

Faced with the biggest influx of people since the end of World War II, Europe was in crisis. Its leaders could not agree what to do.

There were fears the European Union would capsize if the flow was not stemmed. The number arriving in 2015 was quadruple that of the previous year. European systems were stretched to breaking point.

The 1951 UN Refugee Convention had defined a refugee as someone outside their country of origin who had 'a well-founded fear of persecution because of his or her race, religion, nationality, membership of a particular social group or political opinion'.

Many of those on the move now were fleeing wars and were thus eligible to apply for asylum. Others, however, were seeking better lives away from failed states and the ravages of climate change. They did not qualify as refugees and were dubbed 'economic migrants'.

Under the Schengen Agreement of 1985, border controls had been abolished in mainland Europe. This allowed people to move freely between countries and relied on each member state to trust others to control who entered the Schengen Area. The first country of entry for an asylum seeker was supposed to register the application and take fingerprints, in accordance with the Dublin Regulation in EU law.

But the influx of refugees and other migrants had overwhelmed controls in the front-line states, and European countries had not developed a united response to the crisis. There was no agreement on a redistribution system so that countries could share the burden. The Central European countries of Poland, Czech Republic, Slovakia and Hungary rejected a proposal to introduce quotas to relocate asylum seekers across the EU. Germany started processing the applications of Syrians within its borders – and became a magnet for refugees. The Schengen Agreement was falling apart.

Populist politicians, media and users of social media were stirring up fear of Muslims taking over Europe. Viktor Orbán, the nativist prime minister of Hungary, expressed concern that Europe's 'Christian identity' was under threat. Advertisements in the Hungarian media claimed 'an illegal migrant arrives in Europe every 12 seconds' and 'migrants threaten our culture'. Hungary, which had been a transit country for refugees, put up fences of razor wire to close its borders with Serbia and Croatia.

*

The wars in Iraq and Syria were not only producing refugees; they were also mobilizing a new generation of jihadis.

On 7 January 2015, two French-born brothers of Algerian origin had forced their way into the offices of the French weekly satirical newspaper, *Charlie Hebdo*, and shot dead twelve people. President François Hollande called the assault on this bastion of laïcité (secularism) an attack on the 'very identity' of France.

'*Je suis Charlie*' hashtags and demonstrations proclaimed solidarity with *laïcité* and freedom of speech. But, although horrified by the murders, some were uncomfortable being associated with *Charlie Hebdo* and the offensive cartoons of the Prophet for which it was notorious.

'*Je suis Ahmed*' hashtags appeared in honour of the policeman, Ahmed Merabet, who was also killed by the gunmen and was a practising Muslim.

The attacks kept coming.

On Friday 13 November 2015, terrorists struck again in Paris. Gunmen entered the Bataclan theatre during an Eagles of Death Metal concert, taking hostages and firing indiscriminately. Three suicide bombers, failing to get inside a football match between France and Germany at the Stade de France in the Paris suburb of Saint-Denis, blew themselves up outside the stadium. Cafés and restaurants were also struck. In total, 130 people were killed. It was the deadliest day in France since World War II.

How could any sane, decent person not be appalled by such horror? I watched the footage on the Internet, filled with anger and sorrow. I sang the refrain from 'La Marseillaise' at the top of my lungs over and over again in solidarity with the French people:

> *Aux armes, citoyens,*
> *Formez vos bataillons,*
> *Marchons, marchons!*

ISIS claimed responsibility for the attacks, saying they were in retaliation for French air strikes in Iraq and Syria. But few Europeans would make that connection.

Suspicion turned towards Muslims in our midst and refugees at the borders. The perpetrators were mostly French and Belgian citizens, but two of the attackers were Middle Easterners who had arrived in Greece masquerading as refugees, and made their way across Europe without being checked.

Trying to calm his citizens, President Hollande said the refugees were escaping from the same people who had perpetrated such violence – conveniently ignoring that most displaced Syrians were in fact fleeing the Assad regime.

Daesh sought to provoke a backlash against Muslims to show that the West was at war with Islam – and to recruit more Muslims to their cause. And with every attack, fear deepened.

There were calls for limits on immigration and restrictions on Muslims – feeding into extremist propaganda of a clash of civilizations. There was not a single narrative as to what drove a young European Muslim to join the jihad. What was undeniable, however, was that the attackers gained more significance in their deaths than they ever had in their lives.

Two French experts on radical Islam became embroiled in an acrimonious debate on the issue. Olivier Roy blamed the Islamization of radicals; whereas Gilles Kepel focused on the radicalization of Islam. Roy noted that only a tiny fraction of European Muslims were involved in extremist violence. He also pointed to the significant percentage of white European converts who joined Daesh. He believed that psychological factors provided a greater explanation than religion and that the phenomenon was best understood as a nihilistic rebellion, by alienated people, expressed in Islamic rhetoric (rather than in the Marxist language of the sixties and seventies). Kepel, in contrast, argued that French-born Muslims were increasingly influenced by Islamist preachers promulgating radical teachings of Islam – and this pushed some towards jihadism.

Following 9/11, Europe's mixed record of integrating Muslim immigrants had been examined. Some argued that Islam was incompatible with Western values. Others, however, blamed government policies. France pursued assimilation, treating individuals as citizens rather than as members of particular ethnic or religious groups, and demanding that immigrants adopt French values and identity.

Yet many of those whose parents and grandparents came from North Africa remained isolated in the *banlieues* (suburbs), were still referred to as immigrants and differentiated from *Français de souche*. And *laïcité*, which historically had kept the Catholic Church in its place, had now become associated with restrictions on the expression of Muslim identity, such as the ban on headscarves in schools and government buildings. In 2005, France had experienced urban riots as a protest against discrimination, racism and unemployment.

Germany and Britain, on the other hand, adhered to a policy of multiculturalism, whereby an immigrant's cultural identity was respected and protected. Germany, needing labour after World War II, had brought in 'guest workers' from Turkey. The government encouraged them to preserve their own language and culture, believing that they would return home. They lived separately from mainstream society, doing jobs that Germans did not want to do and running convenience stores.

Britain, whose Muslim population had come largely from former colonies at the request of the government for workers, was rudely awakened by the attacks on 7/7 in 2005, when four suicide bombers detonated rucksacks packed with explosives, killing fifty-two people in central London. Three of the bombers were British born and bred – sons of Pakistani immigrants. The fourth was a convert originally from Jamaica. The fact that the perpetrators could conduct such attacks on their fellow citizens shone a spotlight on the apparent failures of multiculturalism.

For much of the twentieth century, there were debates between left and right over how to create a better society, the role of government and the reach of the market. However, in recent decades, identity and culture rather than class had become the prism through which people differentiated themselves. There were fewer institutions and associations – such as trade unions – to bring people together and build a sense of social cohesion and solidarity. Government policies assumed that minorities were part of homogenous communities, with fixed, unchanging identities. Resources had been distributed to ethnic and faith-based organizations, whose leaders were treated as representatives and intermediaries with the government. In so doing, this institutionalized the sense of difference.

Many young Muslims, alienated from both mainstream society and the culture of their parents, created third cultures. For some it was hip hop; for others, it was religious observance; and for a small group, it was violent jihad.

Immigration had made European societies more diverse. But in truth, there had never been real public debate in Europe about mass migration, nor how to manage its impact on the national identity of countries whose populations were predominantly white and of Christian heritage.

*

I was looking for ways to help. The first step was to try to find out more about the situation. I had originally thought of walking in solidarity with the refugees. But they were no longer on foot – they were being transported on buses and trains.

Greece had overtaken Italy as the primary point of arrival for migrants. The crossing to Greek islands from Turkey could take less than an hour – and was easier than that from Libya to Italy.

Greece was unable to absorb the migrants. The country's economy was in disarray due to its debt crisis. Unemployment hovered around 25 per cent. And while Greeks showed compassion to the refugees, they did not want them to stay.

The Former Yugoslav Republic of Macedonia had lifted its restrictions preventing migrants from crossing its borders. The route through the Balkans had opened up.

I flew out to Thessaloniki, a city in northern Greece which itself had witnessed forced migration a century ago – and still bore the scars. At the beginning of the twentieth century, Greece had unsuccessfully tried to extend its borders to include all Greeks in the Ottoman Empire. The backlash led to a massive population exchange: around 1.3 million Christians were relocated from Turkey to Greece, and 585,000 Muslims from Greece to Turkey.

At the airport to meet me was Rebecca Fong, the US consul general in Thessaloniki and an old friend of mine from Iraq. In her current role, she had responsibility for monitoring the migrant crisis. Rebecca was a supreme chef, a mad cat lady, and a designer of handbags that she made from bits and bobs found in antique stores, markets and junk shops during her tours in Iraq, Syria and Afghanistan.

I invited Jen Butte-Dahl to join me. She flew in from Seattle where she lived on a floating home and directed a graduate programme at the University of Washington. She had volunteered for ShelterBox over the summer on the Greek island of Lesbos, providing emergency shelter to the refugees washing up on the shores each day in their thousands.

Jen and I had first met in Jerusalem in 2005. I had been working as the political adviser to General Kip Ward, the US security coordinator for the Middle East peace process, observing the withdrawal of Israeli forces and settlers from Gaza. Jen had been working at the US consulate. She was capable and effective – and looked like Nicole Kidman.

Also in our circle in Jerusalem had been Chris Stevens, the number two in the US consulate. Dashing and dynamic, he was much loved and admired by all who came into contact with him. Now Chris was dead – killed on 11 September 2012 in Benghazi while serving as the US ambassador to Libya. We would always remember the man who had lived life to the fullest and embodied the best of American internationalism. His career from Peace Corps volunteer through to State Department diplomat was an inspiration to many. And he had died doing a job he believed in, helping Libyans in chaotic times. Jen was working with his family to establish programmes that continued the work he loved – building bridges between the United States and the Middle East.

Libya was still a mess. ISIS had gained a foothold there, too. As for the peace process between Israel and Palestine, it had long since stalled. Israeli prime minister 'Bibi' Netanyahu had calculated that the political price of uprooting Israeli settlers in the West Bank outweighed the benefits of a deal with the Palestinians. Meanwhile, the Palestinian leadership was weak, corrupt and divided. President Mahmoud Abbas had promised the Palestinians that the way to end the occupation and achieve a Palestinian state was through negotiations – but he had failed to deliver. While Israel thrived, Palestine withered.

Faced with the common threats of terrorism and Iran, Israel and Arab countries were covertly cooperating – despite the lack of a solution to the Palestinian situation, and the expansion of Israeli settlements in the West Bank which made a two-state solution increasingly unattainable. US aid to Israel – along with its financial support of the Palestinian Authority – maintained the status quo, even as the number of Arabs between the Mediterranean Sea and the Jordan River moved to overtake the Jewish population.

*

After a couple of days in Thessaloniki, Rebecca, Jen and I drove in a US consulate car up to Idomeni, near the Greece-Macedonia border. The transit camp that international NGOs had set up to provide medical services and legal help to refugees stood empty. Fighting had broken out at the camp a few weeks before our visit.

Only Syrians, Iraqis and Afghans were being allowed to cross the border into Macedonia. Other migrants had grown increasingly frustrated. Camped out in tents in muddy conditions, some had protested, gone on hunger strike and sewn up their lips. Since then, the Greek authorities had emptied Idomeni camp and began busing Syrian, Iraqi and Afghan refugees up from Athens to a nearby petrol station, and from there to the border at staggered intervals. There was no time for them to make use of the camp facilities.

We spoke with officials from UNHCR and Médecins Sans Frontières who were very frustrated, unable to provide protection or to gain access to the most vulnerable refugees.

'It's more difficult to work in Greece than in South Sudan,' the MSF man lamented. The police kept changing shifts, and each had a different approach.

I approached the border crossing, eyeing refugees walking down the railway tracks and into a tent to have their papers checked.

A flap of the tent lifted and a girl, perhaps eight years old, wearing a red hijab, poked her head through. 'What's your name?' I asked her.

'Raghed,' she said.

'Where are you from?'

'Iraq!' She disappeared again into the tent. Minutes later, I watched her and her family, with bags on their backs, exit the tent through a barbed-wire corridor, cross over the rail tracks and into Macedonia. What terrible things had those young eyes seen?

I turned around. A woman in a black hijab was walking quickly towards the tent with her three children, carrying nothing more than hand luggage.

'*Salaam aleikum,*' I greeted her.

'*Aleikum salaam,*' she responded.

'Where are you from?'

'Syria.'

I wished her good luck. 'May God protect you.'

She flashed me a quick smile. She had made it this far. And minutes later, she too was across the border.

We drove to the nearby petrol station where the refugees were being staged. I struck up conversation with a group of young men sitting in the café. They told me the names of their cities and provinces in Afghanistan. I had visited each place when I had worked with ISAF in 2006, but did not tell them so. Outside in the cold, some Syrian men invited me to sit with them around a table. One told me he was a Kurd and had escaped to Iraqi Kurdistan, across Turkey, then to Greece. He had been on the road for a month. He was running short of money but hoped to make it to Germany. Another, an Arab, told me he was against both the Syrian regime and the Free Syrian Army. 'They are all bad,' he said.

The refugees' hopes and dreams appeared so basic: to live their lives, to feel safe, to feel wanted. One of the Syrians gave me a cup of tea. I declined his offer of a cigarette. He insisted, but I refused. Even there, in the cold unknown, the Syrians tried to show me, the stranger in their midst, the hospitality of home.

*

Refugees from the Middle East were being routed through small towns across the Balkans.

Once in Macedonia, the refugees were put on buses that took them across the country to Serbia. In Serbia, they were then bused to the town of Šid, west of Belgrade, and transferred onto trains headed to Croatia.

Jen and I bade our farewells to Rebecca and took the bus

to Skopje, the capital of the Former Yugoslavian Republic of
Macedonia. We discovered, when we saw a bronze statue of her
in the centre of town, that Mother Teresa was born in Skopje
in 1910. Also there to memorialize her was a chapel that had
glass and filigreed walls, silhouettes of doves on the outside
and a museum displaying memorabilia of her childhood before
she left as an adult for Ireland and then went on to India.

Visiting the city's Holocaust Memorial Centre, we learned
that 98 per cent of Macedonia's Jews had been killed in World
War II. In the basement was a Bulgarian van that had been
used to transport the Jews to the Treblinka extermination
camp.

*

We left Macedonia and headed on to the Serbian capital of
Belgrade, where Jen and I rented a car and drove to Sarajevo.
As we entered Bosnia and Herzegovina, the roads soon turned
into small lanes. We passed through deserted villages of
pockmarked houses. The land was arable – but in many places
neglected. Horrors had happened in those hills.

After booking into our hotel in Sarajevo, we walked the
stone-flagged, narrow alleys of the Baščaršija, passing the
churches and mosques that stood as evidence of the peaceful
coexistence of Muslims, Jews, Orthodox and Roman Catholics
in former times.

It was in Sarajevo in June 1914 that Archduke Franz Ferdinand
of Austria was assassinated by a Serbian nationalist, setting in
motion the train of events which led to World War I. The
Central Powers of Germany, Austria–Hungary, Bulgaria and

the Ottoman Empire were pitted against the Allied Powers of Great Britain, France, Italy, Russia and Japan, with the US eventually joining the Allies in April 1917. Around 17 million people were estimated to have died in the war by the time it ended in November 1918.

When I looked at what was happening today in the Middle East, I could not help but wonder if we were sleepwalking into World War III. The civil wars and ISIS were entangling regional and international powers. What happens in the Middle East does not stay in the Middle East.

As we sat in a restaurant eating *pita ispod sača* (a local speciality of thin pastry, meat and onion, baked in an oven), it was hard to contemplate that, just over twenty years ago, Sarajevo had been besieged for 1,425 days. More than 10,000 of its 500,000 citizens were killed, mostly by Serbian shells or snipers.

The city, once so devastated, had since been rebuilt. Tourists were back on its streets. But those who had experienced the war would forever bear the scars.

Conflicts in the Balkans in the 1990s had left a quarter of a million people dead and two million displaced. We went to an exhibit on the massacre at Srebrenica. In July 1995, Serb forces rounded up over 8,000 Muslim men and boys, took them away and murdered them. Dutch UN peacekeepers had proven incapable of ensuring a safe haven. Some young Muslim men had been radicalized by the slaughter.

*

It was snowing as we crossed the Bosnia-Croatia border and found the refugee transit camp at Slavonski Brod (thanks to

the precise directions of a UNHCR official). I had sent an
email earlier in the day to the police at the camp, but they
could not find it when we arrived and I worried that we would
not be able to get in. My fears were unfounded. The Croatian
police were friendly and helpful.

The UNHCR man took us on a tour of the camp in the
freezing cold evening. It was minus 7 degrees Celsius. I was
wearing a big coat, gloves and a hat, with a scarf pulled up to
cover my nose – but still I was cold.

The refugees had been transferred from Serbia to Croatia
by train. At Slavonski Brod, they disembarked and entered
a tent where they were fingerprinted and processed before
being allowed to travel on to Slovenia, in a deal worked out
between the two countries. Around 3,000 refugees were passing
through Slavonski Brod each day.

The UNHCR man took us to a large tent, where NGO workers
were handing out cups of hot tea, satchels to children, and
warm clothes and blankets. They identified the most vulnerable
refugees and gave them extra care. They ensured that all the
children were well wrapped up in coats, hats and scarves.

Most of those I talked to were from Syria but some were
Iraqi. They had all fled to Turkey, where along the coast a
shadow economy had developed around smuggling people
to Europe. Life jackets, inner tubes and rafts were on sale,
and transport was provided to remote launch sites. From
Turkey, they had taken boats to Greece, and from there they
had been transported by bus and train to here. They had left
behind their homes and possessions, bringing with them only
the bare essentials.

I admired their resilience and good spirits. There were groups of young men, some related, some who had got to know each other on the road. There were couples with young children. I observed very few old people, teenage girls or unmarried women. A couple of mothers looked exhausted. One sought a place to breastfeed her baby.

'Weren't you afraid of the sea?' I asked a Syrian man.

'Yes, I was very afraid,' he replied.

He, like others I spoke to, had used his savings to pay a smuggler to transport him and his family in a small dinghy from Turkey to Lesbos. The going rates seemed to be $1,000 to $3,000 per person.

The words of the British-Somali poet Warsan Shire reverberated in my head:

> *... no one puts their children in a boat*
> *unless the water is safer than the land.*

The trip was perilous, with thousands drowning. But still they came.

'How long will we be here?' the Syrian man asked me. I knew from the UNHCR official that it would only be a couple of hours, and told him so. The processing was quick. Little official information seemed available. But the refugees sent messages back and forth over Whatsapp with relatives and friends who had made the trip before them. When I asked where they were headed, most had their eyes set on Germany, encouraged by reports of the warm reception there.

We followed the refugees out of the tent and back into the bitter cold, where they stood in line. Each refugee was handed a plastic bag containing food and a bottle of water before they boarded the train bound for Slovenia.

The railway tracks conjured up such terrible images of Nazi Germany and the deportation of Jews to the death camps. Yet, this time, it was Germany that was taking in refugees, accepting a million in 2015 – half of whom were Syrian.

*

Amid all the chaos and uncertainty, Angela Merkel, the German chancellor, stood strong. In her new year's address, she urged Germans to welcome refugees and not to listen to the racists who harbour 'hatred in their hearts'. She acknowledged that coping with immigration would be difficult but pledged that, if handled right, the challenges of today would be 'an opportunity of tomorrow'. Germany's population was declining. It needed immigrants. *Wir schaffen das*, Merkel repeated. We can do it.

There were heart-warming stories of Germans greeting refugees at railway stations and hosting them in their homes. But during the New Year's Eve celebrations in Cologne, gangs of Muslim men sexually assaulted hundreds of German women. In response, thousands of members of a German anti-immigration movement, Patriotic Europeans Against the Islamization of the West (PEGIDA), participated in protest rallies. Refugees were now associated not only with terrorists but also sex pests.

In his January 2016 address to the diplomatic corps accredited to the Holy See, Pope Francis acknowledged the 'great wave of refugees' and how they appeared to be 'overburdening the system of reception painstakingly built on the ashes of the Second World War'.

He recognized the concerns about 'changes in the cultural and social structures' and the 'fears about security' but insisted that 'there should be no loss of the values and principles of humanity, respect for the dignity of every person.

He urged Europe to 'find the right balance between its twofold moral responsibility to protect the rights of its citizens and to ensure assistance and acceptance to migrants'. But this was easier said than done. .

The European Union was struggling with financial crises, economic stagnation and unemployment. The influx of refugees aroused populist, nativist and anti-immigration sentiments which far-right parties were capitalizing on. The impact on European politics was proving to be profound.

CHAPTER 12

And even though it all went wrong

Britain

June–July 2016

The refugee crisis in Europe was being used to galvanize support for the exit of Britain from the EU. Nigel Farage, the leader of the far-right UK Independence Party, was filmed standing in front of a massive poster of Syrian refugees at the Slovenia-Croatia border. The implication was clear: unless the UK left the European Union and took back control of its borders, the refugees would flood into Britain. There was continuous media coverage of clashes at 'the Jungle' – the makeshift camp in Calais – between the French police and migrants desperate to reach the UK.

I did not believe that the majority of Brits would fall for what I regarded as racist fearmongering. After all, in May

2016, London had elected Sadiq Khan to be mayor. With 1.3 million votes he received the largest personal mandate of any elected official in the history of British politics. I saw Khan's election as a counter to the narrative peddled by ISIS and populist politicians that Muslims could not live in the West.

In his acceptance speech, Khan said he was 'proud that London has today chosen hope over fear and unity over division'. The son of a Pakistani bus driver, he had grown up on a housing estate, then become a human rights lawyer and a Labour party politician. Khan summed up his identity in multiple ways: 'I'm a Londoner, I'm European, I'm British, I'm English, I'm of Islamic faith, of Asian origin, of Pakistani heritage, a dad, a husband.'

Generation after generation of immigrants, my Eastern European grandparents included, had come to Britain's shores, abided by our laws, adopted our customs, and contributed to our society. And improved the food.

*

You can come early for the Tish, Stephen Shashoua messaged me. I had never been to a *tish* before so I did not know what to expect. I turned up at Victoria House on Bloomsbury Square in London to find myself among fellow wedding invitees who were black, brown and white; of the three Abrahamic faiths, Buddhist and non-believers; bearded and clean-shaven; in heels and in flats; from North America, Europe, Africa and Asia. Stephen, dressed in a salmon-pink suit, sat between two of his closest friends. One by one, they told stories of their friendship with Stephen: of cars skidding and crashing, of yoga and pilates. After each story, everyone raised their glasses, said '*L'Chaim*' and drank a slug of whisky.

Stephen Shashoua was a Yale World Fellow, one of sixteen extraordinary individuals selected each year out of thousands of applicants to spend a semester at Yale on a leadership programme that I directed. Stephen, a Canadian of Iraqi Jewish origin, was marrying Rachel Johnston, a British woman of Scottish background. I was not sure that either believed in God, but both were spiritual and their heritage was important to them.

To any Iraqi, the name Shashoua was immediately recognizable as that of a distinguished lineage of Jews. Faisal, on being appointed king of Iraq by the British in 1921, had rented Qasr Shashoua – a grand house on the banks of the Tigris in Baghdad's Adhamiya neighbourhood – for a couple of years while a new palace was built for him.

But to everyone else, Shashoua was the guy with the difficult-to-pronounce surname who they called Zeus or Steve; the man committed to interfaith dialogue who could always find common ground and would bend over backwards to make people feel included and loved.

After the storytelling was over, we went into the ballroom and took our seats for the ceremony. The chuppah was brought out, with four friends each holding a pole. Under this canopy, Stephen stood beside the kippa-wearing female rabbi. Then Rachel appeared in a beautiful ivory dress (which she had designed herself), escorted by the kilt-wearing Johnston men with their hipster beards. Friends read out the *Sheva Brachot* (seven blessings), some in Hebrew, most in English. In their vows, Stephen and Rachel chose each other as life partners and expressed their love and commitment to the stars and the moon. They took from different traditions, reinterpreting rituals for their time and purpose. It was beautiful and special.

The master of ceremonies was a large bearded man called Abdul-Rehman, who wore a kaftan and spoke English with a Canadian twang. He walked back and forth with his microphone. He said he had been a bit worried about Stephen: he had left it late to marry and there was speculation over his persuasion – he was, after all, wearing a pink suit. 'We Muslims,' Abdul-Rehman went on, 'we marry young, we marry often.' There were howls of laughter. He introduced the bride's Scottish family: 'We Muslims and Jews, we are well into beards. But I have to hand it to the Johnston brothers. They have some impressive beards!'

And when a friend, who might have been a Scot or a Jew, an atheist or a believer, gay or straight, took the stage with his guitar, the whole room sang along to the chorus of Leonard Cohen's 'Hallelujah'.

*

Rory Stewart told me to meet him at 7 p.m. in Parliament, as he did not know what time the vote would take place. I did not know what vote he was referring to. But I turned up at the Houses of Parliament and was amazed at how easy it was to get into the building. I put my handbag through the X-ray machine and walked through the body scanner. I was through in minutes, wearing the badge I had been issued around my neck.

I walked down the long hall, turned left and waited patiently in the octagonal Central Lobby, sitting on a very deep seat with only my ankles dangling over the edge, as MPs rushed back and forth. I glanced down at the tiled floors, then up at the arches decorated with statues of kings and queens, then at the panels over each of the four exits depicting the patron saints of the United Kingdom: St George for England, St David for Wales, St Andrew for Scotland and St Patrick for Northern Ireland. I looked at the metal grilles on the windows, which were displayed in the Central Lobby to bear testament to the suffragettes who had campaigned to ensure the franchise was extended to women. The grilles had originally served to ensure that MPs would not be distracted by the sight of women in the Ladies' Gallery. A lot had changed since those days.

Tom Tugendhat spotted me and reached down to pull me up off the seat. I had met Tom my first evening back from Iraq when he had cycled me home on the back of his bike. Now retired from the army, he was a Tory MP. He could not stay to chat for long as he had to get home to look after his young son. We promised to have dinner together in the near future. Whenever I was back in London, Tom would summon the clans – diplomats, soldiers, development experts and aid workers who had served in Iraq and Afghanistan – for 'wine and swine' at Gastronomica in Pimlico. The banter was always free-flowing – no one to impress, no one to explain things to.

Rory appeared and walked over to me. Lots of people called out to him, and he acknowledged them and introduced me, explaining that we had worked together in Iraq and Afghanistan. Rory had been in the media a lot during the winter floods earlier in the year, donning wellington boots and an anorak to go and fill sandbags in his constituency in the north of England. We went to the members' bar and waited for him to be called to vote on what I discovered was a terrorism bill. I asked Rory how he'd known what to do when he became an MP. Was there a handbook? Was he given training? He said it was all a bit of a mystery, but new MPs generally followed the example of the other MPs. And there were party whips to ensure discipline.

But still no call came to vote. We went to the canteen in the Commons. Rory chose a healthy pasta. And I, who had eaten a healthy breakfast, went for roast beef and a very large Yorkshire pudding with gravy and horseradish. Still no call to vote came, and Rory declared we could leave.

We took the tube to South Kensington and went to Janet's, a quirky retro bar, where we continued to drink wine into the evening. Rory spoke about his work as a junior minister for the environment. It was deeply frustrating, he said, because George Osborne – the Chancellor of the Exchequer – and the rest of David Cameron's Conservative government were not prioritizing the environment. And civil servants blocked every attempt he made to do things. He wanted to make a difference in the world but felt frustrated. He had come to realize that where he had had most influence was with his NGO in Afghanistan – Turquoise Mountain, an art school that nurtured and restored Afghan heritage. He told me that, as a junior minister, the only change he had been able to implement was the introduction of a five-pence fee on plastic bags.

I reminded him that this was a significant success and was reducing the number of plastic bags in circulation.

Rory's father – who had been his hero – had died the summer before, aged ninety-three, and he still missed him and spoke to him in his head. His father could not understand why Rory wasted his time with politics and bureaucracy. He thought he should be a public intellectual.

'What should a young man do?' Rory asked. 'Becoming an MP seemed the most obvious choice for someone dedicated to public service.' His father had never found a job he loved more than his colonial service experience in Malaya during his mid-thirties – despite going on to become the deputy head of MI6. Rory pulled up on his phone a photo he had taken at an exhibition on the British Empire at Tate Britain. It was of a painting of Captain Colin Mackenzie sporting Afghan dress – wearing it like an award for his skill in carrying out secret missions in the nineteenth century. 'I wanted to be him,' Rory confessed, before admitting that he knew that dream was futile. We lived in a different age.

Rory often thought of his time in Afghanistan and Iraq. How was he to find such a sense of purpose again? T.E. Lawrence, after his World War I service, returned home and enlisted in the Royal Air Force, before dying in 1935 in a motorbike crash. A.T. Wilson, after governing Iraq, became an MP. In the run-up to World War II, he had become an admirer of Hitler. But when war broke out, he joined the RAF, stating – as Rory recited by heart – 'I have no desire to shelter myself and live in safety behind the ramparts of the bodies of millions of our young men.' He was killed in a plane crash in northern France in 1940.

I reflected on how out of the Second World War had come the European Union, an ambitious peace agreement that had stopped countries warring, created the largest economy in history and enabled us to study, travel and work in each other's countries; and Pax Americana, which had maintained world order for the last seventy years.

But despite our generation trying so hard in our post 9/11 wars, we had not brought about a better peace nor inspired a better order. The Middle East was unravelling and Europe melting down. And America was withdrawing from its leadership role in the world. It had all gone so wrong. The whole concept of an international community was fading. What were we bequeathing the next generation?

I confided in Rory that I really did not know what to do next myself. I missed the strong sense of purpose I'd felt when working in the Middle East. I wanted to come back to the UK, but did not know what I would do here. Few of us who dedicated our careers to international development ever found a way to contribute our skills and experience to the communities from which we once hailed.

We spoke about our mutual friend Minna Järvenpää, who we had thought would become a UN Special Representative of the Secretary-General, or president of Finland. She had been the mayor of a town in Kosovo during the Balkans conflict and then had spent years in Afghanistan with the United Nations. Rory had determined to go into politics to try to prevent us embarking on unnecessary wars again. Minna had decided to go off to an ashram in India. 'How can we fix other countries if we are so broken ourselves?' she had asked. 'We need to deal with the conflict within if we are to become more effective at promoting peace in the world.' We thought she would be gone for a couple of weeks, or a month at most. But Minna finally emerged from the ashram two and a half years later, calm and radiant. She now ran yoga therapy for peacemakers out of an old villa near Florence in Italy, and spent the winters in India. She believed that all who worked in conflict zones were traumatized to some degree. And yoga could help them with their recovery.

'How is family life?' I asked Rory. 'How has that changed you?' He reflected for a moment, and then said that it was the only true happiness in his life at present. He was not fulfilled in his current job. He would give politics a few more years to see if he could reach a Cabinet position and bring about real change. What else could he do? He knew that he would not return to academia. When he had run a centre at Harvard, with all the resources, the best experts and access to Hillary Clinton and General Petraeus, he had not been able to get the policy on Afghanistan altered. He speculated that even the Secretary of State and the general had been unable to change things, because power had become so diffused.

Rory was writing a book about his father, Scotland and identity. He had conducted extensive research, walking the borderlands between Scotland and England. I described to him how I had spent a week walking Hadrian's Wall from east to west the previous year. On the walk, I discovered that the boatmen who had gone along the River Tyne supplying the Roman garrisons had been bargemen from Basra, and that the auxiliary archers had been Syrians. Globalization was not new. Our worlds had intertwined for centuries. There was no getting away from the Middle East.

Rory had written books about Afghanistan, Iraq and intervention. He enjoyed writing – but it did not give him the thrill of being in Baghdad or Kabul. He'd thought about repeating the twenty-month walk he had made across Afghanistan and Pakistan, and writing about what had changed in the world as well as in himself in the intervening years.

'Isn't it the human condition to be dissatisfied?' Rory mused. He'd even thought about going to live in a monastery. Perhaps life's purpose could simply be to contemplate the meaning of life.

*

John Jenkins met me for dinner at an Italian restaurant on Northcote Road in Clapham. He had finished his tour as the British ambassador in Saudi Arabia and had since retired from the Foreign and Commonwealth Office. He was recognized as the best Arabist of his generation of British diplomats. Yet he was angry and disappointed. 'I spent nearly my whole career in the Middle East. Look at how things have turned out.'

Our conversation turned to Iraq. 'Iraq could have worked,' he said. 'Iraq was headed in the right direction. I keep wondering if there was more we could have done in 2010 to block Maliki continuing as prime minister that might have prevented all of this...'

If Maliki had been replaced after he lost the elections, then the conditions would not have been there for ISIS to rise up out of the ashes of al-Qaeda in Iraq and wreak havoc in Iraq, Syria – and Europe.

JJ picked up his wine glass and quoted Shakespeare's Brutus:

> *There is a tide in the affairs of men.*
> *Which, taken at the flood, leads on to fortune;*
> *Omitted, all the voyage of their life*
> *Is bound in shallows and in miseries.*
> *On such a full sea are we now afloat,*
> *And we must take the current when it serves*
> *Or lose our ventures.*

JJ was frustrated with Obama. In his view, the president had misjudged the Middle East and what America could influence. Obama's 2009 Cairo speech about a 'new beginning' looked in retrospect like a cruel illusion – not the promised dawn of a new ethical order. It had been neither backed up by practical policies nor given adequate resources. Obama now argued that the Middle East was no longer important to US interests; that there was little the US could do to fix what was broken there; and that US efforts to do so would inevitably lead to war, the loss of American soldiers and the diminishing of US power and reputation. Obama's unwillingness to project power was frightening America's friends and emboldening its enemies. 'Nature abhors a vacuum,' JJ pronounced. And Obama, with his signalling of 'leading from behind' and pivoting the focus of US foreign policy to Asia, had created one that was being filled by Russia, Iran, Daesh and militias.

JJ described how Russia had used military force to change the situation on the ground in Syria in favour of Assad. Putin was deliberately poking Obama in the eye for being timid. Despite declaring the use of chemical weapons a red line, Obama had not carried through with his threat of repercussions after Assad gassed around 1,400 people in the Damascus neighbourhood of Eastern Ghouta in 2013. He had backed down from military strikes on regime targets – after David Cameron failed to gain parliamentary support for military action – and had grasped Russia's last-minute proposal to remove Assad's chemicals.

Confident that there would be no pushback from the United States, Putin was prancing around the international stage. Russia was deliberately seeking to weaken the liberal world order, using aerial bombings in Syria to flood Europe with refugees and providing financial support to far-right parties in the West.

One of the reasons that Obama had not taken action in Syria was so as not to jeopardize his chances of reaching a nuclear deal with Iran, which he viewed as the US exit strategy from the Middle East. The US assumption that the deal would change Iranian behaviour seemed naive, JJ asserted. While it had warded off the risk of nuclear proliferation, it had done nothing to curb Iran developing its missile programme nor its support for militias across the region in a strategy it described as 'forward defence'. Through the fight against ISIS, Iran had increased its influence over the governments of Iraq and Syria, and developed land corridors across both countries. Israel was deeply concerned. Saudi Arabia and the Gulf countries felt threatened and encircled, and feared that the US was dumping its traditional allies and realigning with Iran. Lacking the military capacity to balance Iran, the

Gulf countries had taken to supporting proxies to push back
on Iranian expansionism. Saudi Arabia was bombing Houthi
rebels in Yemen, convinced they were supported by Iran.

'Obama does not engage with other viewpoints. He twists
them, makes straw men and cuts them down,' JJ complained.
Obama made out that those who opposed his do-nothing policy
on Syria were proposing a full-scale invasion and occupation.
'Nobody was arguing for this,' JJ continued. What he and
others had proposed were ways to complicate and frustrate
Assad's mass murder so that he would be forced to reach a
political deal with the opposition.

Obama trumpeted his foreign policy as 'don't do stupid
shit'. But that was neither an overarching set of principles
nor a strategy. The narrow focus on counterterrorism did not
address the root causes of conflict. And the reluctance to lead
infuriated America's allies in the region.

'US presidents are expected to do something when 400,000
people die in a civil war, refugees flood into other countries
and militias take over states,' JJ said. 'There are serious things
wrong in the Middle East, things that are nothing to do with
the West. But we can influence outcomes. We are just not
committed enough to doing so.'

The choices were not simply invasion or inaction, he
stressed. Each case was different. Intervention had saved
many lives in Iraqi Kurdistan in 1991, in Kosovo in 1999
and in Sierra Leone in 2000. Non-intervention had led
to genocide in Rwanda. The failure of the international
community to respond to the civil war in Syria would be a
blot on our collective conscience. Furthermore, for years

to come, we would be plagued with the fallout of refugees, terrorism, militias and regional instability.

At the end of the evening, and after we had drunk two bottles of red wine between us, JJ declared, 'I have to get away from the Middle East. It is making me ill.' He confided that he was going to keep bees in Kent.

*

I took a train from Clapham Junction out to Guildford. General Graeme Lamb met me at the train station and drove me in his wife's battered Land Rover to their home in the Surrey countryside.

It soon became clear that Lambo was voting to leave the European Union. He saw it as a failed project, and one from which the UK should disentangle itself. And he simply loathed Jean-Claude Juncker, the president of the European Commission. I argued that the EU needed reform – not abolition. But nothing could convince Lambo. His mind was made up. So was that of his wife, Mel. But their two daughters were voting Remain.

Our discussion moved on to the refugee crisis. The UK government had committed to taking in 20,000 Syrian refugees over a five-year period. Lambo's mother, a fiercely independent woman in her eighties whose language was as salty as her soldier son's, lived on the Isle of Bute, an island off the west coast of Scotland with a population that had declined to under 7,000. The community had offered sanctuary to fifteen Syrian families. I wondered how they were faring in such a remote place and whether they could bring themselves to eat haggis. Lambo's mother had not yet had any interaction with them but noted different food stuffs being stocked in the local shops. It would only be a matter of time before the kids were speaking with a Scottish brogue.

The refugees would bring new blood and new skills to Scotland. I told Lambo that I had called out a plumber when my boiler had broken. An old man with a long white beard had appeared immediately. He seemed able to fix everything. Turned out he was an Iraqi – a Kurd from Kirkuk. What were the chances of that? I could not believe the coincidence! Now whenever there was an issue with my house, he would come himself or dispatch a young Iraqi or Syrian to fix it.

Lambo told me he was never going to write about his military experiences. He did not look backwards and did not reminisce about war. He had burned all his notebooks – every single one. 'Why did I stay in the army for thirty-eight years?' he asked rhetorically. 'It was all about people. I was always in the very best of company, with people who were striving to achieve the same goal. It was all about service, something greater than self. And the least important of everything was pay. You don't define your life by what you earn, you define it by what you do.'

I asked after Harry Parker, the soldier I had met a few years earlier in Battersea Park when he was trying out his blade-runner prosthetics. Lambo told me that Harry was doing well. He had got married, had a child and written a novel, *Anatomy of a Soldier*, in which the trauma of losing his legs to a roadside bomb is narrated by the objects around him.

*

I had never attended Prime Minister's Questions before. But with the build-up to the monumental vote on whether Britain should remain in the European Union, I thought it would be interesting, so I accepted Tom Tugendhat's invitation to join him in the members' chamber, sitting up in the balcony looking down on David Cameron.

I was struck by the warmth and camaraderie in the chamber; the jousting, the joshing. I had never felt favourably disposed towards Cameron. But there, in the flesh, answering questions left, right and centre, he was impressive. He had pressed ahead with his pledge to hold an in/out referendum, determined to stop Tories 'banging on about Europe' and to settle once and for all the 'European question in British politics'. He spoke of how remaining in the EU was good for Britain's security, jobs and economy.

Cameron was obviously concerned by polls showing increasing support for UKIP and its anti-EU and anti-immigration platform. He disparaged Nigel Farage, saying he would destroy Britain and turn it into a 'little England'.

'If you love your country, you want it to be strong. Britain will be strong in Europe, influential in Europe. Vote to remain in Europe,' Cameron declared with passion.

The Labour Party was supposed to be pro-EU. But I would never have known that from the lacklustre performance in the Commons that day of its leader, Jeremy Corbyn. Corbyn had never been enthusiastic about Europe. Back in 1975, as a local councillor, he had voted 'No' in the referendum on Britain's membership of the European Community.

Around two-thirds of the Members of Parliament supported Remain. But how about the rest of the country?

*

On 16 June 2016, Jo Cox, an up-and-coming Labour MP who was a passionate campaigner for the UK to remain within the EU, was murdered in her hometown in Yorkshire by someone who opposed her political views. It was a terrible shock; such things just did not happen in Britain.

I had never met Jo, but she was close to a number of my friends and we had corresponded over email about how to stop the killing in Syria and deliver humanitarian aid. We had both supported the Nobel Peace Prize nomination of the White Helmets – unarmed Syrian volunteers who were digging people out of rubble, providing first aid, rushing the wounded to hospitals and giving victims burials. We had planned to meet up for dinner.

I joined thousands of admirers, friends and family of Jo Cox in Trafalgar Square on 22 June, on what would have been her 42nd birthday, to celebrate her life.

Raed Saleh, the head of the Syrian White Helmets, flew in from the Middle East to honour Jo. Malala Yousafzai, the young Pakistani activist, described Jo as a champion for women and children. Malala also noted that after she had been shot by the Taliban and needed a refuge, it was Britain that took her in. Representatives of the Archbishop of Canterbury, the Jewish community, the Muslim Council of Britain, the Hindu Council UK and the British Humanist Association all took to the stage together.

Speaker after speaker described how Jo had made each and every one of us want to be a better person and to do more for others. She was a campaigner, an activist and a politician. She had such compassion for all, and in particular the disadvantaged and immigrant communities. She truly believed that we achieve far more together than we can alone.

Her husband, Brendan, asked that Jo's death lead to something good in the world. He said that if she had been alive today, she would be rushing around campaigning for people to vote to remain in Europe, as she hated the idea of building walls between people. Jo wanted the world to be a better place. She believed in tolerance and respect, and spoke out against extremism. Her killing, he said, was an 'act of terror' designed to promote hatred.

Children from their son's class came on stage to sing 'If I Had a Hammer'. They were white, black and brown – the faces of modern Britain. And the crowd joined in with them, hammering out the call for justice and freedom.

Jo's favourite musical was *Les Misérables*. And the cast of the London production of the show took to the stage to sing her favourite song for her, for us, for Britain and for the world... *Do you hear the people sing? Singing the songs of angry men?*

Jo was the best of British in her values, her activism and her internationalism. She made the world a better place. In her maiden speech in Parliament she noted that we all have so much in common, and that what unites us is far greater than what divides us. Jo lived for her beliefs – and died for them. Gemma Mortensen, a close friend of Jo's and a Yale World Fellow, urged each one of us as we grieved Jo's death, to pledge to take forward her legacy, to hope and not to fear, to love and not to hate. We all – in the most un-British fashion – joined hands, sobbing and laughing, held our arms up high, and committed to 'love like Jo'.

*

The following day, 23 June 2016, 17 million people – 52 per cent of the electorate – voted to leave the EU in a referendum with 72 per cent turnout. Despite experts warning that Britain's economy would suffer and its position in the world would be diminished, over half the country had voted to leave.

Three-quarters of Brits under twenty-five voted to remain. But the majority of people over fifty voted to leave. London, Scotland and Northern Ireland voted to stay in the EU. But England as a whole and Wales voted out. Across the north of England, where whole communities had once worked in coal and steel, the vote was overwhelmingly Leave. The Labour Party was out of touch with the working class and no longer represented them.

While London celebrated its diversity – embodied by Mayor Sadiq Khan – in other parts of the country, people feared their identity was under threat from too much immigration.

Having led the campaign for the UK to remain in the EU, Cameron immediately resigned as prime minister.

Farage heralded the vote as a 'victory for real people'. However, the Leave campaign had never expected to win. There was no plan. The pledge – on a bus – to spend the £350 million a week that the UK gave Brussels on the National

Health Service turned out to be neither true nor doable. No one knew what Brexit meant. Would there be another referendum on Scottish independence? Although 55 per cent had voted to stay within the United Kingdom in the 2014 Scottish referendum, 62 per cent of Scotland voted to remain in the EU. Would a border need to be reinstated between the south and the north of Ireland? Would this lead to a referendum on a united Ireland?

The country that once ruled a quarter of the world now seemed to be struggling to govern its four constituent parts.

I took an Uber across London. My driver was originally from Pakistan, had been in the UK for five years and had so far managed to save enough money to buy two houses. He wanted to buy eight more before he retired. Much better to buy property than shares, he told me. He had trained as an engineer but made more money as an Uber driver.

'I voted Leave,' he divulged. He explained that Asians had to go through an application process to get visas for the UK. They worked hard and paid their taxes. He compared this with Eastern Europeans, who he said came to Britain in their hundreds of thousands to live off benefits – and strained our already overstretched public services. I had no idea if there was any truth behind his allegations. There were plenty of stories of Eastern European migrants working hard in agriculture and construction. I was confident that immigrants were in fact net contributors to the economy.

The driver asked me how I had voted. I told him Remain – that I felt both British and European.

'So you are European? When did you move here?' he asked.

'I didn't move here. I was born here. In England.'

He looked at me in the mirror. 'Why did you say you were European?'

I realized we were talking at cross purposes. I saw being European as part of my cultural identity, an idea that I subscribed to.

'How long has Britain been part of Europe?' he asked me. I paused, wondering how to respond to the question. Before I could get an answer out, he said: 'Forty-three years! It's only forty-three years!'

'Look at where we are geographically located,' I hit back. 'Britain is in Europe. We aren't in Africa or Asia. We're in Europe. For centuries, there was fighting between the different peoples in Europe. There were two bloody world wars in which millions were killed. And it was in the aftermath of these wars that the European Union was created, the most successful peace treaty of all time, which brought an end to fighting between Germany, France and England.'

I then sat sulking in the back of the car.

After he dropped me off, I went online to read the *Daily Mail* and *The Sun*. For years, they had mocked Brussels, making ludicrous claims that the EU was banning the sale of eggs by the dozen and insisting on straight bananas. They were jubilant at the outcome of the vote.

I realized I did not know half the country. I was not from a wealthy background, but by virtue of my education I had become an expert, an elite, who embraced and benefited from globalization. I was totally out of touch with the sentiments of those who said they did not care if Brexit harmed the UK economy because they themselves did not have anything to lose.

Nor had I realized the scale of immigration to the UK, particularly since the 2004 accession to the EU of central and eastern European countries. There were now 3.3 million EU citizens living in Britain, with 270,000 arriving in 2015 alone. It was a shock for me to recognize that I was far more concerned with the plight of Middle Eastern refugees than I was with the fears of many of my fellow citizens.

*

Four days after the Brexit vote, England suffered a humiliating defeat at football to Iceland, a country with a population so small – 300,000 – that they needed an app to prevent accidental incest.

*

On 6 July 2016, Sir John Chilcot finally made public his findings on the Iraq War following a long investigation that began in 2009.

The report concluded that the UK 'chose to join the invasion of Iraq before the peaceful options for disarmament had been exhausted. Military action at that time was not a last resort.' In March 2003, Iraq did not present an imminent threat, the danger posed by Iraq's weapons of mass destruction was exaggerated and the strategy of containment could have continued. Planning for the aftermath of the overthrow was 'woefully inadequate' and the intervention 'went badly wrong with consequences to this day'.

Tony Blair's reputation was irreparably tarnished. If not for the Iraq War, he would have gone down as one of the UK's most successful and popular prime ministers.

Blair had catapulted to the centre of the political scene in 1997 as the young fresh-faced Labour leader, winning a landslide election to end eighteen years of Conservative rule – and he went on to win two more. It was Blair who championed Cool Britannia, a new national identity based on great culture and music that replaced what he described as the 'post-Empire malaise'. Blair's new ideas raised the national spirit, inspiring hope for the coming millennium. He promoted Britain as a country with a special relationship with America, punching above its weight on the global stage and serving as a bridge between Europe and the US.

In his statement to the nation on 9/11, Blair said: 'This is not a battle between the United States of America and terrorism, but between the free and democratic world and terrorism. We therefore, here in Britain, stand shoulder to shoulder with our American friends in this hour of tragedy. And we, like them, will not rest until this evil is driven from our world.'

What was clear from the Chilcot report was that Blair had been motivated by his belief in the vital importance of being a good ally to the US. In the build-up to the invasion of Iraq, Blair wrote a memo to President Bush saying: 'I will be with you, whatever.'

Blair took the country to war against the will of the majority of Brits. The Iraq War was held up as evidence that elites did not have greater knowledge or better judgement than the general public. And along with the financial crisis and unregulated immigration, it paved the way to Brexit.

Among the litany of the mistakes and oversights of senior British officials, Chilcot made mention of those involved in implementation on the ground: 'Service personnel, civilians who deployed to Iraq… showed great courage in the face of considerable risks. They deserve our gratitude and respect.' That was not much solace.

For forty-eight hours, I was wheeled out in the media as Exhibit A, the anti-war Brit who had gone out to Iraq to apologize for the invasion, had received no briefing before leaving the UK, was put in charge of a province and narrowly escaped death in her first month.

I spoke alongside family members of the 179 British servicemen and women who had been killed in Iraq.

One father kept repeating: 'They died for nothing.'

*

I was invited to give the sports day speech at my old prep school, Ashfold, in the Buckinghamshire countryside. The headmaster introduced me in the marquee on the spot we used to play British Bulldogs, close to the pool where I had learned to swim. He told the pupils that I had been one of the first girls to go to the school – and was remembered for my football skills.

When I stood up to speak, I noted that around 40 per cent of the pupils were girls. I told them that I hoped they were called by their real names, as I had been dubbed 'Fred Blogs' so that the opposition would not know there was a girl on the football team.

I regaled them with stories of my time in Iraq, of surviving bombings and living with American soldiers on an airfield. 'Ashfold prepares you for anything,' I concluded. 'Dream big.'

Afterwards, I wandered around the school with Hugh Taylor, who was the chair of the governors and had been a contemporary of mine. As we passed through classrooms, memories flooded back of tales of Brits sailing their little fishing boats across the Channel to evacuate our forces stranded in Dunkirk, of watching the Battle of Britain on a big screen and of reading about the adventures of great explorers.

We climbed up the stairs, passing the library, which seemed to have shrunk, until we reached the corridor known as 'Matron's landing', with the matron's sitting room, the sick room, the communal bathroom and my room – not much larger than a cupboard – next to that of my mother's, who had once been the matron. It looked like something out of *Downton Abbey*. The staff lived in the nooks and crannies on the top floors of the 400-year-old Jacobean country house.

We emerged once more into the glorious summer day and poked our heads into the chapel before strolling through the woods and along the dirt track, reminiscing about the assault course, walking on the frozen lake and riding our bikes.

But the school grounds that had seemed to go on forever and had once marked the totality of my world now seemed quite small.

*

Carl Bracey and I unleashed his small wooden sailing boat from its mooring and pushed it out into the estuary at Hayle, a small town on the west coast of Cornwall. We hoisted the jib and then the mainsail. But there was not a whiff of wind to take us out.

Carl handed me a lifejacket to use as a pillow as we each stretched out on the boat, staring up at the threatening grey clouds. The forecast was for rain, but the weather in Cornwall is quite unpredictable.

'What do you think our purpose in life is, Carl?' I asked him.

'To have fun,' he replied without hesitation. Then, after a moment, he added, perhaps for my sake: 'And if you can help some people along the way then that's good.' He was a GP, and planned his leisure time and holidays better than anyone I knew. And whenever I was back in the UK, we went out sailing together.

We lay for half an hour, deep in our own thoughts. This was not turning out to be much of a sail. We'd had many an adventure over the twenty years we'd known each other: walking across the Sinai with Bedouins, sailing the Greek islands, and our epic trip to Jura where we had been dropped by boat at the top of the remote, sparsely inhabited Scottish island (where Orwell finished writing *1984*) and had walked the length of it, running out of provisions after failing to catch fish or rabbits.

I looked out and could see ripples on the sea. I suggested we start the motor and go out further to find some wind. Carl pulled the cord a couple of times before the engine roared and we headed away from the coast. He cut the engine again, and before long we felt a little wind on our faces. We smiled at each other. Carl turned the helm into the wind and I pulled in the jib. We were sailing.

It took us an hour or so of tacking back and forth before we turned into St Ives harbour. We pulled down the sails and motored in between the other vessels until we found a place to moor, then clambered across the four small boats next to us and climbed up the metal ladder onto the jetty. We walked down the cobbled streets, past the restaurants and shops, to a café on the beach front, situated alongside chalets. For breakfast, I ordered a bacon bap and orange juice, with which I was soon soaked after a seagull dived down to snatch my food and missed.

In the evening, we drove to the small town of Mousehole and sat on the harbour wall, eating fish and chips – well-coated in salt and vinegar – and drinking beers. About a hundred or so people had gathered to hear the all-male Cornish choir sing.

'We welcome all those who have come from far away,' the conductor said. And then the men began to sing. The 'Battle Hymn of the Republic' roared out from their mouths. 'Glory! Glory! Hallelujah!' the audience sang along to the chorus.

Then there was a song in Cornish. Seagulls squawked and circled overhead. I looked out across the harbour at the little boats, blue, green and red, dangling from lines to prevent them from drifting.

No matter how far I travelled, nor how long I was gone, I still felt deeply attached to Britain. I had friendships here that stood the test of time and distance. The smells, the sights, the birdsong still held that gravitational pull.

The sun had gone down by the time we reached the last song. It was Leonard Cohen's 'Hallelujah'. The lyrics of loving and losing, of trying and failing, resonated more than ever. Tears streamed down my face.

By the end, everyone in the harbour was chanting in unison. Hallelujah.

EPILOGUE

The sun also rises

I awoke to the sound of cockerels greeting the rising sun. I quickly packed my small red rucksack, put it on my back and strode down the cobbled streets of Saint-Jean-Pied-de-Port. I stopped in front of the medieval church of Notre Dame du Bout du Pont to fill up my water bottle at the fountain. Then I passed under the Porte d'Espagne onto the stone footbridge over the Nive river.

A few pilgrims were ahead of me, bags on back, sticks in hand. I followed them up the steep country lane. Before long, I was enveloped in such thick fog that I could not make out anyone in front or behind me. I trudged on for a couple of hours, up and up, barely able to see beyond my feet.

I turned off the tarmac onto a well-worn grassy track. The scallop-shell marker, the symbol of the Camino de Santiago pilgrimage, indicated the way. I paused to drink and to stretch my legs before striding off again.

Then the fog thinned out and the sun broke through to reveal glistening emerald slopes. I could see for miles in every direction. Wild boars crossed in front of me. Cows grazed. Sheep shuffled after each other. Horses with shaggy manes trotted in the distance. Eagles soared overhead. I sat on the ground for a while to savour the view. The uphill slog to the top of the Pyrenees had been worth it.

There was no border crossing between France and Spain. The signposts simply changed language: pilgrims went from *pèlerins* to *peregrinos*.

Many *peregrinos* spent the night in the *albergue* (hostel) in Roncesvalles, a small village on the Urrobi river, famed as the site of the defeat of Charlemagne. I visited the monastery and observed Catholics crossing themselves in front of the thirteenth-century statue of the Virgin of Roncesvalles in the Collegiate Church.

I walked on to the village of Burguete where I checked in at a small hotel. I showered and changed into the one pair of trousers and the long-sleeved top that I had brought with me. Afterwards, I sat outside in the garden drinking water. Seeing I was alone, two women invited me to join them. They told me they were American, sisters-in-law, and walking all the way to Santiago de Compostela. They were both in their forties. One, a mother of four adult children, was searching for what to do next in life. The other was a fitness instructor who showed me photos of her dogs. We consumed almost a whole hog and several bottles of rosé and red wine, which flowed like water, before we retired to our rooms. I did not see them in the morning as they were up before dawn, determined to complete the Camino in record-breaking time. I was slow to rise, as it had taken me ages to get to sleep due to the pain of my leg muscles spasming from the eight-hour walk.

The next day was less hilly, but it was another twenty miles to the next hotel. I walked around fields of wheat, through forests of beech, and along hedgerows sprinkled with wildflowers. In the villages, the windows and walls of homes were adorned with potted geraniums. But I only spotted retired folks and wondered whether many of the villagers had left for the the cities in search of employment.

I walked for a while with a young Danish man, who carried with him his Bible and a guidebook. He was an agricultural consultant. His girlfriend had recently dumped him, he told me. The day before he departed, she'd said she wanted to try again. He felt confused and lonely. He asked about Brexit. The British vote had stirred up the right wing in Denmark, who blamed all the country's problems on the EU – and Muslims for failing to integrate. The Dane said what was needed was a Marshall Plan for the Middle East. Western countries needed to invest in the region and integrate the refugees there rather than in Europe. The Dane had been exempt from military service by drawing a high number in the lottery system that determined who would serve. He told me he would have put on a uniform if he had drawn a low number, but his views on the military had since changed after reading the Sermon on the Mount. 'To end the cycle of revenge, one has to turn the other cheek,' he told me.

After stopping in Zubiri for a 'pilgrim's lunch' of salad and stuffed peppers, I walked on for another hour in the burning heat to Hotel Akerreta, a medieval house outside Larrasoaña. I filled the bathtub with hot water and bubble bath, and climbed in gingerly. My blisters stung. My joints moaned. But soon I was immersed in the water, watching the steam rising.

I smiled. It had been a good day and I was thoroughly exhausted. I thought about the pilgrims I had met. The doctor who was born in Sri Lanka and served in the British Army. The young female Chinese pilgrim, a student studying in Madrid, who had translated from Spanish into English for me when a local tried to explain that there was a quicker route. I wondered how far the two American women had walked that day and where they were spending the night.

It was so easy to strike up conversation with pilgrims with a simple '*Buen camino*'. Everyone seemed to trust each other, bonded by the shared experience of walking long distances, and the common afflictions of blisters and backache. Everyone had a story to tell.

I climbed out of the bath and dried myself. I threw my dirty socks into the lukewarm water and knelt to scrub them with a bar of soap. I pulled the plug to let the water drain out. Then I rinsed my socks under the tap, wrung them out and hung them over the chair to dry overnight.

*

James, son of Zebedee, grew up in the Galilee and was one of the first disciples to join Jesus – and the first apostle to be martyred. He was beheaded for his faith on the orders of Herod, in 44 AD. Legend has it that, after his death, his remains were brought from the Holy Land to the Iberian Peninsula, where he had once evangelized.

For centuries, pilgrims had made their way by various routes to the tomb of St James in Santiago de Compostela. They walked the way for faith, penance and salvation. As with those who made the journey to Rome or Jerusalem, pilgrims to Santiago could receive indulgence to reduce punishment for their sins.

Prior to Christian pilgrims, these paths were trod by Celtic tribes headed to land's end, Cape Finisterre, on the Atlantic coast of Galicia, to watch the sun set over the ocean. Today, thousands continue to walk the way to take stock, or simply as a challenge and for fun.

I was walking to reflect.

I wanted to get away from the persistent sense of gloom, the discombobulating drumbeats of disaster that pervaded the media.

I was seeking a sense of peace on the Way. One step at a time. Hour after hour. Day after day.

The Iraq War would always be part of my life – but it no longer defined me. Writing *The Unravelling* had not only helped me process the war, it had also enabled me to explain it to others. Now friends and strangers had something to talk to me about. We could connect.

An Iraqi journalist, Qais Qasim, translated the book into Arabic. Iraqi readers reached out to me over Facebook. I penned a foreword to the second edition:

> *Dear Iraqi reader,*
> *I imagine you browsing books on Mutanabbi Street, and sitting in Shahbandar café,[1] reading your latest purchase.*

---

1 In 2007, a car bomb on Mutanabbi Street killed thirty people and wrecked Shahbandar café. Among the fatalities were five of the sons of the owner,

And I sit down at the table next to you, and order numi Basra tea.[2] And you look up from your book, surprised to hear a foreigner ask for such tea, and you strike up a conversation with me, and ask me whether I had ever visited your country before.

And I smile, and say yes, many years ago, back during Iraq's darkest days.

And I ask you what you are reading. And you tell me it's a book by an Iraqi author, who writes on the human condition and is heralded as the modern-day Ali al-Wardi.[3] And you tell me with pride about the cultural renaissance that is taking place in your country, and how across the Arab world there is a thirst to read Iraqi poetry and prose, fiction and non-fiction.

And with tears welling up in my eyes, I tell you how happy I am to be back again in Iraq, invited to speak at the Baghdad literary festival.

I hope that day will come before too long.

I reflected on the American soldiers I knew. They had set out to transform Iraq – and had been transformed by it. At war, many had seen their better selves, learned what they were capable of doing and been prepared to lay down their lives for each other. There was not a day that went by when I did not see a post on Facebook commemorating a soldier who had been killed in combat on that date. I noted soldiers setting up organizations to help enlisted veterans get into university, supporting their

Mohamad al-Khashali. He has since rebuilt the café in their honour.
2 Tea made from dried limes.
3 Ali al-Wardi (1913–95) was an Iraqi social scientist.

translators' resettlement in the US and raising money for wounded warriors. I observed soldiers active in civic life, standing for election, committed to making America a better place – to make it worthy of the sacrifice of those in uniform.

I recalled the friendships formed on the battlefield through sweat and tears, and loss and loss and loss, in an effort to give Iraqis a better future – the only purpose that made any sense as to why we were there. When I thought back to the war, I remembered our dedication to each other, the commitment to the mission, the selflessness, the trust, the better angels of our nature.

*

When I set out on my travels through the Arab Spring, I had been confident that the uprisings would bring about better futures for the people of the region because the instigation for change came from within.

How naive I had been. I had had no inkling of the miseries to come from the breakdown of state authority – nor the blowback on the West with terrorism and the massive migration to Europe.

The pathologies that afflict the Arab world run deep. The uprisings challenged the way in which states are governed – but regimes proved incapable of reform. They countered or collapsed.

The Arab state is in crisis. Carved out of the wreckage of the Ottoman Empire a century ago, some states still struggle for legitimacy. In the face of demographic pressures, climate change and globalization, regimes are no longer capable of providing security, employment or basic services. The social contract between rulers and ruled has frayed. As regimes reverted to repression, the hopes for peaceful transitions to transparent and technocratic governance were dealt a mortal blow. Yet such securitized responses will inevitably produce further division, discontent and radicalization. Unless regimes reform, future generations are bound to mobilize again in protest – and their grievances will foster the next iteration of insurgency.

The Middle East persists in a paradoxical relationship with the West, humiliated by its power yet seeking its assistance.

Refugees and terrorists are not contained in the region. What happens there affects us.

So we should engage – but to do so with greater understanding of the root causes of instability in the region, respect for the cultures and empathy for the people. We need to be willing to learn from the past, have the humility to listen and the patience to build trust.

We should revise our foreign policy, and reform our institutions, to promote reconciliation rather than arms sales; to invest in reconstruction rather than in dropping bombs; to mediate between different groups rather than endorsing proxies; to strengthen the rule of law rather than autocratic rule; to help build a new inclusive regional security architecture rather than an alliance against Iran; to encourage the development of a free trade area rather than imposing tariffs; and to provide greater opportunities for learning and exchange rather than banning Muslim visitors.

Furthermore, we should help reform the global order to incorporate the rising powers and to generate consensus over new international norms to prevent wars and govern trade.

But instead, policy makers in the West oscillate between advocating for military intervention to resolve the crises we contributed to creating; and calling for disengagement in the hope that the problems will go away.

*

I arose early, ate breakfast and packed my belongings into my rucksack. Before long, I was on my way, hiking through the Arga Valley. In the late afternoon, I walked through the Portal de Francia into the old city of Pamplona. Basque flags hung down from buildings alongside declarations in English – 'You are not in Spain or in France' – in case visitors did not recognize the Basque symbol of the white cross over a green saltire on a red field. The place was buzzing with young people drinking beers, eating tapas and smoking at bars. The bulls were not running through the streets that day.

It was a Sunday. I entered the cathedral, majestic in its gothic way, and sat listening to the old men chant the rosary. I watched the faithful few walk twice around the church following the banner held high in front of them – a ritual that had been passed down through the generations.

Pamplona had been conquered by the Visigoths, the Arab Umayyads and the Franks. Empires rose and fell; they came and went. But through all the political churning, wars and plagues, a stream of pilgrims had continued walking, coping with adversity, trusting to find shelter and food, and believing in salvation.

I remembered back to when I was a student at Oxford – the Cold War ended, the Berlin Wall fell, Mandela was released from jail, apartheid was abolished and the Middle East peace process began. Francis Fukuyama declared the 'end of history'.

It was liberal democracy from here on out, the promise of an optimistic future.

On my first visit to New York in the mid-nineties, I had taken the ferry to Ellis Island and stood at the Statue of Liberty with my arm held aloft. 'Give me your tired, your poor, your huddled masses…' the inscription read.

America! The land of opportunity, freedom, and new beginnings. The last best hope for the world.

I had visited the United Nations and read aloud the charter.

> *We the peoples of the United Nations determined to save succeeding generations from the scourge of war… to reaffirm faith in fundamental human rights, in the dignity and worth of the human person, in the equal rights of men and women and of nations large and small…*

It was such a heady, hopeful era. Dictatorships were replaced by democracies. A billion people were lifted out of poverty. Civil wars ended in negotiated settlements, supported by peacekeeping forces approved by an activist and united UN Security Council.

However, in its response to 9/11, driven by fear and anger, America undermined the very rules-based international order that it helped establish and led. It went abroad in search of monsters to destroy, using military force rather than diplomacy as the main tool of international engagement. Defence meant offence. The country that heralded human rights and freedom not only invaded and occupied Iraq, it held thousands without due process, tortured detainees in Abu Ghraib and Guantanamo Bay, abducted suspects in one country and sent them via extraordinary rendition to another, and sanctioned assassinations even in countries where it was not at war. Tens of thousands of innocent civilians have been killed as 'collateral damage' in the obsessive hunt to eradicate terrorists. More enemies have been created than taken off the battlefield.

America no longer stands as the shining city on the hill. It has spent billions of dollars on security and intelligence to protect the homeland, trampling over long-treasured civil liberties. Yet the expenditure is not in proportion to the threat. Since 9/11, fewer than a hundred Americans have been killed in the US by Muslim extremists whereas tens of thousands die each year from drug overdoses, gun crime, and traffic accidents.

Today, it feels like the optimistic 'new world order' that we thought would go on forever is in fact coming to an end.

*

I dined at Café Iruña in Plaza del Castillo, where Ernest Hemingway had once hung out, describing the city and its San Fermín festival in his novel, *The Sun Also Rises*. I ordered *ensalada Iruña, pescado del dia* and *flan* – and a bottle of wine. And I started writing on my iPad the thoughts that had been ruminating in my mind while walking.

Brexit and Trump are wrecking balls, laying bare things that are fragile and failing. The policies pursued by elites have kept us forever at war in the Middle East, led to the financial crisis, increased inequality and failed to adequately regulate migration.

This has contributed to a loss of trust in the establishment and provoked a populist backlash from those who feel that their concerns have been neglected.

No better idea of government than liberal democracy has come along. But big money and powerful players make ordinary people feel ignored and humiliated. While capitalism has created wealth, it has also increased inequalities, with elites getting richer, while those left out and those left behind see their wages stagnate and their opportunities disappear as jobs locate elsewhere or became automated. The recklessness of bankers led to the 2008 financial crisis – yet the government bailed them out while ordinary citizens lost their homes.

In the absence of leadership, parties and policies to pursue communal good, identity politics is polarizing people and driving us further from each other. Many are fearful of the future and of the end of their way of life, nostalgic for a golden age that never was, yearning for someone to restore a sense of familiarity and order. Walls are going up. Bridges are coming down.

Modern technologies are speeding up change and diffusing power. While new media has increased access to information, it has also fragmented the public sphere. Opinion has become the new fact, with trust the victim. The same technologies that enabled people to mobilize in protest against governments have also been used to surveil citizens and recruit jihadis. Positive messages of unity compete with extremist views and video nasties. The fringes no longer occupy the outer edges of society but are magnified in social-media's echo chambers of bots, trolls and fake news. The valley of open-mindedness is shrinking.

But borders and barricades cannot protect us indefinitely. Cultures will continue to collide and collude as they have done through the centuries. Structural forces driven by technology and globalization will continue to shrink the world. Corruption, unemployment, climate change, demographic pressure, terrorism and migration require not only local and regional responses but also international cooperation.

I finished the bottle of wine and paid my bill.

Wandering through the streets of Pamplona, bubbling with locals, pilgrims and tourists, young and old, enjoying the warm evening, I came across an open-air concert. I sat to the side on the steps of the cathedral and listened for a while to the songs in Spanish, Basque and English. Some of the audience were dressed in their Sunday best; others in walking clothes with windswept hair. Children danced to the music.

I stared up at the stars, and quickly made out Polaris and Ursa Major, viewed by people all over the world though ascribed different names and myths: the Great Bear, the Big Dipper, the Seven Sages, the Drinking Gourd, Odin's Wagon, the Great Cart, a funeral procession, the point of navigation for sailors, the direction of freedom for black slaves in America escaping to the north. For me: the Pole Star and the Plough – my moral compass and the heavy effort required to follow it.

The post-war journey I had taken in search of home had been a long one and full of adventure. Through it, I had found hope and humanity; I no longer felt alone. We are all travellers on this voyage through life, dealt different cards to play and with diverging paths to take, shaped by the people we meet, our loves and losses, struggling onwards, ever onwards. We are connected to each other in the most fundamental way by our common quest for meaning, significance and happiness.

Each one of us can make the world a little bit better by how we live and what we do each day. It is the small deeds, those individual acts of kindness, the selfless gestures, the respect for another's dignity, the willingness to listen, that foster the trust essential for cooperation, collaboration and coexistence. Empathy is everything.

My students make me optimistic about the future. They are locally active and internationally concerned; of different traditions but of a common future; citizens of somewhere as well as citizens of the world. They have respect for the cultures and beliefs of others. I admire their innovation and entrepreneurialism. I watch them amplify the voices of the less advantaged, seek to address the structural barriers that perpetuate inequalities, strive to strengthen civic bonds in their communities, and promote peace. The millenial generation is striding forth determined to leave the world a better place than they found it.

This is not a time for cynicism or despair. Out of a crisis will come opportunity.

The future is not preordained. There is much work to be done to make it less violent and more just.

A new world is struggling to be born.

Acknowledgements

I am grateful to so many wonderful people in the Middle East who received me in good faith, who treated me with kindness and respect and who shared their food and views with me.

Some of my accounts of travel started out as blogs and articles in foreignpolicy.com, *Atlantic* and *Politico*.

For feedback on drafts I would like to thank: Yuval Ben David, Derek Berlin, Ben Buchan, Anthony Cosio-Marron, Ben Davis, Alex Djerassi, Robert Ford, Claire Hajaj, Greta Holtz, Jolyon Howorth, John Jenkins, Nancy Jenkins, Ken Pollack, Graeme Lamb, Mel Lamb, Hamish McNinch, Finbarr O'Reilly, Alysoun Owen, Clarisse Pasztory, Corey Pattison, Leanne Piggott, Ramzy Mardini, Isabelle Savoie, Justin Schuster, Victoria Wakely, and Laura Ziv.

Special thanks to Daniel Ziv and Annisa Maryam who hosted me in Bali among rice fields and white herons, providing me the tranquillity to edit.

I am grateful to my agents Clare Alexander and Kathy Robbins; to James Nightingale at Atlantic Books; and to Gemma Wain, for copyediting.

And finally my thanks to Yale's Jackson Institute for Global Affairs for seeking out practitioners as well as academics to teach; to Yale World Fellows for their confirmation of our common humanity and dedication to making our world a better place for all; and to my students who are the hope for the future.

Index

A note about the author

Emma Sky is a Senior Fellow at Yale University's Jackson Institute. She worked in the Middle East for twenty years and was made an Officer of the Order of the British Empire for services in Iraq. Her first book, *The Unravelling*, was shortlisted for the Samuel Johnson Prize, the Orwell Prize and the CFR Arthur Ross Book Award. She lives in New Haven, Connecticut.